IN | APPROPRIATE

Interviews with Canadian authors on the writing of difference

Edited by **Kim Davids Mandar**

Introduction by **Daniel Heath Justice**

Ian Williams
Ayelet Tsabari
Sanchari Sur
Eden Robinson
Jæl Richardson
Waubgeshig Rice
Amanda Leduc
Chelene Knight
Mahak Jain
Wayne Grady
Alicia Elliott
Farzana Doctor
Michæl Crummey
Arif Anwar
Angie Abdou

Gordon Hill Press – Guelph, Ontario

Copyright © 2020 Kim Davids Mandar

All rights reserved. No part of this work may be reproduced or used in any form, except brief passages in reviews, without prior written permission of the publisher.

Cover and book design by Jeremy Luke Hill
Proofreading by Carol Dilworth
Set in Dual and Linux Libertine
Printed on Mohawk Via Felt
Printed and bound by Arkay Design & Print

LIBRARY AND ARCHIVES CANADA CATALOGUING IN PUBLICATION

Title: In | appropriate : interviews with Canadian authors on the writing of difference / edited by Kim Davids Mandar.
Other titles: Inappropriate
Names: Davids Mandar, Kim, 1969- editor.
Identifiers: Canadiana (print) 20200220446 | Canadiana (ebook) 20200220543 | ISBN 9781774220085 (softcover) | ISBN 9781774220092 (PDF) | ISBN 9781774220108 (HTML)
Subjects: LCSH: Authors, Canadian—Interviews. | LCSH: Multiculturalism in literature. | LCSH: Cultural pluralism in literature. | LCSH: Ethnicity in literature. | LCSH: Race in literature. | LCSH: Cultural appropriation. | LCGFT: Interviews.
Classification: LCC PS8101.M8 I5 2020 | DDC C810.9/3529—dc23

Gordon Hill Press respectfully acknowledges the ancestral homelands of the Attawandaron, Anishinaabe, Haudenosaunee, and Metis Peoples, and recognizes that we are situated on Treaty 3 territory, the traditional territory of Mississaugas of the Credit First Nation.

Gordon Hill Press also recognizes and supports the diverse persons who make up its community, regardless of race, age, culture, ability, ethnicity, nationality, gender identity and expression, sexual orientation, marital status, religious affiliation, and socioeconomic status.

Gordon Hill Press
130 Dublin Street North
Guelph, Ontario, Canada
N1H 4N4
www.gordonhillpress.com

Table of Contents

Editor's Preface – Kim Davids Mandar	vii
Introduction – Daniel Heath Justice	xi
Ayelet Tsabari	1
Mahak Jain	15
Wayne Grady	31
Sanchari Sur	39
Alicia Elliott	49
Arif Anwar	65
Michæl Crummey	73
Ian Williams	85
Angie Abdou	93
Jæl Richardson	107
Farzana Doctor	119
Waubgeshig Rice	131
Eden Robinson	141
Chelene Knight	155
Amanda Leduc	169
UN Declaration of the Rights of Indigenous Peoples	183
UN Declaration of the Rights of Disabled Persons	197
Selected Bibliography	201

To Tahirih, whose life of study, art and activism
continues to inspire my work

Acknowledgments

First, thank you to my family and friends who have supported this foray into the world of published writing and my re-engagement in academia. Any life change brings stress and a need for trustworthiness and encouragement. To my teachers, writing group colleagues, writing workshop friends, and grad school allies: you have been a godsend of epic proportions.

Next, this project wouldn't have been possible had Jeremy Luke Hill at Gordon Hill Press not placed his faith in me, or if my friend and classmate, Anna Bowen, had not invited me to the wonderful podcasting project (with Dan Evans and Tamara Jong) of *Bookish Radio* at CFRU. I offer my sincere gratitude to Jeremy Luke Hill for his tireless dedication to literary community building in Guelph, and the free flowing coffee at his table. His effort to sustain the Vocamus Writers Community and launch Gordon Hill Press with Shane Neilson continues to build on a precious legacy. That, and his edits and feedback, have made this project come to life.

Of course, the authors who said "no" to being a collaborator for this book taught me many things. I thank them for entertaining a response to the invitation, their candor, and their subsequent encouragement in saying that they believed this project held merit and value. To Dr. Cecil Foster: your time and conversations, while not appearing in these pages, were valuable components to the process at hand. I value you as an elder in this community who has contributed and continues to contribute much to deep thinking.

I also appreciate the network of people who will pick up, read, consider and share the insights from these pages. If the project is to be of any benefit, it will because of your choices and your actions. I have been silently communing with all of you as this project has unfolded over the past months. I encourage you to research the many writers who have, over the years, published thoughtful work on this topic. I also recommend that you attend the Festival of Literary Diversity and other events where you can hear from diverse writers first hand, that you volunteer in local literary spaces, and that you experience how exploring diversity might enrich your personal world and, as a result, our collective, evolving world.

Also, a brief note of empathy for everyone who is discouraged by our slow learning process when it comes to writing with respect. Inclusion is a painstakingly slow process fraught with difficulties. We know this. I send you compassion as we exercise patience; healing as we recover; and hopes for safety, friendship and humour.

Finally, to the writers who agreed to make this collection, given the constraints, the risks and the learning involved: you inspire me and invoke in me a deep respect for your work, your humanness, and your willingness to craft a community in which I feel honoured to belong.

Kim Davids Mandar

Kim Davids Mandar

Editor's Preface

Kim Davids Mandar holds degrees in applied linguistics and music therapy. She is now a full-time MSc student at the University of Guelph, writing a thesis on the role of theatre in building intercultural sensitivity. Her Certificate in Creative Writing from the University of Guelph is a capstone course away from completion.

As a first generation settler on Turtle Island, I have been told many stories. The cells of my body and the spirit that animates it hold many more. Which of these narratives will hold the most sway in my actions is a choice that presents itself to me every day.

In navigating those choices, I found myself, in September 2018, invited to conduct and edit this compilation of interviews about writing "the Other" in Canadian fiction. How do the storytellers of today make choices in crafting the narratives that are peddled in the marketplace? How might those narratives influence us? Concurrent with my MSc research, which explores the ways that humans develop intercultural competence, I eagerly accepted the work.

The subject of writing "the Other" has been a controversial one in the past few years. In May 2017 Canada's literary elite called for an "appropriation prize" shortly after Canada was rocked with the controversy about whether Joseph Boyden had the right to base his authorial prosperity on Indigenous stories and present himself as a representative Indigenous voice. More recently, Camilla Gibb's novel *Sweetness in the Belly*, shortlisted for the Giller in 2005 and winner of the Trillium Book Award in 2006, evoked criticism for the movie rendition, where Dakota Fanning was cast as yet another white protagonist in an "exotic" setting.

In addition, Heather, of Chapters Indigo renown, selected the novel *American Dirt* by Jeanine Cummins as one of her "Heather's Picks" novels. This selection boosted international sales of the book, but it also sparked immediate criticism of the superficial nature of the Latinx stereotypes upon which it relies. Protests swelled in op-eds and on social media. As ripple turned tsunami, both publisher and novelist issued justifications and apologies. The publishing house reported reviewing their processes and hiring practices; there was a staged learning forum where promoters and author publicly confessed their ignorance, listened carefully to criticism, and professed being schooled in a new awareness that will change the way they choose and read fiction. On my twitter feed, Artistic Director, radio host and author Jael Richardson responded by inviting thought leaders and all interested folks to the Festival of Literary Diversity (FOLD) in Brampton, presumably to continue their education.

I checked out FOLD for myself in 2017, at the encouragement of my creative writing teacher, and I decided to volunteer, to get an immersive experience. I was embraced in a warm and enthusiastically motivated team, one with vision and dedication and skill. Deep in my bones, I felt at home. When Alicia Elliott interviewed Eden Robinson for the Last Lecture at FOLD 2017, I felt like I did when I used to sit in my auntie's kitchen as a child and listen in on adult conversations. I would absorb and mine the shared insights for their treasure of social secrets, honest frustration, arguments and laughter. I could relate to the feelings expressed in a way that was different from my typical everyday conversations. Multidimensional. Human. Real. Meeting these authors, in the FOLD environment, changed my relationship with Canadian literature.

Soon after accepting to do this project with Gordon Hill Press, I saw a Tweet from Jael Richardson: "Writers of colour & Disabled writers have been reading other people's stories about us for so long that a lot of our before-the-page work is spent severing what we know about ourselves from what we've read before reconstructing truer versions of ourselves on paper. #diversecanlit". I was stunned to read something that resonated so closely with my own personal experience. Was I the only one who was late to the conversation? Were there others, like me, who were waking up to these truths? I felt confirmed in the belief that inviting authors to explore this reality in conversation could be illuminating. I cherished a hope that it might be of service to a more equitable writing practice.

Kim Davids Mandar

The pages in this collection hold conversations with insightful Canadian fiction authors. As you read, I invite you to consider the role of fiction in our society, the roles of the writer, publisher, educator and booklover. Consider the social context into which these stories inject themselves and the implications of your choices in reading material for both yourself and others. Consider how power shows up and is channeled within the current system. Consider your role in the current system.

We need to make these considerations, I believe, because we partake in the essential oneness of humanity, and of all living beings, which exists within a spiritual matrix that transcends and sustains all life. I believe the most powerful force operating within this system is love. I believe that we have much to learn about love. It is from this lens and positionality that I engaged in this topic of discourse. It is from this bias that I derive my passion for exploring the practice of respect in written work. I believe we can, together, improve in this aspect of communication and its subsequent effect on social development.

The interviews themselves are not, of course, comprehensive. Only so many voices could be fit into one volume. I approached those who I felt might wish to contribute ideas to this discussion, whose work dives into diversity, and who were within my range of literary connections. Some of the authors I invited declined, some generously participated. I say generously because the investment of time and energy without financial remuneration is a sacrifice. It is both energetically demanding (especially given the topic at hand) and materially demanding. Only some people have the inclination, courage and magnanimity to say "yes" when approached by a neophyte editor such as myself, and a new small press on the Canlit landscape, and to see the project through to completion. I am indebted to these fabulous collaborators for their expertise and their kindness. That said, this collection is a small buzz of conversations in a broad network of possible responses. Not only do these authors have additional insights and evolving perspectives that they could share, but also, these conversations are obviously a few of the many valuable perspectives in the Canlit community. It is my hope that through this publication a little door is propped open for a collective inquiry on the subject of appropriation to continue expanding and evolving.

In my own life, the ideas shared by these thoughtful authors led me to ponder themes of collaboration, conversation, relationship, social awareness, historical knowledge and consequences of the written word. It led to a variety of considerations when thinking about how to share the interviews with you. One choice was to leave the conversations as untouched as possible. Unless the author chose to revise their voice, I didn't feel comfortable to "clean it up" for the project beyond obvious issues of clarity. How could I investigate the idea of making space for diverse voices and at the same time censor those who were speaking? Another decision was to include two appendices at the end of the book, along with a bibliography of related materials mentioned throughout the interviews. I hope they can provide some valuable points of reference as our learning continues.

Finally, if this project has simply been a personal engagement with thoughtful people, then I would be the only beneficiary. While grateful for this privilege, it would be, to me, a failure. However, if reading these pages might stimulate further dialogue, thought and enriched writing practices, what a respectful reception that could be as we collectively learn more about how to leverage the social impact of storytelling. My hope is that we learn how to travel this multidimensional space in a way that increases equity of voice, profit and power. Thank you for reading these conversations, sharing them, using them (alongside the work of these fabulous authors) in teaching situations. Let's reconceptualize together—there is a limitless universe beyond our little roadmaps.

As a recognition of the contribution of all those who agreed to be interviewed for this project, I will be donating all royalties from this work to the Festival of Literary Diversity (FOLD) in Brampton, Ontario.

Daniel Heath Justice

Introduction

Daniel Heath Justice is a Colorado-born citizen of the Cherokee Nation, a novelist, and a scholar of Indigenous literatures, speculative fiction, and animal cultural histories. He teaches on Musqueam territory at the University of British Columbia, where he holds the Canada Research Chair in Indigenous Literature and Expressive Culture.

Imagining Together:
Rights, Responsibilities, and the Question of Appropriation

There are few topics as quick to create confusion, hurt, anxiety, anger, or resentment, and few as easily and unhelpfully caricatured, as that of appropriation. It's an issue that seems to cut to the heart of artistic expression as well as political representation, and everyone, it seems, has an opinion about what it is, what it isn't, why it matters, why it doesn't, or whether it's a thing at all. It seems made for the cultural wars of our times, yet it has a long history. There's no consensus about its definition or its terms, and too often when it enters broader conversation it's in a simplistic and reductive way.

Perhaps that's inevitable, given that the issue of appropriation is inherently one of positionality and power. There's a lot at stake in discussions about representation, especially for those from communities and contexts too often misrepresented to painful, even catastrophic effect.

In | Appropriate

When you, your family, your nation, your faith, your community, or your affiliation group have been defined by outsiders in detrimental, repressive, sometimes violently abusive ways, the question of representation is inextricably entangled in the struggle for dignified survival. This is especially the case for those who have long been on the social, economic, and political margins. Representation matters. And because it does, there's no neutral, apolitical, safe ground on which to stand, especially when writing as an outsider to that context.

To say especially isn't to say exclusively, however, and that's often a nuance missed in these conversations, for even those writing or creating art from within a particular community or context have to grapple with the expectations of representation from others in the community. No one is beyond accountability. Indeed, it's been my own experience that writing from within is layered with myriad concerns, expectations, and anticipations that aren't applied to outsiders without the same level of relational obligations. Given that insiders are held to such a standard, why should outsiders be exempt?

These aren't theoretical questions or abstract issues to me; I've considered them for a long time, certainly from graduate school. Given that much of my thinking of these issues dates to that period, it's probably useful to include that context here, too. I was a pretty anxious graduate student, especially given that I didn't have a lot of generational knowledge to draw on for navigating the academy. My dad finished the eighth grade; my mom finished high school. A few aunts and uncles on my mom's side had undergrad degrees, but I was functionally a first-generation student, and the first to my knowledge on either side to pursue a graduate education. There was much that was esoteric about the academy, especially for a working-class kid from a down-on-its-luck mining town in Colorado, and I keenly felt the divide between what seemed to be my middle-class peers' ingrained multigenerational knowledge and my own constant fumblings through the same system of unspoken assumptions and hidden expectations.

But it wasn't just class consciousness that emphasized the distinctions between our worlds. It was also race. I was born to a Cherokee father and a white mother, but was raised in her hometown far from Oklahoma, where my dad's extended kin were from and where his mom was born; when he was a teenager his mother Pearl died of tuberculosis in 1945 after years of decline in a TB hospital ward in Colorado Springs. Though of mixed heritage himself, Dad was phenotypically Native in a very racist time and place; he lived his life defined by other people's ideas about "Indians," and with Pearl's death and subsequent distance from her family he had little of the cultural or familial knowledge that could have offered a deeper understanding of what it was to be Cherokee. As a result, much of his life as a Cherokee man was defined by other peoples' stereotypes, which impacted and sometimes disfigured his understanding of what it was to be Cherokee, as well as my own. And although I went into graduate studies in part to help correct those understandings, the experience was often alienating, given how deeply racist and anti-Indigenous so much of my education was and how culturally distant my grad student life was from the context of my upbringing.

Representation was a source of constant interest and concern for me, and I would sometimes dump my anxieties on my mentors, who were eminently patient. But one conversation, as I remember it, stood out for its bracing clarity even now. I've long since forgotten the context, but it was certainly one in which I was again talking about my ambivalence about doing work in what we then called Native Studies. After all, I was light skinned; I hadn't been raised in Cherokee community; I hadn't dealt with the kinds of racism my dad had experienced. It all came down to one question: what right did I have to do this work?

My Ph.D. supervisor, Fran Kaye, was a wild-haired, bespectacled leftist from New Jersey (but with Canadian roots) and a specialist in Great Plains and Native literature; I learned a lot from her, especially on this day. She was usually patient with my existential uncertainty, but today she fixed me with a firm glance and exclaimed, "Daniel, you're sounding like a White guy! White people are always saying, What are my rights, what are my rights?" Her voice softened but became even more forceful in its quiet clarity: "What you need to ask yourself is the Indian question: What are my responsibilities in doing this work.'"

Of course this is a simplistic binary, one that Fran herself complicated in her own scholarship and teaching every day as a committed White activist among Indigenous people from all backgrounds. But it carried a powerful truth, one that framed much of my own approach to the work I would subsequently undertake, as well as my support of scholars from a wide range of backgrounds. It's a story I share with my own students every year, Indigenous and non-Indigenous alike. And it's how I come to the issue of appropriation.

Too often discussions of appropriation come from these two approaches—one of rights, one of responsibilities—but with very little overlap; we presume that we're talking about the same thing when we're actually coming from very different cardinal directions, and as a result we end up talking at or past one another. This volume and its contributors bring rights and responsibilities into closer alignment, and while they don't always overlap, they certainly make thoughtful conversation more possible.

But these are always hard conversations, make no mistake. And there are thoughtful, sincere people on both ends of the spectrum, as well as cynical, self-righteous opportunists quick to insist that only one perspective (their own) has moral weight or intellectual validity. The reality, as this collection shows, is nearly always more complicated.

In 1990, Anishinaabe writer Lenore Keeshig-Tobias penned a powerful editorial in the *Globe and Mail* that set the CanLit world afire with indignation, apologetics, and, I think, some measure of reflection. Though now thirty years old, it could easily have been written today. In "Stop Stealing Native Stories," Keeshig-Tobias (then Keeshig) took the entire Canadian state and its citizenry to task for relentless theft of Indigenous stories, perspectives, and experiences. It was far from a call for censorship that her detractors claimed. Keeshig-Tobias was powerfully, firmly calling Canada and its non-Indigenous arts community into a relationship of accountability and responsibility. She connected the theft of Indigenous stories to the entire state apparatus of land stealing, kidnapping, persecution of Indigenous languages, weaponized residential school education, and anti-Indigenous propaganda: "the Canadian cultural industry is stealing—unconsciously, perhaps, but with the same devastating results—[N]ative stories as surely as the missionaries stole our religion and the politicians stole our land and the residential schools stole our language" (Keeshig 35). She pointed out inequities in funding for Indigenous writers compared to White writers; misrepresentations in celebrated films and novels; the connections between the academic looting of Indigenous burial grounds and the extractive treatment of Indigenous cultures by non-Indigenous writers, made possible by decades of oppressive state policy that explicitly persecuted Indigenous peoples' self-expression while valourizing White Canadians' representations of "Indian" life: "Imagine, Canadians telling native stories because their government outlawed native languages, native culture" (Keeshig 36). Long before the Truth and Reconciliation Commission brought the issue of residential abuse to the forefront of Canadian politics, Keeshig-Tobias was one of the boldest voices insisting on the truth of those schools and how they were represented in mainstream Canadian media.

Keeshig-Tobias put forward a firm responsibilities-based argument, but the nuance was lost to many of her critics, who focused almost entirely on the question of rights and claims of censorship, typically the presumed artistic rights of White writers representing "Others" in their work. Black writer M. NourbeSe Philip would also offer a blistering critique of how censorship claims by White writers obscured the issue of racism in the Canadian literary world: "The 'right' to use the voice of the Other has, however, been bought at great price—the silencing of the Other; it is, in fact, neatly posited on that very silence." Importantly, she further notes that "It is also a right that exists without an accompanying obligation, and as such, can only lead to abuse" (NourbeSe Philip 101).

For both Keeshig-Tobias and NourbeSe Philip—and many other writers from long-marginalized communities—the issue of voice is inextricably connected with that of power and resources. They highlighted the absurdity of writers from within the centre of power and authority claiming censored victim status when everything in the culture upheld their privileged access to the means and mechanisms of socially sanctioned representation. Long before gaslighting was part of the interpersonal vernacular, these women identified the ways that CanLit and CanMedia worked to gaslight Indigenous and Black artists and other artists of colour, to blame those at the margins for calling attention to the inequities enriching those at the centre. Their words also brought focus to the impacts of outsiders' assertions of rights over responsibilities, especially for Indigenous and Black people in Canada, who continue to pay a real and heavy price for the stereotypes and misrepresentations of the White imaginary, not the least of which include being killed, surveilled, jailed, institutionalized, unhomed, and displaced in ever-rising and utterly indefensible numbers by the state, its agents, and its citizenry who have so fully invested in the idea of Indigenous and Black inhumanity. Misrepresentation itself may not kill, but it informs the minds and imaginations of those who see certain peoples as being less worthy of life, liberty, and compassion than others, and it certainly motivates abusive and even murderous policies and behaviours.

Defenses of appropriation range from a blanket version of "artists have the right to write/create whatever they want" to more nuanced considerations of how limits on expression empower repressive politics, or that they can even backfire on under-represented communities by leaving them with even less representation. Then there's the "art for art's sake" argument, which presumes that art exists only for itself and outside of the moral values of what is generally dismissed as a benighted and uninformed public. I have little patience for the first argument, which seems to me rooted in, at best, the superficial idealism of first-year philosophy majors and libertarians and, at worst, an Ayn Randish kind of ruthless individualism that sees others only through a lens of objectifying utilitarianism.

The third argument isn't much better, as it disconnects representation from any meaningful context; the presumption here is, of course, that if white writers—or men, or straight people, or Christians, or other majoritarian group—don't do the representing, no one will, a scenario that ignores the reasons for that power imbalance existing in the first place. And rather than look to remedies that would include increasing opportunities for under-represented writers to be foregrounded in the various representational media so that there will be ample people available to speak to issues of specific concern, it simply assumes a situation of eternal stasis with whiteness and White authority firmly embedded at the centre.

The second argument, however, deserves a bit more engagement, as to my mind it's the most complicated. There's no question of the danger posed by state limits on free expression, but what's often called out as "censorship" in these debates isn't that by any stretch— it's anger from people in communities that have too long borne the physical, psychological, and emotional consequences of other people's impoverished imaginations. To conflate indignation from members of an appropriation-targeted community with the myriad violences of state power is a strange move, and one hard to read as anything but intentionally obtuse and disingenuous.

The "art for art's sake" argument, occasionally put forward as some sort of idealized apolitical stance on representation, is one firmly rooted in the politics and cultural values of fin de siècle England and western Europe, including suffocating heteropatriarchy, religious chauvinism, xenophobia, and stultifying intellectual and artistic moralizing. Oscar Wilde and his Decadent contemporaries were rebelling against the dominant values of their time, but they brought their own biases, cruelties, and limitations to their arts as well; there's never been a time when art could be fully divorced from politics, for good or ill, and the more artists have insisted on being above the fray, the more bodies they tend to be standing on to make the claim. Wilde was a brilliant writer who challenged the moral hypocrisies of his age while at the same time callously mistreating his wife and sexually exploiting poor and vulnerable youth; his own version of the admirable "uselessness" of art is a product of a very specific time, one that speaks to but can't—and shouldn't—entirely encompass our own. It's a philosophy that was quite easily co-opted to serve the powerful and enfranchised, especially in the twentieth century, and as such it seems an imperfect if not dangerous guide for artistic creation and production today.

As a fiction writer and scholar of literature I'm enough of a humanist to believe that our arts offer insights into our experiences, and that the work of artists is vital to our health and wholeness as people. Yet as a Cherokee Nation citizen and as an Indigenous Studies scholar, I'm keenly aware that the same Enlightenment that gave rise to artistic freedom, representative democracy, scientific reason, and human rights discourses also fuelled and justified violent global imperialism, institutionalized misogyny, chattel slavery, racist taxonomies, and land dispossession through some of the same rationales and ideas. The Enlightenment has cast a deep and deadly shadow; it has never been an unalloyed good.

Writers never work in a representational vacuum; for many communities, the representational archive is long, deep, and noxious. For me, this is both the challenge and the opportunity of writing—how to contend with that archive and readers' expectations, how to challenge the simplistic narratives and offer something more complex and honest in return, and how to hold up the best of our humanity while grappling with the worst of it. Always those words return: "What are my responsibilities in doing this work?" And always the knowledge that responsibilities take place within relationships, and that relationships require attention and care to be healthy. It can be scary to be in relationship, but when undertaken with care, it can also be beautiful, even in its inevitable imperfection.

No community is a monolith, and no person is ever part of just a single subject position; whether Indigenous, queer, working class, or otherwise constituted in, between, and among these and other categories. Even in our own communities there are disparities of power, conservative and progressive elements, those who seek to control others' stories, and those who seek to express themselves in relation to or defiance of the values and voices in power. We can't pretend that any group speaks with a single voice, but for under-represented communities the answer isn't having more outside voices speak on our behalf, but for more of our own diversity to be foregrounded, more of our own varied perspectives centred. It's not that we need or want a token few to sit in these spaces—we want as many of our own in those spaces as possible. We're complex people and complex communities—our representations should be, too.

And then there's the messy issue of false identity claimants, which brings another entire layer of complexity, pain, and no small amount of pathology to the mix. Although Indigenous communities continue to be the main target for those making unsubstantiated identity claims—with Archie Belaney/"Grey Owl," Asa "Forrest" Carter, Joseph Boyden, Tim Barrus/"Nasdijj," and Elizabeth Warren only the most public among thousands of self-indigenizers in Canada and the United States—many racially, culturally, and economically marginalized communities have experience in this realm, and names like Rachel Dolezal, James Frey, and "J.T. Leroy" are now notorious for their appropriation of identities and subject positions not their own.[1] These are the most egregious and visibly extractive examples of appropriation and the ones most fascinating to the general public, but more frequent, and more insidious, I think, are the everyday artistic and media assertions of authority over peoples' identities and representations through sloppy, unreflective, and uninformed projection.

Critics talk about appropriation as a kind of theft, a hostage-taking of other peoples' stories, experiences, and identities that then deforms them into something unrecognizable and too easily coopted for personal profit and social advancement. Advocates talk about it as a kind of imaginative transfiguration that helps us empathize with other people's experiences, especially those already underserved by the dominant stories and images out there. It's all those things, and others. It's done in innocence as well as with knowing intent; it's done with good intentions and bad. It's wrapped in relations of power, of politics, of economies, of violence. The definitions fluctuate, the impacts vary, but it's always messy and frequently painful. These debates lay bare the inherently contradictory, unmanageable, and uncomfortable reality of our complicated humanity and the implications of power and privilege on our imaginations. I don't know of anyone who really enjoys such discussions. It hurts to face the lies others want to present as a defining truth; it's scary to call one another to account, especially when we care about what they're doing and who

---

1   Cherokees in the US and Métis in Canada are the two Indigenous groups most commonly targeted by false identity claimants. Darryl Leroux's *Distorted Descent: White Claims to Indigenous Identity* (Winnipeg: U of Manitoba P, 2019) is a wide-ranging examination of the phenomenon of raceshifting in Canada, especially in the context of claims to Métis identity; Circe Sturm's *Becoming Indian: The Struggle over Cherokee Identity in the Twenty-First Century* (Santa Fe: SAR Press, 2011) does similar work with Cherokee issues. An excellent study of the cross-cultural phenomenon of literary identity imposters is Miriam Novick's Ph.D. dissertation, "Impostures: Subjectivity, Memory, and Untruth in the Contemporary Memoir" (University of Toronto, 2011).

they're representing. We often want clear and straightforward stories, even when we chafe against their limitations; we want people to reach across difference, but too often witness how that reach is compromised by what we project into that space between us.

This volume is about that messy space between self and other, idea and creation. It's a complicated conversation that leaves a lot of difficult questions unresolved and offers few firm pronouncements of unshakeable certainty. But together the contributions focus less on the affirmation of the right of representation than on the responsibilities of doing work that honourably attends to our complications and contradictions, that takes disparities of power seriously, that expands our imaginative possibilities without ignoring the consequences and contexts of lived experience, that make real space for a broader range of artists to share their rich and challenging visions with the world on their own terms and for their own purposes, and that puts us into a relationship of accountability and, sometimes, conflict.

If we believe that art can do good, it's naïve to pretend that it can't also do harm; you can't have one without the other, just as you can't have rights without responsibilities. In the end, there's no "getting it right," no formula for the precise balance between the artist's call to create with any integrity or honestly and the care to avoid unnecessary harm with what we create. There's only doing our best to listen, to learn, to understand, and then to act in ways that are humane, honourable, and generative, and hopefully, when we stumble, to do better the next time.

It takes a lot of courage to participate in these conversations with genuine openness, as there's a lot of pain, fear, and anxiety around representation; these emotions radiate through the contributions, as does anger, frustration, and, not least, hope. And we surely need art that offers more hope than harm right now. It's not an easy issue or a simple conversation, but as these writers demonstrate, being willing to participate with humility and care is essential if we're truly going to find better ways of living—and imagining—together.

Ayelet Tsabari

January 16, 2019

Ayelet Tsabari was born in Israel to a family of Yemeni descent. She grew up in a suburb of Tel Aviv, served in the Israeli army, and travelled extensively throughout South East Asia, Europe, North America, before moving to Vancouver, Canada in 1998. She is the author of The Best Place on Earth. *A graduate of Simon Fraser University's Writer's Studio and the MFA Program in Creative Writing at the University of Guelph, Ayelet teaches at the University of King's College's MFA in Creative Nonfiction, and at Tel Aviv University.*

K: In *The Best Place on Earth* you crafted such a diversity of characters. Can you speak to how you made those choices, and how you went about writing them?

A: There's a lot more freedom in writing a collection of short stories. It allowed me to attempt things that I wouldn't dream of attempting in a novel. It's just one of the reasons I love the short story as a form. You can write about places you only know a little bit. I would never dream of doing that in a book length form, so writing a collection of stories was an opportunity for me to experiment with multiple viewpoints and perspectives and try things that I always wanted to try.

Often when writing fiction, there's a voice that presents itself to me; it speaks and needs to be heard, and I follow it. Sometimes I would question, later on, "Why this voice?" But there's an initial spark of magic and mystery that happens when you begin to write, and it's wonderful, and I'm in love with it. With the first story, "Tikkun", that's kind of what happened. And then I did question that. I asked myself, "Why am I writing this story from this guy's point of view, and not, say, from the religious ex-girlfriend's point of view? That's a good, interesting, female point of view. Why not tell her story?" And I realized that despite the fact that she's a woman and I'm supposed to feel and to relate to her more, that wasn't the case. The character of Lior and the voice of Lior were much more alive in my head and resonated with me so much more than hers. It was always him.

I say that I questioned why I wrote in his voice, and I did, but I didn't question my ability to write from a male point of view, and I was surprised when someone on social media actually commented on that negatively. He hadn't read the story, but when the trailer came out we included an excerpt from that story, read by a male actor, and someone commented on a friend's post, saying, "Why does she do that? Why does she write from a male point of view? What gives her the right?" or something along those lines. I was stunned by that. Because despite being aware of the issue of appropriation—I mean, obviously; you kind of have to be when your own voice has been appropriated from the time you could read – writing from a male point of view didn't cross my mind in that context. I didn't see it as an issue at all.

When I write from a man's point of view, I do rely a lot on my partner. With this story in particular, because it was first person, and the voice had to be bang on, he did make some helpful suggestions in terms of voice and authenticity. Anytime I write young men's characters, I ask him to weigh in. Also, being a native English speaker—I'm English as a second language—he helps me, sometimes, to hone the dialogue. I would ask him, "Does that sound right? Do you buy this?" and sometimes he does, and sometimes he doesn't. Sometimes he makes suggestions. And I do that whenever I write a character that's very different from me. I guess now we call those "sensitivity readers".

K: There's a lot of diversity within a group: how do you know when you've "nailed it" and written it in a respectful way? Is it more than one sensitivity reader? Is it two? Does it depend who it is? Or do you just have a feeling?

A: It really depends. The question of whether you "nailed it"—man, that's something you ask yourself constantly, even when you're writing about someone who is very much like you, even when you write about your own community. It's still your perspective, and it may differ from others in the community. As a writer, you constantly wonder. It never goes away. We constantly strive for precision in writing; that's a part of the deal. You have to rely on an intuition, I suppose—whether something feels right or whether it still needs to be investigated. There's no good answer. Every story is different.

K: In your acknowledgements for your collection, you acknowledged Camilla Gibb, who was your mentor at the time, and Camilla's background is anthropology. She also answered, I believe, in an interview, questions about cultural representation because she writes about different cultures. Was discussing accurate representation part of your mentorship?

A: She did say once, and I don't remember if she said it to me personally or if she said it in a different setting, "Shouldn't we at least try and fail sometimes?" And I thought that was very astute. It stayed with me, and I've repeated that since: "Shouldn't we at least try?" There's something about the idea that we're all basically human, and that we share some feelings, emotions, struggles, pains, the physical bodies that we live in (although that also, of course, varies). There's something about that that rang true to me, that I found comforting.

K: Why should we try? What's the benefit?

A: Because fiction has the ability to promote empathy. Writing is an act of empathy, and reading is an act of empathy, and I love fiction for that. In part, it's going back to the idea of goodness, I think. And I know a lot of writers who would say fiction is not about goodness, that it shouldn't be; and some of the best fiction is disturbed and dark, with characters that are ethically and morally corrupt, and I agree completely—fiction can do all kinds of things to all kinds of people. Personally, and that's just my own personal affinity, I want people to feel deeply, and I want to feel deeply when I read. That's what I seek, and that's what I want to evoke. Fiction does that, by zooming in closer.

When I talk about Israel in particular, and how when we're reading about war-torn countries or watching news items about them, we see a newscaster standing on a rooftop overlooking the smoky city, and it's so general and one dimensional and shows the people as a mass. Fiction zooms in, and gives voice to one family, to one house, and makes the "other" seem less "other". In small ways, even writing from the point of view of an elderly Yemeni woman in "Brit Milah," a woman whose views are very different from my own, was an exercise in empathy. Yes, I'm Yemeni, but I'm a youngish woman, and the traditional views Reuma holds are very foreign to me. Writing that story through her point of view, and not through the point of view of her daughter, whose views are in line with my own—that was, to me, an act of empathy. To understand Reuma, to try and embody her, and to portray her in an empathetic and authentic way was important to me, and, on a craft level, more challenging to me as a writer, which is a good thing. Writing it from Ofra's point of view, there was no challenge there. I don't think the story would have been as strong.

K: Did you have sensitivity readers for that?

A: I did not. I did not. I'm not sure why. Maybe it was just that I don't know elderly Jewish Yemeni born women who read English? Maybe I was too scared, because I was writing about such a taboo in Jewish society. The idea of not circumcising is very loaded. Maybe because I was writing about elderly women I felt I knew well, older aunties and women from my community. I realize as I say this now that this is a poor excuse. And to be honest, I was really scared of it being out in the world. I was really terrified.

K: What has been the response?

A: The response was amazing—I was blown away. You know, I really thought that this was the one story that people were going to give me heat over, because of the way circumcision is treated in Jewish tradition, I guess in Muslim tradition as well. It's almost not questioned. It's just what has to be done. So I was expecting to get a lot of pushback from people. And surprisingly, and maybe that was because I chose Reuma's point of view, and not her daughter, a lot of elderly Jewish moms—not just Yemeni or Israelis—told me how much it touched them. They said, "My son did this," "My daughter did this," and it was clear that they didn't agree with that choice. But they were just so relieved to find that story, their story, being told.

K: You mentioned the consequences of experiencing your own voice being appropriated your entire life, and not being able to read authentic representation of your own culture. What are the consequences of that?

A: Oh my goodness. Cultural appropriation is a part of a larger issue. It's a reflection of a power dynamic and an imbalance in society. So, it's hard for me to speak of it in isolation. It's a representation and a subset of a larger problem. Growing up, what I found in literature in terms of a representation of my culture and community, and I didn't find much, was often a caricature. As a child I read everything in sight, and I remember the day I picked up a random children's book, and I remember there was a Doctor Tsabari in it, and I was blown away. Blown away! I couldn't believe that there was a doctor in this book that had my last name. That was inconceivable to me. The fact that I still remember that, after all these years, shows you how rare it was for me to encounter a Yemeni doctor—with my last name no less!—in a book. It was such a small act. It was such a tiny thing that this author did, and it was amazing for me.

You know, when writers talk about how, out of fear of appropriation, they choose not to include any characters of colour or any marginalized or diverse characters—this is a great example of why they should. It was a very minor character, but it affected me so strongly. I was so shocked to see that this could happen, that there could be a Doctor Tsabari in literature.

K: So, beyond the shock, what other emotions did it evoke? Was there an outrage, like, "How dare you write about this?"

A: No, I was so pleased! I was so pleased that it wasn't the regular stereotypical caricature, like the primitive, poverty stricken Yemeni grandma, who lives in a poor neighbourhood, and her grandson, trying to be more Israeli, finds her so embarrassing. It wasn't the Yemeni maid cleaning the rich people's homes, or the working man, or the criminal, or the over-sexualized "exotic" brown-skinned young woman. It wasn't what I expected when I saw Yemeni characters portrayed. It was different. And it was a doctor! So, that's a really good example of how a tiny act of inclusion can make such an impact on a child's life.

In literature and in movies, Mizrahi characters, Jews of Arab lands, Jews of middle eastern or east African descent, are often portrayed in a very one-dimensional way. It's always a stereotype. And there were no books by Yemeni authors that I knew of to offset that. It's a reflection of a power dynamic in a larger, systematic problem. This representation—brought forth by White authors—was the only thing I was exposed to. It's very, very damaging. As a child who wanted to be a writer, in particular, it made me think that there was no room for my voice and that there was no place for my family in literature because I didn't see it. It didn't seem possible to write about people like me in fiction.

Earlier on I said that there's a mystery element to writing, where the voices will present themselves to you and you end up telling the story as it comes to you. But the decision to feature Mizrahi characters—Yemenis mostly, but others as well, Moroccans, Iraqis, Tunisians, because this was a book of short stories, I wanted the range—was a very calculated decision. This was a mission. I was writing the book I wanted to read, as Toni Morrison famously said. I was writing the stories I wasn't exposed to. This is my—and I know I'm writing it in English, and I know it's all backwards, but still—it was my way to rectify that childhood experience.

Even after I started writing *The Best Place on Earth*, for example, every time I was writing a female object of desire, I found myself falling back into the old trap: she was White, she was fair-skinned, she was often blonde. I had to catch myself, and that was another shocking realization for me. This is, again, going back to the damage of not seeing yourself portrayed in literature or seeing yourself only as one thing. So, where I could, I went back and corrected that, and to me, that's no different than doing any editorial work. Sometimes we edit for style, sometimes we edit for pace, and yeah, sometimes we edit for cultural appropriation and inclusiveness—that's another element that I think all writers should consider.

K: How can a writer do that? Your Filipina caregiver, for example, was so powerfully written. When you're doing the cultural appropriation edit, sensitivity readers are part of that. Did you do anything else?

A: Yeah. That's another story that I worried about, for sure. Again, I was pleased with so many people telling me how much it resonated with them. What did I do with that one? I spoke to people. And I researched as much as I could, and I tried (I don't want to sound cliché) to be highly aware of what I was doing and of my intention. I identified deeply with the character of Rosalynn and the woman who inspired her. And still, I worried. And I still sometimes worry since it's been published. I worry, and I sometimes question myself. But then I go back to the reactions, to what people are saying. And I'm like, well, obviously this was an important story to be told.

This particular story was something that was haunting me for a really long time before I wrote it. It was based on three people that I knew well. When I write fiction I sometimes take real scenarios, things that are true or factual in their basis, and then let the story take flight. It's fictional, of course; I save my non-fiction for non-fiction. So it was based on those people, and that love story, and the family that was created with three misfits who were living on the margins of Israeli society. It was in my heart—for years. I think I started thinking about it fifteen years ago. Those characters just haunted me. Their story had to be told.

K: You've brought up your creative non-fiction writing, and your memoir is coming out—*The Art of Leaving*. How does writing difference well in these two genres compare? Is there a different process in fiction, do you think? Are the stakes lower in fiction for accurate representation, or respectful representation, than they are in creative non-fiction? This question brings up the idea of audience—does the marketplace consume fiction differently than it would consume a creative non-fiction product?

A: Yeah, I do think people experience it very differently. Sometimes I resist that, and I wish that they wouldn't. Especially since people often assume that fiction isn't really fiction. And then, you write non-fiction, and people think it's too bizarre to be true. There's always that doubt.

K: That's so weird, isn't it?

A: It's so weird! I've had so many people ask me, "Who are you?" out of my fictional characters—or even just making assumptions like, "Oh, so you were a trouble-maker in the army," after reading say, "Casualties", and I'm like, "Oh, no, no—I mean, yes, actually, I was a trouble-maker, but I was a very different trouble-maker. I just wrote about another trouble-maker"—I know, it's shocking [laughter]—"but actually I was nothing like her."

On one hand, the boundaries start to blur, but on the other hand people really seem to want boundaries. And a part of me wishes there were none, just so I could protect myself from the exposure [laughter] that I'm going to experience in six months when my entire life is going to be on display. What the hell was I thinking [laughter]?

I never considered there might be appropriation in my act of writing memoir. It's so interesting. Like, I'm writing my story, how can I appropriate anything here? This is my story, this is my life. But then, there's always the concern about other people's privacy. And what I did was, I sent relevant essays to people—not to everyone, only to people who were in touch with me and I could easily locate and who wanted to see them. None of them corrected me. None of them had any issues. One of them corrected my Italian [laughter], but that's it. But, I'm still terrified. Especially when it comes to family, because my story is entangled with their stories. I'm aware of that, and I try as much as I can to protect them, but there's only so much I can do.

K: Michael Crummey's Henry Kreisel lecture was broadcast on CBC on *Ideas*. In this lecture, he described his experience of going to a literary festival in the United States and somebody asking him where he was from. He said, "Newfoundland". and the person responded by saying, "Oh, I know Newfoundland." They had read a book called *The Bird Artist*, which was set in Michael's hometown. When he heard that, he was crestfallen. He told them, "Okay, you know nothing about Newfoundland from that book."

A: And who wrote that book? Someone's who's from Newfoundland?

K: No, someone in the United States—a novelist.

A: I have a very similar story. A book was written about the Yemeni community—a book of fiction—and there were errors in it. And things that just didn't feel true to the spirit of the community. That's what I was saying before too, that I would never dare to write an entire book from Rosalynn's point of view, even though I identified so strongly with this character. I wouldn't. Again, the short story, the shorter span, allows for a little more freedom. I could never do that in a novel form. A novel digs in such a deep and broad way into the lives of people. How can you get it right? How could someone who is not Yemeni possibly get it right? There are just so many subtleties, so much depth and history, to a community. To any community. Like, maybe if you've lived amongst them for a long time, and studied them. Maybe, maybe.

I've been asked about that book several times in lectures that I've given—mostly in the United States—because people loved it. It was so "exotic". And I have a hard time controlling my face [laughter]. So, one time someone asked me, "Oh, did you hear about this book?" and I was like, "Yeah..." [laughter], and she said, "You didn't like it." And I said, "Well, it's not really about liking it or not liking it. It's just there were many misrepresentations in it and things that didn't ring true," and she said, incredulous, "But, as readers, how are we supposed to know that?" And I said, "Exactly!"

And this is a great example of how harmful cultural appropriation can be. This is the damage it can do. On one hand, Yemeni Jewish stories haven't been published in the White-dominated book industry in Israel, and as a result none have been translated into English, so there really isn't any true representation of that experience available to readers. And then you read this book, written by a White writer, and you think, "Now I know Yemeni culture and Yemeni people," and you don't—you don't.

K: And it's fiction, right?

A: It is. Though it's research-based—she's done a lot of research, obviously.

K: So, even though something is a work of fiction, we readers expect it to be accurate—we expect the representation to be true to life. That suggests something about our responsibility as writers. You spoke about the mystery and the magic—that "spark". If there's a writer, an artist, who feels very strongly that they have that magic flow happening, in order to channel and write someone from a completely different experience than themselves, would you say, "Go for it—write it"?

A: [big sigh] I might, if it were a short story. Though I'd recommend using sensitivity readers and asking themselves why they want to tell that story. If it's a novel, I would gently suggest not, to be honest.

The real question is whether you can do it well, and I find it very hard to believe that many people can. If it's done well, and people from this community love it, then great, but how can you really judge that? I think it's rarely done well.

K: How can we judge that? Because, I mean, as a student—if it is a learnable skill—there must be a way to judge it? You said one criterion is that the people from that community love it.

A: I imagine that would be a really big one. I think about Camilla's book, *Sweetness in the Belly*. She chose wisely, I think. Her main character was not Harari. She chose to write in the first person from the point of view of a White girl who lives amongst them, which is a perspective she knows from being a White girl who lived amongst them. I thought that was a good way to approach it. That said, she created so many characters. Almost everyone else is Ethiopian or Harari. From what I know, people from the community loved the book, and were really pleased that it exists in the world. It was obviously done well, but it's a grey area. I'm not suggesting any, "This is how you do it," because I'm not sure either.

K: Well, none of us are. That's why we're doing these interviews.

A: Exactly. That's why we're having this conversation. The bottom line is, it has to be done really well. And, unfortunately, especially when it's an entire novel, from the point of view of a character who is very different than you, and not just very different, but also marginalized and you're of the dominant culture, there's a lot there. It's usually not done well. So that's where it's at. But filling your book with beautiful, complex, sensitively written characters who are different than you is something we should all do.

K: There was an instructor that I met through an online writing community who is from South Africa, and she was suggesting that I pick up one of her novels, and I did, and I was excited, but then she realized my family was from Cape Malay. She kind of paused, and then she backpedalled and said, "I didn't mean any disrespect when I wrote about Cape Malay." And I said, "Okay." I was so innocent and naive about this. And then, when I picked up the book, there was actually a paragraph disclaimer in the opening pages about Cape Malay too. And I thought, "Whoa, what am I going to find in this book?" Then I read it, and I realized why she had done that, and I was actually okay. I don't know how I would have digested it if I hadn't had any of those warnings, or if I didn't know her as a writer and a teacher. But, to be honest, I still don't know how I feel about it. It was a very small representation. It was an elderly couple who were undereducated. It was, come to think of it, such a caricature, in a lot of ways. And, at the same time, I struggle with being Canadian and with whether I even have the right to be offended by this, because I wasn't raised in the South African Cape Malay community. So, I guess that brings me to the question—whose permission do we need, if any? Do we need to issue these kinds of warnings, caveats?

A: I don't know. I've heard that said before—the getting permission thing. And seeking permission doesn't protect you from others who may take offence, because how does one seek permission from an entire community? It's really very complex. Like the hippie that I am, I keep coming back to just, "Be good, be kind, be aware," but I know that's not enough, and we all want some sort of a road map or a guideline, but there just isn't any. There are some people who are trying to do this, who are teaching classes about writing difference, providing exercises on how to check your bias when you write. So, there are some resources out there. Because, I think, if we end up not writing any characters that are different from ours, that's also a problem.

And again, I'm going back to seeing that Dr. Tsabari in a book written by someone who was not Yemeni, and what a profound experience that was for me. So, even just as minor characters, being aware that your doctor doesn't have to be a default White person.

Yeah, populate your book with diverse characters, especially if you live in a place that is very diverse. That's sort of the flip side of this debate. I wouldn't want that. I read Grace O'Connell's book recently, *Be Ready for The Lightening*, and one thing that I really appreciated about the book is that she had several characters of all various backgrounds in this book. And of course she would. The book is set in Toronto! I know Grace, and she's intelligent and compassionate, and I feel like she knew what she was doing. And I think it was well done. And then, the other thing, if we're talking about the default White character—I had a very nice interviewer, very educated and open minded interviewer, ask me once, "Why is your character of Mizrahi background? It doesn't serve any purpose in the story."

K: What?! What did you say to that?

A: I said, "Why not? Is the default character a White person? Can only White characters just be?" And she was like, "Oh my God." She was taken aback by her own bias. And she immediately apologized. And I think that's okay—that we can make mistakes, that it's important also to accept that we all make mistakes. We all have biases. We all fall into traps all the time because we're human. I've said stupid things that I regretted, that confronted me with my own biases. And she recognized it, and she was really taken aback by her own lapse.

And the other thing too, because I think it's an interesting thing that has something to do with where I'm from: I've been asked why I don't have Palestinian characters in my work.

K: Yes, I have an article here you wrote for the *National Post.* And you have such a great answer, can I read it back to you?

A: Yeah, please.

K: You said,

To those who questioned the underrepresentation of Palestinians in my book, I explained that it was indicative of how segregated these two communities are within Israel. Palestinians were not in my schools, my places of work, my circle of friends. In fact, I didn't make Palestinian friends until after I moved to Canada.

A: Yeah, that's right.

K: Is that definitive as an answer? Or, did you consider including Palestinian characters anyway?

A: I did consider it. That's the thing. I actually do have one minor Palestinian character in the book, and I did consider having more of them. I knew that I wasn't going to write from the point of view of a Palestinian. That, to me, felt strongly, intuitively, like something I shouldn't do. I knew in my bones that this wasn't my story to tell. Again, it's going back to power dynamics, right? That said, I considered adding more Palestinian characters in the book. I had some ideas, but in my experience that's not how fiction works. It was forced. It wasn't organic. It wasn't meant to be. Especially since, as I said, the communities were so segregated when I was growing up. But a part of me also resented even being asked. Because here I am writing a book filled with characters who haven't been represented traditionally in literature. I was trying to contribute something to literature, to Jewish literature, to world literature, and the focus had to be on what was lacking. And there are so many books of short stories, Canadian short stories, that are entirely White. I've read many of them. Why is that not a question to these authors?

K: So, we've talked about power dynamics ,and that's so tricky, right? I'm tripping over that now. It's paralyzing. I was in South Africa for two months last year, researching, and I can't even open that box of journals, books and recordings. I bought hundreds of dollars worth of books, and I have tons of photos and footage and interviews and notes, and I've just zipped it up and thrown it in my garage, because I don't know what to do with it. I feel like I don't have the right to any of it. I can't dive into it yet.

A: Why don't you have the right?

K: I don't know. I just feel the power dynamic thing. I feel like we don't even know the power dynamics until we're in the middle of it all sometimes. If I'm sitting in Guelph writing about my family in South Africa, all I have is what I've been told here and then maybe that two month little window while I was visiting. But the culture is in flux, and the dynamics are powerful—it's like the ocean there. It's so beautiful. I love it, and I feel like I have to live there to even try to do it. And again, it's about those power dynamics. I just don't trust myself to be able to embody an authentic view.

A: Yeah. When I was starting to write, I worried that I didn't have the right to write about Israel. And I was born and raised there. Like, who am I to represent the nation and the people? Who am I to be the voice of Mizrahi women? And I think that's just our insecurities as writers, often. Obviously, there are times when this is a relevant question. But I don't think we should be thinking in those terms, or taking on that burden. Yes, I had a mission to rectify my own childhood experience, to create those stories and characters that were missing from literature, but I'm not representing an entire nation. I'm not representing a people. I'm not representing a community. No one can take that on. That would be paralyzing. So, it helps to remember that we're trying to write our own little truths. You have a voice, right? Your story matters. I understand you've never lived there, but this is your background. That's also a story. That's also a point of view. That's also a perspective.

I remember a few years ago I was working on research for a book that I ended up abandoning. It was about this tragedy that happened to Yemeni immigrants when they came to Israel. It's a sadly common story in the world: children were kidnapped and basically given for adoption to members of the dominant culture who were "obviously more equipped". The parents were told their children had died. They weren't given death certificates or shown any bodies. It's a horrific trauma, an open wound that really shaped my community, and it's still being silenced and denied, and I felt passionate about it. And then I had a child, and I couldn't do it. I just literally could not write it anymore, because I was sitting at my desk sobbing. It's still going to be part of my work, but not in the way that I had intended.

Then I found out, one day, a few years later, that someone was trying to write a novel about it, in Canada—someone who's not from my community—and I felt angry. It felt like that person was exploiting my community's tragedy. And then I shared my feelings with some writers of colour, and someone said to me, "Why are you the person to write it? Your family didn't experience it either." And it gave me pause. I was like, "Okay, so what are we saying? Am I only able to write the things that I've experienced?" This is narrowing fiction down to a point of... like, I don't want it to go there.

It's a depressing thought to me when it comes to fiction. And I don't agree with that person, but I thought it was an interesting question. It shook me a little bit. And that was after I had already decided that I'm not writing it. But I suddenly worried—was my choice to write about it exploitative as well? But if it was, maybe I'd still be writing it. I decided not to write it in the end because it was too painful. And if anything, it disappointed some people in my community when I told them. Some were even mad at me for not writing it. They want it to be told. But who has the right to tell a story? It's a really interesting question.

K: If the story merits being told, then we get to that question of who has the right to tell it.

A: If the story needs to be shared, first of all. I think that's an important question, and then well, why? Why does this story need to be told? And then why are you the person to be writing it? Why do you want to write this?

K: Where do you think this is going to go, with fiction? With global migration, we have increasing interaction and influence between cultures. How would you teach writing difference, if you were to do that?

A: Interestingly enough, a lot of my students over the years have been writers of colour, so often the issue of appropriation has not come up, and writing difference is something that comes naturally, I find, to writers of colour. They have a diverse cast of characters in their books. Also, I'm teaching mostly creative non-fiction, so again, it hasn't come up as often. But it has in the past, and it's really sensitive. I remember there was one White student who was writing a novel that was taking place in a war-torn country, and she was very defensive when it was brought up by me and other students. It was in my early teaching days, and I found myself a little bit unsure of how to deal with it. I'm knocking on wood here, but I've been fairly lucky with students: the issue of cultural appropriation has come up more as a general conversation that we've discussed, but not so much in people's work. But, I'm ready for it. In the past couple of years I've been collecting some resources in case I do need to tackle this head on.

K: You said that you didn't feel like there was space for your voice in what you were reading when you were growing up. And then, you came to Canada, and you found your voice. How did that happen? How did you find your voice?

A: At first I wasn't ready at all to write my stories, Israeli stories even, definitely not Mizrahi stories. In the beginning, if there was any Mizrahi character, she didn't have any ethnicity and her background was incidental. There was something about feeling not very grounded, sort of afloat in Canada and unrooted, that drew me towards the Arabic community in Vancouver. The Jewish community was very White and very Canadian, and I didn't really find my place there. Being surrounded by Arabic culture—the language, the music—it all felt very comforting to me and connected me back to my own Yemeni roots, to my own Arabness, as they say.

So then, whenever I came back home I started to spend more time with my grandmother and ask her a lot of questions, and I think that kind of planted the seed. And from there I started to see that there was something there to be told. It connected me back to my identity. Funnily, being away from home, brought me back to it. And there you go, that's my entire book in a nutshell [laughter]. It was a very long journey, and it meant that I didn't write at all for many years, because I was just feeling lost in between identities and languages too, which is a whole different story.

K: Is it different for you to write in Hebrew?

A: I mostly write in English, now, but yeah, part of the journey was having to sort of be reborn in a new language. It's that tremendous, the way I see it. It's a huge shift. So, it all came together in a very strange way—being away and living in this new language but being very drawn to my roots and where I come from at the same time. And I think there's something about being away sometimes that gives perspective. You can see where you come from in a different light. It's like using a telephoto lens. You can see better from a distance, with greater clarity. It was a very good place to start writing fiction, that distance and that yearning at the same time. It was fertile earth to grow stories from.

Mahak Jain

January 23, 2019

Mahak Jain is the author of the picture book Maya, *a CBC Best Book of the Year, a Kirkus Best Book of the Year, and winner of the South Asia Book Award. She completed her MFA in Creative Writing at the University of Guelph. Born in Delhi, Mahak has also lived in Dubai, Massachusetts, New Jersey, and Montreal. She currently resides in Toronto, where she is a Professor of Creative Writing. Learn more about Mahak at www.mahakjain.com.*

K: When you consider the topic of writing difference respectfully, what comes to mind?

M: I think we need to break that down into two parts, because I have a set of thoughts about how to think about this as a writing educator versus personally in your own writing, and then, finally, how to think of it just as a concept, independent of your own writing or your practice as an educator.

K: Sounds great. Please begin wherever you feel most comfortable.

M: As a concept, one of the things that does come up around writing is whether or not you should write about difference, whether or not you have the right, and what are the power dynamics that go into who writes about what. So, conceptually, completely in a void, I don't really believe in having rules or policing content. The reality, though, is that you can't pretend that as a writer you're not part of the world or part of a community and that you're not, in some way, impacted by the world in which you live.

So, what I take from that is, you do have to be examining what you're going to write about. You need to engage with the reality of the world. That in itself, I know, is something controversial to say, because some writers believe that art is independent of the world.

I don't think that we should police content, and I don't think that writers should be afraid to write outside of their own experience, because I think the act of writing can really broaden your perspective on the world. The reality, though, is that writers don't live in a void. To pretend that the world in which we live, the world which we have absorbed in our own selves and deep parts of our consciousness, is somehow not going to come out in our writing and thereby perpetuate that world—I'm talking specifically about in its worst forms—is a fantasy.

I hesitate to say to somebody, "Don't do that," because it's a much more complicated process, but as soon as somebody refuses to engage with the fact that the world is not the perfect place they'd like it to be, as soon as they refuse to engage with that idea, then I'm a bit suspicious of what's going to come out on the other end of that process.

K: Conceptually speaking, would you say this is a definitive position?

M: No. On the one hand, I feel like in a conversation around this topic you can kind of answer it in a very glib way, in a very short-hand answer, in a one-sentence answer. That's one way of doing it. The other one is that you go on about it forever and ever, and it's hard to find a middle ground. You can either say too little about it, because it's too difficult to say everything, or anything you say is not enough to resolve the question. It really is that deep a question.

K: Yes, so true. Can we move into talking about your writing, then?

M: Sure. I do, right now, write primarily or only about South Asian characters. But I have thought, "What would happen if I were to tell diverse stories within that community?" South Asian is such a big term. I have questions about, "Well, do I have the right to tell the story of somebody of a different class, race, power structure in that big community. Do I have the right to tell the story of somebody who has been disadvantaged by that community?"

I'm reluctant. And I think partially my reluctance has to do with the reality that I would be writing from that perspective in an entirely textual way. I'm not in my own life engaged with a community outside my own in any meaningful way, so I would be coming at writing about that difference from a purely analytical and textual mode, which I feel is, in some way, abdicating responsibility.

For example, in my life, if I had become so deeply engaged with the issue that it touched on me not as a writer but on me as a person, then I would say, "Oh, I have a point of view. I have something to say, because I live it in some way." But, in writing we sometimes talk about how we use objects as metaphorical symbols, and then if you carry the object throughout, you can do something with it, and that's kind of what it would end up being, right? It would end up as a particular background and a particular person being treated entirely as a textual object, not in any way as a real, breathing individual impacted by the world in which we live, because I don't engage with that reality in my world.

I'm speaking hypothetically, because I'm currently not writing in this way. I'm working in a mode that I'm familiar with and that I know. But I am aware of these issues, so I think if I do decide that I'm writing about individuals who, I feel, have been more greatly disadvantaged by this world than I have been, then I have to think about, "Why am I doing that?" and "What do I gain?" and "What does that person gain (or lose)?" And if I have everything to gain, and that person or that community has nothing to gain, then that's sort of perpetuating the injustices of the world and using those injustices for my benefit.

K: So, it becomes an exploitation.

M: I think so, yeah. But it's tricky, because at the same time I know that a lot of writers feel, "Oh, I'm witnessing this, or in some way I'm being asked to think about it, so, therefore, I should be allowed to explore it in my writing." But for me, I have to ask, have you really, entirely captured what it is that you're exploring? If not, then you have a perpetuation rather than the breaking down of these harmful narratives that we carry within us, without realizing it, about how certain people are with respect to other people.

K: Are writers allowed to make mistakes, and are we allowed to be imperfect and in process when we publish something?

M: Writers have permission to write whatever they want. They can sit in their rooms and explore the hell out of whatever idea interests them. When it becomes very different is when it becomes part of a market, and all of a sudden there's profit to be made, and then there's a question of, well, whose stories are you profiting off of?

In | Appropriate

This conversation—it's very different when you're having it in a void versus when you're actually considering real world implications. And I don't know why, but there are writers who want to continue to perpetuate this idea that writers live in a fantasy world, or that a text sort of exists in a world as a separate entity, whereas a book is only a possibility as soon as someone's reading it. It actually requires engagement to exist as an entity. Otherwise, it's just an object. For it to be a story, someone must read it, and, therefore, it is necessarily part of a world, a community. It's not a surprise to me, though, that some writers want to choose when this applies to them and when it doesn't.

K: Right.

M: So one of the basic parameters for a book to exist is that it becomes a part of a community. For an author to then say, "Well, I don't want to deal with the fact of that community," doesn't make any sense. And that's when I start to become suspicious, is when you want to exercise the right to take advantage of this power you have as a writer, but you don't want to deal with the consequences of your writing, or don't think the consequences apply to you. And that reads like entitlement. You're completely entitled to the benefits, but you're in no way held responsible for the problems that come with it

K: So, here's an example—I was at a rehearsal and having dinner with my friend. Her husband is a filmmaker, and he recently read and loved a novel by an American author about North Korea. And he said, "You know, I can't get novels from North Korea, and even though this author doesn't live there, I really enjoyed reading his book, because it wasn't filled with the stereotypes I perceive on popular media." He really enjoyed the humanizing complexity of the characters, but he also said that he has no way of knowing whether it's accurate or not. He just enjoyed the book.

M: I think the book you're talking about is *The Orphan Master's Son* by Adam Johnson. It received a great deal of attention because it won a Pulitzer Prize, and I remember people asking then, "Who is this writer who wrote this book?" So, I think what's really complicated here is, well, if it's good enough, does any of that matter? Because, obviously, if it won the Pulitzer Prize, let's accept that as a useful standard, and trust that the book is well written on the craft and technical level and that it does wonderful things in terms of what you would expect from a book. So, this is where I think people especially get confused about how to deal with this because, well, it's valuable. It's valuable because it's well written.

K: My friend perceived it as valuable because it actually derailed the stereotype that he held. It made him think more deeply about people he will probably never meet in his life. The novel humanized these people and made them more complex for him.

M: I'm not sure. To me, the book, as an idea, not in terms of its content, perpetuated the stereotype that somebody of a Korean background is not capable of telling their own story; therefore, we need this external person to come in and tell that story, when, in fact, I can name another writer right now who lives in South Korea and has spent the last ten years of her life, I think, getting as much information and research as she can so that she can write about North Korea. So why hasn't this filmmaker heard about her? Why hasn't he sought her out?

I think he probably read this book because it did win the Pulitzer Prize, but also because it's written by a man who is White—and I don't mean him specifically, I don't know anything about Adam Johnson—I just mean that the world, and I'm getting back to the realities of the world here—it does privilege narratives written by certain individuals. Right?

K: Absolutely.

M: So, again, people want to say, "Well, it's so important to me. It's so valuable to me," and yes, I have no doubt that it was. I've read books and loved books that have been important to me, but that in some ways are also problematic. But we have to be careful not to allow that to cloud our perspective about the realities of the world. The reality is that your friend is wrong. This is not the only book about North Korea. There are other books written by people who are more, you might say, adjacent to the issue, and are more invested in the issue and in the people involved, but, for whatever reason, he didn't read them. He read this book. He didn't do the research.

People are also just lazy. It's much easier for people to read one book, and then it's done. And just listening to the story, it disturbed me that he said there's nothing else being written. That's not true. That's a myth. And it's sad, really. It suggests that only this one person is capable of telling the story of people who are autonomous and have their own perceptions and point of view.

K: Thank you for introducing this idea of the responsibility of the reader, because it's not only the responsibility of the writer. Clearly, we make choices, and that drives the market, and the market is a big part of this system.

M: Yeah, I mean that's why I want to return to the fact that a book doesn't exist in a void, and a writer doesn't exist in a void. I think writers really want to believe that they're some kind of a special specimen. They accept the fantasy that, "I'm writing my book alone; therefore it exists 'outside' of the world," when it doesn't. All of it operates within the machinery of the world, as does the reader. The writer doesn't exist without a reader; a reader doesn't exist without a writer.

K: And writing itself requires support. I mean, the publishers have a role too. Everyone has a role.

M: Yeah. It's a network, and that's why it's a very complicated issue, because when we talk about this topic, we tend to talk about it in an isolated manner, like, "What is the responsibility of the writer?" and leave it at that. Either it becomes too broad a concept, or it becomes too isolated to just one person. Sometimes you'll have books come out, and one writer becomes the target of everybody's ire for having done "appropriation" badly, when it's not really one writer. It's an ongoing cultural concern.

K: And the concern will be shifting as well, because culture is dynamic. And you're talking about power dynamics, and that's what this is all about, right? It's about awareness and sensitivity and exercising our roles within that social power network. So, what is the moral component around this? How do we negotiate that responsibility?

M: Yeah, well, I think (and this is more from the perspective of an educator) a lot of times, especially with writers who are just starting out, they're less in control of what it is they're putting out into the world. That is, everything still feels like an accident. Who knows where that idea came from and whatever. Whereas, the more I write, the more I gain experience with writing, the more I realize that, yes, there is a spontaneous quality of writing that happens, but at the same time all writing is an artifice.

And so it's really important to remember that writing is constructed and that it's possible for your subconscious, without you realizing it, to construct a narrative for you. As you get better at writing, you take greater control of what's coming out and shaping it and polishing it and presenting it in the way that you want it presented. There's a lot more direction.

Here's a real story: it's about a writer who was a public school teacher, and he had a lot of students at his school who were Black, and so he decided to write about these students. But the way he depicted them, they were represented as these over-sexualized Black boys whose primary interests were crime and drugs, and it was a simplistic portrait. When he was critiqued for this in workshop, he argued that, well, that's how it is, that's actually what I saw and what I witnessed.

I think in a writing class it's important to remind students that everything you're doing is artificial in the sense that you're constructing it. That same man could have constructed an entirely different narrative, because effective writing is about believability and manipulation. Writers are extremely manipulative. When a writer is able to be very convincing about the truth of something (like Adam Johnson), it no longer ends up being only an issue of responsibility but also one of skill. If you're able to do that, if you can use all your skills to create whatever you want and convince somebody of a truth or of its reality, what that really says is that all truth in a text is constructed, and therefore has been constructed by somebody—by you. So, you have to examine yourself. Why is it that you're constructing this particular thing?

People would, I think, like to believe, "I'm not constructing anything. I'm seeing the world, and I'm just representing it." But as soon as you enter the realm of the text you realize that everything is constructed. I actually think this is why a lot of writers say that they understand the world better when they write it, because it helps them see the artifice that also exists in the world around them, the narratives that are constructed by the world, by a culture, by power dynamics, which, as you say, are constantly shifting.

K: In your short story, "The Origin of Jaanvi", you wrote about Thalassemia—the blood disorder. What was your research process into writing that accurately, because it's not something that may be affecting you personally?

M: I do think of that story often when I think of writing outside my perspective: one, because it was written from the perspective of a man, a middle-aged man; and two, because it was written from the perspective of a middle-aged man who has a disability. He has a blood disorder, an invisible disability, one that people aren't able to recognize immediately. I know that writing it, I had discomfort. Not if I should do this, because again, as I said earlier, the question of "should" is complicated. But it was more a matter of, "Have I done it justice? Have I put everything that I can of me into this? Have I done my due diligence?"

And that's not the only story I've felt that with. There's another short story that I've written from the perspective of a young woman suffering from an alcohol addiction, and again this question of why?

Why does she need to be an alcoholic? Why am I doing this? Who is it serving? And, if I have done this, have I just completely given in to stereotypes?"

K: How do you answer those questions for yourself? Where does that lead you?

M: For me, the research takes two forms. One form is the actual information, which you can easily find, the data about the subject matter. But the other form is an emotional research, which has more to do with the body. Then I can think of the character as a real person. There's a real person in the world who suffers from this illness and walks around with it. How does it impact their body? How do they inhabit it,? How do they live it? It's not empathy from a distance, in the way that we were talking about it earlier, where it takes the form of, "I care about this issue. This is unfair." It's more to do with becoming and inhabiting that body.

And, so I try very, very hard to live it for a time, so that I can feel that I'm writing from an authentic place. That being said, I think that's not a very satisfying answer, because I can imagine someone (say it's the teacher that I talked about earlier, who was a White man writing about a Black student) being like, "I'm living in that body"—it didn't really show in the writing. Are you really living in that body? Where does it ache? Where does it hurt? What does the body run into? I remember when I was writing "The Origin of Jaanvi", I realized that if he's suffering from Thalassemia he's also going to be tired. A little more tired and fatigued than everyone else. And because I have chronic pain, I was thinking a lot about what his fatigue would feel like"—How does it feel to live in the world and do a lot of work and also engage with all the other things in his life, such as his marriage, and what does it mean to be a brown-skinned man and all of those things, and how does that all come together in that body?"

I think, for me, not ever forgetting that it's not a textual object, but a real live person with a body that feels things and senses things that is impacted by the world is really important, and that's true for the other story I mentioned as well.

K: So it's taking it right into your lived, everyday, imagination experience.

M: I suppose so, in terms of stakes. Because the reality is that I don't have a stake in it, right? I don't know somebody with that disorder, and I'm not connected. When somebody has Thalassemia Major, it's fatal. They have a short life span, and living with it is very difficult. My character doesn't have that. He has Thalassemia Minor, so he suffers from the disease as well, but not in the same way. I knew there was no way that I could myself, personally, cross the bridge of writing about Thalassemia Major without investing myself in it some deeper way. I know what it's like to have chronic pain. I know what it's like to have similar sorts of physical challenges, but I don't know what it's like to have a fatal disorder. I haven't done the work myself to make my mind and my body engage with what it's like to live with that knowledge, what it's like to be in that body with that knowledge and living in the world, because I think that somebody with Thalassemia Major experiences a great deal more stigma than someone who doesn't, including perceptions of whether your life is valuable if you have the disease.

So that's just a whole other set of questions that I couldn't explore. I knew who I was writing about, and I knew what I was writing about, and I knew the limits of that. But the only way that I could have a stake in it myself was to force myself to live in the body of it as much as I could.

For the story I was writing about the woman who suffered from alcoholism, I didn't drink a lot, but I did make it manifest in my body with my imagination, if you can understand that. Earlier we were talking about characters as textual objects versus individuals with bodies in the real world. For me this imaginative and cognitive process is a huge part about how I proceed with writing difference for myself and how, in a classroom, I would encourage others to think about what they're writing about.

K: I've talked to people who say the field is open. I think you mentioned it earlier, when you said a writer can write whatever they want. And their point is that people don't have to read it if they don't like it. They do it however they do it and with whatever intentions they have or for whatever purpose they have, and then they say there's enough people in the world for everyone to have their own audience. Would you say that's fair?

M: Well, again, that's speaking in a void. There are billions of people on this planet. Not all of them have access in the same way. A lot of that has to do with a history of colonization and continued exploitation of certain parts of the world.

This perspective sounds to me like a fantasy, wanting to believe that we're in no way engaged in a capitalistic market that actually surrounds the whole world and affects the whole world, that we can somehow manage to be completely exempt from this system that decides so much of everybody's life. This just isn't true. Sure, you can put that book out there, and they don't have to read it, but how come that book gets the financial support and the machinery of a whole industry? Isn't that actually saying that you have to read it? The message behind that is saying, "This book is more important than that one." It's implicit.

K: Yeah, I totally agree with you.

M: This is what I meant when I said that this conversation can easily be boiled down to one sentence, and for me that sentence is, "Writers need to stop believing and acting like they're in a void and are therefore entitled to do whatever they want and treat this world as their playground."

K: Is becoming more aware and connected to the responsibility that comes with the power of the pen a learnable skill? Is it a natural tendency? Is it both? What can we do in the classroom and in our writing groups to foster greater accountability this way?

M: It's not a natural tendency. Having been around writers in a graduate program, in an undergraduate program, having taught writers, having been around writers in conferences, it's definitely not a natural tendency. Because at a certain point what we're talking about is what it means to be human. Because, for me, in the classroom, I actually see a great deal of parallel between how we talk to one another about each other's writing, and how we treat one another as human beings in the world.

In a workshop setting, when you're running a workshop, you're automatically bringing together people who have very different viewpoints, who have very different priorities, and who see the world from very different positions of power. So, immediately, you have to ask that room to learn how to respect one another and also to understand that you're not an expert or an authority on someone else's point of view. But at the same time, you have to know that people will bring into that space all sorts of different views that they haven't examined about the world, about other people, and that's the space it's going to end up being.

I think this is a question about thinking more deeply about pedagogy. And some of that has to do with the fact that, if an institution only hires and employs instructors of a certain background within certain power structures, then it's choosing consciously to perpetuate a certain type of teaching and a certain type of perspective in the classroom.

So that's in terms of institutions and what they decide to make systematic or not. In terms of individual instructors, are they themselves engaged with a concern about responsibility in the world? Now, this is the problem, right? Because I'm arguing that writers do have responsibility and need to stop pretending like they don't, whereas another writer will tell you, no, they have no responsibility to anybody else in the world. The only responsibility they have is to the word. I'm arguing that the word doesn't exist in a void, and you have to accept my premise in order to be able to take part in what I'm proposing, which is perceiving the way you're teaching in the classroom very differently.

If you're coming at everything you see from the position that we hold attention within ourselves about what impact our word has on the world, then it automatically transforms our writing and teaching. And there are writers who are also thinking about how is it that we can change the dynamic in a workshop or in a writing classroom so that the focus is no longer on validating certain perspectives, which happens when you say, "Oh that's so well written," or "That's so great," and more on what happens when you say, "What was your intention here? What was your goal?" making the conversation more about where each writer is individually coming from.

K: Like, skill and craft?

M: Well, the traditional pedagogical approach to creative writing looks primarily at skill and craft and says, "You did that well. You didn't do that well." The writer is usually not allowed to respond or participate in a discussion of their work. An alternative involves engaging in a conversation with the writer, asking, "What are your intentions? What are you trying to do here?" And it forces the writer to have a conversation with their material and with what that material is representing. Personally, I believe you need both. For any writer to succeed, you need both.

But like I said, I think a lot about bodies. I think that in writing, in the world of writing, we often get too cerebral in discussing what's happening on the page. Every person is expected to come to the classroom and pretend that they haven't brought their body with them. We're just talking about the text, about if it's been written well, when the reality is that the body actually makes a difference. Every person has had different painful and ecstatic experiences in that body, and they've experienced the world very differently in that body.

So a lot of the problems that you sometimes see in workshops, say where a male writer writes about a female character in a way that the other women in the class find really problematic and disturbing, come because what we're really talking about there is bodies, and we want to pretend we're not. We want to say, "It just wasn't believable," or "That was offensive, why are you doing that?" when really we should be asking, "Okay, writer who wrote this, you're trying to capture this experience in your writing—what research have you done on the bodies of women to make you think that you are an authority on this subject? What do you know? And if your research contains only viewing women as objects, then that answers the question." Or, preferably, remember that when you're thinking about how to represent women, you're actually thinking about specific bodies that exist in the world, and you should take into account how those bodies are going to perceive this representation.

These responses from readers, which may offend the writer, are valid responses, because by virtue of writing something you've asked readers to engage with your work, what you've chosen to represent of the world. Therefore, you also as the writer must engage with perspectives that don't agree with you. This is where the question of race arises, and people say, "You shouldn't have written about this other culture, or this other race." And writers are like, "I don't care what people of that race think, even though I think it's totally okay for me to write about that race."

K: Right.

M: They want to engage with the body of a textual object, but not of a real-life object, as if there's no relationship between those two things.

K: What makes good research, then? If that writer, in your example, would like to enrich that writing and continue on the path that they've started in response to that workshop feedback, is there a place where they can go with that research to make it better?

M: We're assuming here that the writer means well, right? We're assuming that they really want to do their part and be responsible. Some time last year, I was at a recording for this podcast called *Food 4 Thot*, and they were talking about the subject of appropriation, and they were discussing a female writer [Hanya Yanagihara] who wrote a novel [*A Little Life*] from the perspective of four people, and either all four of them are gay, or some of them are, I don't know. And this question of appropriation never really came up much around her book, but in this *Food 4 Thot* podcast, the hosts are all gay on the podcast, and they were talking about how they felt about this.

And they talked about there being three levels of engagement writers can have. There's the first level, where the person doesn't care at all. They're like, "I'm going to do whatever I want." There's a second level, where the person means really well and is very concerned about how this group of people that they're not a part of is being treated in the world, so they decide to write a book. And what the podcast hosts said about that second person is, "Great, go vote, or donate money instead." And in fact, I agree with that. I think that if you're concerned because you have all the privilege and someone else doesn't, and that makes you feel bad, and you don't want it to be like that—well, that sounds very political. Use your political power to change that.

But they argued that this writer [Yanagihara] was working from a third level of engagement. She'd been part of or adjacent to a queer and gay community for something like ten years. And she had interviewed, she had done her research, but also at a certain point, she had increased the stakes for herself—that is, if harm was done to this community, harm would be done to her as well. She wasn't in living in a vacuum. Her life had become entangled with the lives of those she was depicting. That's different. What that is, and I don't remember if Alicia Elliott used this word in an essay she's written on the subject of empathy and appropriation, or if they used this word in the podcast, but that's love. I think it might have been Alicia Elliott who said that there's a difference between writing from a place of concern...

K: Empathy and Love?

M: Yeah, she talks about the difference between writing from a place of empathy and a place of love. So, empathy is the thing that's like, "Okay, go out and make a donation. Go out and cast a political vote. It's great that you're empathetic." But, love is when you're so deeply invested in the outcome, that you have a stake in the game, you know?

K: Yeah.

M: You have something to lose. And that's like the question earlier, like, who does this benefit? If you have nothing to lose but everything to benefit from writing a different perspective, that should actually point you to the fact that it's because you're in a place of power.

But, if you have something to lose—say by writing from the perspective of an Indian woman, about the stereotypes that people have about India and being Indian, so I'm deeply concerned that every single time I write something I might be perpetuating this dangerous belief against my community—then the consequences actually affect me in the world. And so, that's a very different kind of engagement that immediately forces me to be engaged with it in a moral way. It asks me to. It demands it of me.

K: Right.

M: But, when you're not at all impacted, then your engagement never asks that of you. And if you're in a position of power, sometimes nobody else is asking that of you either, because you're seen as entitled to say whatever you want.

K: Exactly. And talking about skin in the game, this is a hard project for me to be involved in at all. Sometimes I wake up and think, "Why did I say yes to this?" And then other times, I'm like, "This is so important."

M: Yeah, well, it's different. I mean, the publisher who you're working on this with is a White man, right?

K: Yeah, he is. So, his wife is African-American, and their children (both biological and adopted) are all, I believe, mixed race.

M: So he sounds like he's motivated to explore this subject matter, but I think it's different in terms of skin in the game—like, as soon as I say, "Writers do have a responsibility," it will always be read through the lens of the fact that I'm a woman of colour. It won't be read through the fact that I'm making some sort of moral and philosophical statement. Versus if a White man said that, it would actually be very different, right? He would be lauded, in a way that I wouldn't be. There's that stereotype of mothers versus fathers. When the mother does her responsibility with the kid, it's like, "You should do more," while with the dad, it's like, "You're so amazing!"

K: I know what you mean.

M: So, I think there is different skin in the game for you as an editor. I understand that.

K: Talking further about this, I'm intending to write about my heritage. I went to South Africa last year to do research, and this work is helping me consider my way forward. You see, I have a relative here in Guelph. I've known him and his family for decades. We're socially connected, and were neighbours and everything. He's from the same neighbourhood in South Africa that my dad's from, that I'm writing about. It turns out that this relative's uncle is one of the foremost novelists from that neighbourhood. There aren't very many, but his uncle was one of them. So I'm trying to encourage him to write the stories that I hope my descendants will be able to read, and he won't do it. It's not because he thinks the stories are sacred and shouldn't be shared or written down. It's because he doesn't feel he has the skill.

M: Right, so the question is, do you have the skill as a writer?

K: Should I be writing these stories with him? I don't want to do that, because I feel like he's going to defer to me too much, and I don't want to alter the way he would do it, because it would be much better from his perspective. But he won't do it.

M: Okay, so let's pretend this isn't a question of appropriation, because I'm not sure it is. Let's just say there's a writer, and they're like, "I have interesting tales from my background. I don't have the skill to write them, but there's a writer who thinks these are really good stories and should be written," and you just look at those two individuals separately. To me, what I see is a writer who has the capability of transforming that material into a written work. And I don't see any issue with that. But you're in the stage of your writing where you're sort of finding confidence in your own abilities and stuff, right?

K: Yeah, in my identity and voice. Because I feel like my identity is not tied to one culture at all, not to one neighbourhood or one aspect of my history.

M: Whereas I can imagine another writer who says, "I know I'm good, and I know I'll do a good job." And that's it. That's where they would stop. And I think some of this conversation is that you and the thing that you're engaging with are complicated by your relationship to your own voice. And that's okay. That may just mean that you're not ready for this project yet.

K: There's also the question of the responsibility of the audience—people who are purchasing books, people who are the marketplace, people who are becoming more conscious. What is the role of the audience in helping to advance this aspect of writing difference more respectfully?

M: Well, we talked about this a little bit earlier. I mean, there was this trend for a little while on the internet where people said, "I will only read books by people of colour this year," or something. I don't know if that's a very impactful way of going about it, by putting all the burden on readers. And I think it's unfair, too. If anything, we should know by now how powerful the marketing industry is, how powerful advertisements are, how powerful social media is, and how much that impacts the decisions about what people buy. There's a reason that stores like Barnes and Noble and Indigo charge money to publishers for displaying some books right at the entrance. The reason it costs money is because they know that it works.

I think it's very easy for the publishing industry, which really has a ton of power and influence, to say, "Well, it's the reader's responsibility.

In | Appropriate

It's the readers who aren't interested." This is a lie. It's actually not true. It's been proven to us since the 1950's in terms of advertisements and marketing, that organizations have the ability to influence what readers become interested in. And why they're choosing not to is the question I'm more interested in.

Wayne Grady

January 28, 2019

Wayne Grady was born in Windsor, Ontario. His writing has appeared in such literary magazines as the Tamarack Review, Quarry, Event, *and* Queen's Quarterly. *He has published two novels—*Emancipation Day *and* Up From Freedom. *He has taught creative nonfiction in the MFA program at the University of British Columbia, and now divides his time between Kingston, Ontario, and San Miguel de Allende, Mexico.*

K: There seems to be some confusion around the idea of writing difference, some hesitation that can kind of create a paralysis, for writers of fiction as well as creative nonfiction.

W: Yes, and since I write both, I've really noticed it.

K: How would you like to begin?

W: Well, a couple of things come to mind. One is that I think it's a different question for fiction and nonfiction writers. I think fiction writers tend to explore unfamiliar territory, new territory, imagined territory, and creative nonfiction writers are writing primarily about their own experience in the real world, as in memoir, for example, or travel writing, or personal essays. They don't always feel able to project themselves into another character. In fact, when I was teaching creative nonfiction, I actually forbade them to do that, because I said that when you're writing from the point of view of someone who isn't you, you're writing fiction. I'm not sure I believe that now, but it was a good starting point for a class discussion.

But my primary stance on any kind of writing is that no one can tell us what we can or cannot write. People can refuse to read what we write, or to publish what we write, but as writers, really, we have to feel free to go where our instincts and our imaginations take us. In fact, we're encouraged to go where our imaginations take us. Otherwise we'd just write stories about sitting in our studies or watching television or having coffee. Not all of us want to do that. We don't want every novel to be about a person's own narrow, unimagined life. Some writers do that, but I don't think we really want to impose that as a standard. So, while I agree that there are cultural areas and personal sensitivities that we have to keep in mind, we must do so without censure. So, that's where I start, where I come from.

And the other thing I would say is that I am less troubled by the point-of-view question than I would be if I were all one race. I'm mixed race. I'm half White, half Black, and I feel that I have licence to write White or Black characters. At the same time, because I was raised White and thought I was White until I was forty-five years old, my cultural background and my psychological background are as a member of the White community. I'm very aware that I'm trying to adjust to that and come to terms with that in my work as well as in my life, and I think our society as a whole is trying to come to terms with that dichotomy.

Esi Edugyan asked me on stage at one of the festivals how I self-identify. I kind of hummed and hawed about that, because I really didn't know how I self-identified except as mixed, which is not identifying with either side of the person I am. But I did admit that when I wrote *Up From Freedom*, I wrote it from the point of view of the main character, who is a White male. So I assumed I felt more comfortable writing from the point of view of a White male. I don't think of that as not having permission to write from a different point of view. That's just the point of view, for that novel, with which I felt most comfortable at the time. One of several things I was trying to do with that novel was to create a White male character who was forced to listen to a Black female character.

K: You have said that in one of your drafts you had alternate chapters between Virgil and Tamsey, but that when you did that, Tamsey's voice was largely internal, and that's why you ended up making her narrative in third-person, because you wanted Virgil to have to listen to her, you wanted her to express herself through spoken word, through dialogue. You wanted him to actually listen to her spoken words.

W: Yes, I wanted Moody to have to shut up and just listen to her.

K: It's interesting to me that when you did write from her point of view in your initial drafts, that it was largely internal. Can you speak to that choice in terms of authenticity in writing?

W: Well that's a question of literary technique. When you write from one person's point of view, you can only write what that character is thinking and feeling and saying. You can't write something that the character doesn't know, or something that happens off-stage. It's very limiting. So that wasn't a question, for me, of appropriation of voice. It was about how to do it best to make the novel work better. But I also found that in writing Tamsey in close-third-person, I was actually letting her speak in a voice of her own.

It was quite cumbersome to have two main characters with two points of view going back and forth, which made the whole novel then become about two odysseys that come together in the end. That would have made it a six hundred page book. So, what I opted to do was to follow Moody's journey to the point where he meets Tamsey and then hook into Tamsey's story and have Tamsey tell her story to Moody. And that actually worked better for me, because then I realized that what I had to do was to get Tamsey to talk to Moody.

Now, Tamsey, coming from a background of slavery, having been a slave all her life, was not a person who would be naturally comfortable talking about herself to a White person, especially to a White male. Her previous experiences of White males would not have been, shall we say, conversational. So, having her talking and telling her story to Moody was a short-handed way of saying she was a very strong, confident and forthright person, and was moving ahead, away from slavery and towards freedom. It seemed important to do it that way, rather than have her say, "Oh, I'm a very strong person, a forthright and self-confident person." It's the old, "Show, don't tell," mantra. It worked better for the novel to have one point of view and to have Tamsey talking out loud, to Moody. And, also, it worked out psychologically better, because it forced Moody to listen to her. One thing I believe very strongly is that a lot of the problems between antagonistic characters and antagonistic groups of people come from one side not listening to the other side.

K: Yes.

W: Men don't listen to women. Whites don't listen to Blacks. Colonizers don't listen to the colonized. The history of race relationships, for example, has been that even Whites who are sympathetic to Indigenous people seem to feel they can help them by telling them what they're going to do to help them, instead of just shutting up and listening to what they actually want. So, that's what was going through my head as I was making this decision in the book about voice.

K: That's really beautiful about your process. Now, we're talking about writing difference in general, so it isn't confined to race and gender—it's any kind of difference. It could be age, ability, many things. So, in terms of the idea that we should feel free to write anything that we wish and not to be constrained, because this is fiction and because we're artists and this is what we do, can you speak to the context and the role of fiction in contemporary society to create social change and impact power dynamics?

W: I once was talking to Lee Maracle about how she felt about White writers writing Indigenous characters. I thought she would say, you know, "Don't do it. Write your own stories." But she didn't. What she said was that Indigenous stories are there for everyone, that no one owns them. The only thing she asks is that the teller get the story right, tell it with respect, and add something, make the story their own. And that's a mandate that every writer, whether of fiction or non-fiction, should follow. Get it right. Make it your own. If you're going to write from the point of view of a character who's not you, do your research, get the story right.

One of the things I learned from writing so much creative nonfiction and then moving to fiction is that getting fiction right is just as hard and involves just as much research as writing nonfiction does. Right now, for my next novel, I'm writing about a character who has colon cancer, and I've never had colon cancer. I don't know what it's like to have a really serious illness, so how do I get the story right? Well, I know several people who have had cancer, so I'm talking to them. I'm getting stories about what it's like on a daily in one case on an hourly—basis; what kind of treatment they are getting, what the big problems are, what the little problems are, what bothers them most about it. Is it the pain, the loss of dignity, the loss of privacy? But generally what constraints having that condition puts on them. When I write that character, I want someone who has colon cancer to read that story and say, "Yes, he really got it right. He knows what he's talking about." Otherwise, it's just bad fiction. The problem wouldn't be that I was appropriating the voice of a person who isn't me. The problem would be that it just wasn't very good writing. And that, to me, is the bigger crime.

K: Do you have ways of checking or measuring whether you've gotten it right? How do you know when you're done?

W: Well, you're never done, for one thing. I show it to people who have better insights into that condition than I do. Merilyn, my wife, who's also a writer, had something like ten or twelve outside readers for her last book. She had a nurse in the novel, and she knew a nurse and asked her to read the manuscript before she sent it to the editor, to make sure she got the nursing stuff right. Part of the novel takes place in Mexico, and even though we live half the year in Mexico and are fairly sure we know how to write about it, she had a Mexican friend read that section to make sure she had that part right. And so on.

I didn't do that with *Up From Freedom*, because the novel involves a fugitive slave in the mid-nineteenth century, and there's no one alive today who was a runaway slave in 1850. But I did a lot of reading, and I also related some of my characters' experiences to things that have been part of my own life: Moody becomes a fossil collector, for example, and I worked fairly extensively with paleontologists when I wrote my two nonfiction books about dinosaurs. For the rest, I have to rely on my imagination. What was the relationship between Moody and Tamsey like? How did it work? No one can tell me that. I can get the history right, but historical accuracy isn't necessarily the goal in a work of fiction. Still, I don't want to get simple things wrong, and oftentimes getting the nonfiction parts right will open a door to new insights for the novel, and it's really nice when that happens.

K: Do you think that fiction writing has the same role in social dynamics as nonfiction or journalistic writing?

W: In fact, I think it has an even greater role in determining people's attitudes. I think people read fiction wanting to believe that it's nonfiction. There've been psychological studies that have proven that. It's that whole "suspension of disbelief" thing on the part of the reader. Readers positively want to suspend their disbelief. They want to believe that what they're reading is reality, and they will believe that fiction is reality even when what they're reading goes against what they know to be the truth in "real life". There was a study conducted at Washington University in the States in which two psychologists gave a class of history students a story, and told them in advance that the story was a work of fiction. In the story, George Washington was not the first president of the United States—he was the second president of the United States. After the students read the story, they were given a series of questions, and one of the questions was, "Who was the first President of the United States?" and something like sixty per cent of the students who had read the story said that they didn't know.

K: Wow.

W: And these were history students at Washington University. But we know this from the history of the novel as well. Back in the first decades of the novel, writers went to great pains to convince their readers that what they were reading actually happened. The novel *Pamela*, for example, published in 1740, was purportedly based on actual letters received from a servant girl, even though Richardson made the whole thing up. Defoe claimed that *Robinson Crusoe* was based on the real adventures of a man who who'd been marooned on an island in the Caribbean. Novelists went to extraordinary lengths to disguise the fact that what they were writing was fiction. Readers didn't trust fiction in those days. Now, as that experiment at Washington University showed, it seems readers trust fiction more than they trust nonfiction.

And we still try to convince our readers that we're writing true stories. Unless we're writing really bizarre science fiction or pure fantasy (and maybe even then), we still make our novels conform to what most people understand as reality. We still, if we write a novel that takes place in Toronto, want to make sure all the streets are where we say they are, that the buildings are where we say they are, that the nonfiction parts of fiction are accurate. We can't have people meeting at the corner of two streets that readers know don't meet—that kind of thing. And all of that is to create this illusion that what we're reading is something that actually took place, or is taking place even as we're reading it. Janet Malcolm has said that people believe fiction more than they believe nonfiction because it's the only account there is. When they're reading nonfiction, every character in the book could have their own version of the story, whereas in fiction, there's only one story, and it's the one you're reading. That's why I think fiction has played a very important role in cultural history, in determining how people conduct their lives. I think fiction writers have a very important and serious role to play, and we should be aware of that.

K: I'm curious about the ethical role, then, that a writer plays in terms of the context their work is distributed within, and also the role of the system and the marketplace.

W: I think that all artists have an ethical role to play. In any genre, in any discipline, we have a very important ethical role. I believe it was Shelley who said that poets are the unacknowledged legislators of mankind. Think of that: legislators. The people who make the rules. That's an important role. But I don't think it stops there. I think we're also the recorders and witnesses. Nadine Gordimer was very specific about her role as a witness to the abuses of apartheid in South Africa. This is part of what I meant earlier about getting it right. If we're going to be legislating and recording and witnessing, we'd better make sure we get it right, because, as I said, people are going to read it and believe it and act on it. And also, a hundred years from now, someone's going to read our work and think that's what society was like in those days. And so we want that to be right for the people who read and believe us now, and for those who read us (and we all believe our work will still be read a hundred years hence) in the future.

K: How are these questions influencing the world of publishing these days?

W: In Phillip Roth's last full novel, *Exit Ghost*, he makes an interesting observation about the direction in which literary publishing and literary criticism were heading. He lamented that we've come to a point where a writer's biography has replaced objective criticism of the writer's work. People will like a book or dislike a book or publish a book or turn down a book based on what they know of the writer's personal life, and not so much on how well the book is written. We've moved away from art for art's sake—and that may not be a bad thing in itself—but have entered the era of the politically correct novel, and that cannot be good. Roth said, and I agree with him, that this is a shame, because it's really the work that matters. Plus, it gives writers whose biographies we don't know a disadvantage, and sometimes it gives writers whose biographies we do know a disadvantage.

K: Yes.

W: Both of us could mention the names of writers who have suffered because people know too much about their personal lives. I remember a teacher telling my eight-year-old daughter she shouldn't read Raold Dahl, and look what happened to Gunter Grass's books when it was discovered he'd served in the SS during the Second World War. Literary criticism becomes something else when it steps outside the book and makes pronouncements based on things that aren't in the book. And that's sort of what we're talking about when we're talking about writing about "the Other", that if we didn't know the writer's ethnic background or physical background or gender we would be making pure assessments about how well or how poorly the writer captured that "other" reality. I think that would make some books rise in people's estimation, and probably would lower other books in people's estimation. So, there really is an important aspect to this kind of discussion.

K: I guess, from an educator's perspective, there's the product and the process of learning how to write. Often this issue of accurate and respectful representation of difference doesn't become an issue until after something is published, when it's out there in the world, and then it can become difficult for a writer. Do you have any advice or insight about that long-term process of evolving as a writer? Is there room for evolution in today's market, in today's writing world?

W: That's an interesting question. Publishers don't necessarily stay with a writer throughout the writer's career, as was once the case. You're only as good as your previous book. In fact, you're really only as good as the sales of your previous book, if you're publishing with a major publisher. Book Net now can tell a publisher exactly how many copies of your last book were sold, and publishers can easily base their acceptance or rejection of your work based on those figures. I think that was more prevalent a few years ago. Now I think an editor who really loves your work can go to bat for you and get it accepted, even if your previous book did less well than had been hoped. I wouldn't necessarily call that evolution, but there's been some improvement and some easing in the process.

I'm now working on the edits of my third novel, and I think it's a stronger novel than my first one. I know all writers think their new book is their best book, but this one certainly didn't take me eighteen years to write, as the first one did, and I think the voice in this third novel is closer to my own voice and is a stronger, more confident voice than the first two. I'm confident in taking more literary chances with this book in terms of structure and style and, actually, germane to our discussion, getting into the heads of several characters who are not me—the poor guy with colon cancer, for example, but also his daughter. I think that the confidence my editors at Doubleday have shown in me has given me the freedom to develop as a writer. And fortunately that can count for more than sales figures.

Sanchari Sur

February 15, 2019

Sanchari Sur (she/they) is a 2019 recipient of a Banff Centre residency (with Electric Literature), and a 2018 Lambda Literary Fellow in fiction. Their work can be found in Toronto Book Award shortlisted The Unpublished City *(2017), PRISM international, Humber Literary Review, Room, ARC Poetry Magazine, and elsewhere. She is a doctoral candidate in English at Wilfrid Laurier University, and the curator/co-founder of Balderdash Reading Series (est. Jan 2017).*

K: Can I read something back to you, that you wrote for the Invisible Publishing blog?

S: Sure.

K: This is from November 8, 2018: It says—

As someone who also writes fiction, and one who often writes of Calcutta, there is no nostalgia there. Ask my characters why they drag me to Calcutta. The Calcutta they take me to is a recreated Calcutta, a Calcutta of my characters. Some would argue it's not even Calcutta anymore, changed to Kolkata in 2001. Here, I am creating an alternate space, an imaginative space pieced together from memory and imagination.

So, yes. There is a longing. A longing to tell a story.

When I read that, it spoke to me a lot about what we're exploring in this project, because sometimes, as a woman of colour myself, I feel obliged to represent and write about a certain history or a specific community perspective, and I feel a lot of pressure about that. And I'm wondering, in your opinion, and in your experience, is there something about maintaining a connection to the past that's not desirable in telling stories? Like, something that's limiting or that begs less than a helpful representation, or perhaps unwanted responsibility on the part of the writer?

S: For me personally, I haven't felt that pressure, mostly because my desire to stay connected to India has always been there from the beginning, so it's not an external pressure that I've felt as a writer. I still visit India every few years. I still have friends there. I keep in touch with my family—my extended family, I mean—and I often write about my city of birth, again, not on purpose. It's usually culled from stories that I've heard over the years from my mother, from my grandparents, from my own memories of when I lived there until the age of nine, and from when I kept going back while I was living in Dubai and then later in Canada. I've been back multiple times. But, again, my memory of Calcutta is very fragmented, very short term. There's no continuity there. I was there until I was age nine, and I've not lived there for a considerable amount of time after that.

K: Does this topic, then, this idea of writing accurate or respectful representations, does it play at all in your approach to your work?

S: It does. I'm very worried when I'm trying to represent characters who may be different from me, either through class, disability or racial background. Because I think, as a writer, I have some sort of moral responsibility towards my characters. This might sound strange, but it's something I brought up in a creative writing workshop I was teaching at Naked Heart last year: if you cannot think of your characters as people, then they're not going to interact back with you. So I like to think of my characters as actual people, as actual lived realities. I think that's helped my writing process a lot. It makes me more mindful of how I'm interacting with my characters on the page and how the representations are coming out on the page.

K: So then, as a writer who's invested in that, and has an awareness of a moral responsibility and perception, what allows you to get to the point where you feel comfortable, or where your character feels like a real human being, so much so that you feel you're able to write authentically from the perspective of "the other"?

S: A lot has to do with just being self-aware of the different politics in writing and in representation in general. There's a lot of gender and identity politics right now, and nobody can say, "Oh, I don't know about this." There's no excuse to be ignorant. We're all so connected through the internet and social media. My own research goes into areas that are outside of myself. I'm often (I wouldn't say forced) in a position where I'm almost compelled to think about my characters in a certain way.

Of course, there are certain characters that I'm still not comfortable writing, like, I'm still afraid to write about a Black person or an Indigenous person in fiction, mostly because I think I may not be able to do justice to such a person. Even though I do have friends who are Black or Indigenous, I may not even have the right, to a certain extent, to write that.

My characters are usually gender queer, non-binary, people of colour. And usually South Asian, because that's the kind of cultural writing I feel I'm able to do the most justice to with my knowledge base, my experiences in life, my interpersonal relationships, and even the kind of community work I've done all my life—volunteer work, or in the writing community as well. So, I'll stay in that spectrum, writing about person of colour characters who may or may not be queer, which intersects with other parts of their identities, but they often are characters who have a South Asian basis in cultural identity.

K: What informs that assessment of whether we do have this right?

S: First of all, I think nobody has the right to tell you what it is that you can or cannot write.

K: I think I read that in a piece you did for *PRISM*.

S: Yeah. So, I don't think anyone has the right to tell a writer to do that. The responsibility falls on the writer to figure out if they have the right or not. I think it's more of a personal ethical dilemma of where to go and how to go.

I also believe that mere research is not enough. I used to believe that it was enough, but sometimes it doesn't translate that way on the page. I'm talking only about fiction writing at this moment. I think you have to have interpersonal relationships. You have to build community. You have to build allyships with other people who are different from you before you feel you can maybe attempt representing them in fiction. The thing is, and again, this may sound really weird, but I don't choose who my characters are. They come to me. The novel that I want to start working on, it came to me as a novel, and the characters came to me whole, and the main person who came to me is this Irish Canadian gay man. So, I mean, he's very White. I didn't pick him. He came to me. So I don't know how to frame that.

K: How would you go about writing that in a way that you feel comfortable? Is it easier because of the way it came to you, whole?

S: Well, the narrative came to me as a whole, but his voice was very distinctive. And I think I understand him because he comes from this queer background, but also because he's in academia, so I connect with the character at a different level. I've never felt discomfort writing him. I don't think I've reduced him in any way. And right now I haven't really begun to write the novel. Right now he only exists in a short story. But it's his voice that's in the short story. He's the protagonist. I don't know how it will be with the novel—we'll see. But he's in a relationship with a guy who's of South Asian origin, so the South Asian connection is there. Again it's not on purpose. It just happened to be that way.

K: You're also bringing up this reality of writing other gendered characters. This idea that you mentioned about building community with these friends that are from different perspectives—do you have friends that are Irish academics, South Asian, male, etcetera?

S: I have friends who are academics and who are white, and my character was conceived way before my sister started dating this guy, but my sister is dating this guy who is part Irish Canadian settler. His family has been here for generations in Canada. So that's my experience. I feel like I can wait for the character to tell me more about themselves, but it will come out with that process of writing the novel. Right now I only have a moment in the character's life, when the character was going through a dilemma. And that's the dilemma that ended up being the short story. But I know this is meant to be a novel. It's not meant to be just a short story.

K: Will you have sensitivity readers who will read your work before, or as part of that editing process?

S: I don't know. Here's the thing—I mostly feel like sensitivity readers exist for White writers. Because people who usually ask whether they can write this seem to be White people, in my experience.

K: Why do you think that is?

S: I think because there's so much flack against what you can or cannot write. There was a huge backlash last year with this guy, I forget his name, who wrote a poem in the voice of a homeless man [Anders Carlson-Wee's "How-To", published in *The Nation*]. I think it was a White man, and he used a specific kind of dialect in writing the poem, and there was a whole conversation about how he wasn't allowed to write the poem.

For me, poetry is a different situation, and that's why I don't consider myself a poet. I think fiction allows you things like writing in dialect, more easily than in poetry, because poetry is often considered non-fiction as well. So, as I said, I believe that anyone can write whatever they want, and it's up to them, to their personal ethics, if they feel they've done justice or not. But I think the most important thing—there seems to be a lot of guilt, a lot of White guilt, which seem to exist among a lot of White women writers on online spaces, who are like, "I don't want to mess up," but sometimes it feels performative. They'll get sensitivity readers and then say, "I've ticked the box, so now I'm allowed to get away with this narrative," or whatever.

I think there are a lot of politics at play around the question of ethics. There are certain things that I wouldn't talk about or write about, such as Indigenous myths, for example, because I don't think I have the right to those stories. But there have been White genre writers who have co-opted them for their fantasy and science fiction stories. So I think, again, it depends on the writer.

I feel like if somebody has to ask, "Am I allowed to write this?" they probably don't have enough knowledge on that particular topic, or that particular identity, or about that particular person, or whatever they want to write about. And that's why they're asking that question, and hoping for a validation of some sort. I don't think there are easy answers to this question.

So, I don't know if I'll actually use a sensitivity reader. I know I'll ask several people to read and give me their feedback, but I think, again, an important thing to remember is that it's okay to make mistakes. There's too much of a call-out culture, where no mistakes seem to be allowed. I mean, the whole point of a mistake is that you learn and you strive to do better. I don't know how else to move forward. You have to take that into account. I mean, that's also life, that's not just writing.

K: What role do you think real world contexts play in the writing of fiction? Are there social consequences that a writer should try to keep in mind as a sort of filter?

S: I can't speak for other writers, but I know for me I'm always aware of who's going to be reading my work, and who I'm actually writing for. So I think in that sense it does matter—the social context matters to some extent. But I also don't believe in writing something for the sake of writing. I found this critique among queer stories, which is that we should write more joyful queer stories, and I see the value in that. I think it's important to represent queer characters in the context of joy, but not every story I want to tell from a queer perspective necessarily has to be connected to joy. And so, again, that's a personal thing for the writer to figure out. But definitely, I don't believe anybody should be ignorant to possible real life consequences. And I think this can only happen if you treat your characters as actual people—to respect them like you would respect a person in real life. I think that kind of mitigates the possibility of consequences a little.

K: Do you think that writing fiction can play a role in social change and power dynamics in society?

S: I guess in the long term it could, depending on the kinds of stories that are circulating. For example, if I grew up reading about queer salvation, seeing or reading about queer characters that are independent and happy and able to conquer the world, perhaps I would grow up with a stronger sense of self. So in that way, definitely, because I guess you see more of yourself, especially if you are Black, Indigenous, or a person of colour, and you haven't seen yourself (or anyone of a specific marginalized background) enough in writing from a positive light. It's harder sometimes, for a child, when you're not seeing yourself in a positive light and then you grow up almost feeling like you don't exist. So in that sense, yeah, writing fiction can make a difference in the long term. But it has to happen more. It has to happen more consciously. That's why you need different stories out there.

K: What's the role, do you think, of the marketplace? Because writing doesn't exist in a void—we have the readers, the audience (which you've mentioned). We have publishers and editors. We also have the platform of the internet and social media, which gives us more access to one another. So what do you think the role is of the marketplace and the reality of a writer having to earn a living, having to appeal to an audience?

S: I think it's important that your work sells, obviously. Nobody's writing in a void. But writing for a prefixed audience has its limits. Writing certain things just because your publisher thinks it will sell is limiting.

I can't write something that I'm not personally invested in, so I don't know how that would work for me. It's funny, there was this television show on Netflix (it's called *Friends From College*), and the second season was about this biracial guy, and he's a writer, and he's very serious. He's a literary fiction writer, and he's won all these big awards, but his agent says, "Your work's not selling, and we want to push you into young adult," which is really hard because he's not invested in it. I thought it was interesting, because personally I don't think I could do that just because something could sell.

K: Why do you write fiction?

S: I don't know. I've been making up stories since I was a kid, and I've been writing fiction for a long time, since I was twelve. So, I don't know why. I also started writing poetry when I was six. I enjoy fiction a lot more than poetry. I think fiction is forgiving. I think fiction allows me to be, allows me to experience things that I haven't or to live vicariously through my characters. Fiction also makes me feel safe. I don't know how to explain it. I love fiction. My research is also mostly on fiction. I'm not a huge fan of poetry. Although I read a lot of poetry and review a lot of poetry—I prefer fiction over poetry.

K: Do you think there's a distinction (in this area of representation of difference) between fiction and, say, creative non-fiction?

S: In creative non-fiction a lot of it can be first person, a lot of it is very personal. Yeah, I don't think you can create in the same way. With fiction you can make up anything, and you can go anywhere. That's mostly not true of non-fiction, unless you're Carmen Maria Machado, I guess, and expertly break genre boundaries. The understanding is that it's a personal experience that you're writing from. I think there's more at stake with creative non-fiction. Like I said, fiction is much more forgiving. There are a lot of things I'm not comfortable writing about, which is why I don't think I'll ever be a good creative non-fiction writer.

K: Have you ever received negative feedback related to representation in your fiction writing? Or have you ever been unsure of writing something? Have you removed something because you felt it was inappropriate? And, if so, how did you make that decision?

S: Yeah, I did receive negative feedback once when I read a short story. The thing is, it had actually been received positively before. It was a short story that was published in *Matrix* magazine (which no longer exists). It was edited by Lucas Crawford. It was a trans-specific issue, and the character was a trans female character who's also Bengali, like me, and Hindu, but she was a trans female character, and it was the first time I had written a trans character. I didn't write it because, "Oh this is hot, and I want to explore the trans body," but I remember reading it in a different setting, and there were a lot of people who were uncomfortable with the representation—"Well, you're not trans, how can you write this?" There was a lot of aggressive behaviour that I experienced in that group, and nobody came and told me directly. Rather, they behaved passive aggressively towards me. I had to go and reach out to people and ask, "Okay, what is it that I did wrong?"

The feedback was that I focused too much on the trans body. But the thing is, the way the piece is set up, there's no other way to write that piece. And the reason I focused so much on the body was because I was also writing about myself. And the reason I made it a trans female character and not a trans male character is because I didn't want anyone to know I was writing about myself.

Here's the thing: I didn't feel that I had to justify myself for writing that character, because the feedback that came back to me was that it wasn't a misrepresentation. The representation was right. It was very accurate, but how dare I write it because, "You're not a trans person." Well, you don't really know me. You don't know where I'm coming from, so I found that entire situation very problematic.

If I'm misrepresenting something, I'm always up for discussion. But, again, I don't think anybody can tell me what I can or cannot write. And this is true for any writer—nobody is allowed to tell you what you can or cannot write, but if you mess up, you should be open to criticism. Once you write something that's out in the world, it's a product that's out there and it's subject to scrutiny.

K: So then, in response to that process and being open to that criticism, to that feedback, very respectfully, do you think it had an impact on what you might write next? Or, would you choose to write that piece again?

S: The only thing I took from that was that I made the piece longer and more nuanced. But the character still exists in another story. And yeah, I've taken the feedback into account, but you can't make everybody happy with your writing. Not a hundred percent of the people are going to like what you're writing, or agree with it.

There was this one person who came up to me and talked. They were in high school, and they said, "Thank you for writing this," and they told me how they were dating a girl so that they could get away with being who they were. They were performing heterosexuality at home. And they were from a South Asian background. That made me feel good. I'm not writing for the people who are criticizing my work. I'm really writing for kids like myself who didn't see these characters growing up.

And so, for me, that's more important than the negative criticism that came my way. Because nobody asked me why I wrote this. They just decided to vilify me based on what they thought they knew about me.

K: It's not an easy task to begin with, but then, being public brings on all these other things to contend with. I'm glad you're still writing.

S: Well, I did stop writing for two months, because I was just so depressed. It took me two months to process what had happened. But then I talked to a lot of people, and I talked to my mentor, and my partner, and everybody put this situation into perspective. I realized that I wasn't in the wrong. I let up on myself. It was what it was.

K: When you're instructing and helping to guide emerging writers, does this idea of appropriate representation or respectful representation come up?

S: I'm not a creative writing teacher. I've only held two creative writing workshops. But, yeah, this question did come up. My workshop was actually about the ethics of writing as well. What came out of that workshop was that the question to ask is, "Am I destroying the humanity of my character? Am I denying the humanity of my character?" And, if you're unsure about that, then maybe you shouldn't be writing this character. Then it should be a resounding, "No." I think that's a guiding light for me, personally, when I'm writing a character.

K: Do you think this is a skill we can learn, or is it something people just generally have or don't have, in terms of being able to craft characters that feel like fully rounded humans on the page?

S: I think it's a craft. Of course, you still should have some propensity towards writing, but you can definitely teach yourself. I'm a self-taught writer. I've only been writing fiction—"good" fiction—since 2016, so definitely. The whole point is to be as self-aware as possible, and being as aware as possible of your positionality and where you stand in the privilege pyramid, and how much space you're taking up as well, as a writer. It can be hard, especially if the writer is a person of colour and has other sections of marginalized identities, because that just makes their own position very precarious. It's not easy work, but definitely necessary work. It can be learned if you're open to learning.

K: So, in your experience, how have you become a better fiction writer?

S: A lot of my fiction writing is tied to me becoming self-aware of who I am as a person, and what my blind spots are, as well as connecting to things I'm not comfortable talking about yet. The closer I come to knowing who I am as a person, the better I get as a writer. And another thing I've found is that my academic research resonates a lot in my writing—it comes out in my writing in unexpected ways. I feel that the more I learn about things, the better I get as a writer. The more I'm aware of just general things, the more I study things that I'm passionate about, the more I educate myself, the better I get as well. I don't think you can separate those things. I also think that you have to be as honest as possible to yourself. I feel that even if a person is really terrible as a person, I feel that they should be honest with themselves and say, "I'm terrible because of these reasons, because I do these things," and I think that it's very much connected to being self-aware.

K: What is your PhD research in?

S: It's in English Literature—it's South Asian Canadian Women's Literature, specifically. Again, my interest has always been in South Asian Literature in the diaspora. Even when I was a kid, I was reading a lot of South Asian writers, and I was really looking for South Asian writers as well, so that's just sort of translated into my academic interests, right from my undergrad. I'm looking at representations of subaltern bodies in the works of South Asian Canadian women writers and how that challenges the happy idea of Canadian multiculturalism.

K: Do you have any insights from that work that you feel relates to our conversation today about representation? Do you feel, for example, in your exploration of that literature, that representation of difference has been done well?

S: Well it's not so much representation of difference, but representation of all kinds of subaltern bodies. Are you familiar with the subaltern?

K: No, can you please educate me?

S: Well, according to Gayatri Spivak, a subaltern is a person who has absolutely no voice at all, but her research comes from a South Asian kind of background, because the character she talks about is a woman who kills herself, doesn't leave a suicide note, and so she says this person is completely voiceless, and that we can't really engage with the silence of the dead woman. Of course that idea has been challenged. The challenge is ongoing too. I actually identified four kinds of subaltern bodies in the work of South Asian Canadian writers: there's the body of a Muslim person, a trans person, a disabled person, and the true subaltern according to Spivak, a person who has died. I'm looking at the representations of those four kinds of subaltern bodies and seeing how those representations challenge the happy notion of Canadian multiculturalism. This idea that multiculturalism is a good thing because it unites everybody is a problematic idea, and the representation of these four different subaltern bodies in the work of the people that I've chosen, challenge that idea. The idea of a happy unified nation is a myth—it's incomplete and problematic.

Alicia Elliott

March 1, 2019

Alicia Elliott is a Tuscarora writer living in Brantford, Ontario. She has written for The Globe and Mail, CBC, Hazlitt *and many others. She's had essays nominated for National Magazine Awards for three straight years, winning Gold in 2017, and her short fiction was selected for* Best American Short Stories 2018, Best Canadian Stories 2018, *and* Journey Prize Stories 30. *She was chosen by Tanya Talaga as the 2018 recipient of the RBC Taylor Emerging Writer Award. Her first book,* A Mind Spread Out On The Ground, *was a national bestseller.*

K: Can you please begin by sharing what's important to you about the topic of writing difference?

A: Well, I think that it's something that a lot of young writers (and established writers as well) have struggled with. As attitudes change around what's acceptable, or as people who didn't have voices before are now able to speak to things that they couldn't speak to before, it kind of gives feedback. For the longest time, before social media in particular, there was kind of a wall between readers and writers, where they couldn't know necessarily what you were writing about them, or thinking about their work, because there was no space for it. Unless you were writing a review in an established place or platform, there was no way to know. And most of the people who were reviewing were from very particular viewpoints, and they didn't necessarily have the lens to give specific critiques around how accurate representation was.

In | Appropriate

Social media has changed that a lot, and it's changed the conversation around what's a good way of writing difference and what isn't. So, these kinds of conversations are very much in the minds of writers these days, and I think that a lot of people are, yes, intimidated, but also aren't really sure what their responsibilities are.

Some of them might be wanting an easy way to do this, like, "Is there someone I can just send this to, and they can give me the go ahead and then everything is all good?" But, they don't know what a work of fiction or a work of art could mean to a specific community, how it can impact the community. I think that having some sort of tool to help guide writers in the right direction, to have them start thinking about how they should do this, how they should approach it, what their responsibilities are, and about the power differential as well, would be helpful.

K: Yes.

A: Most writers are like, "I'm a writer. How much power do I have? [laughter]." But, realistically, you do have power in your words. How you portray people, readers will automatically assume that a writer has done their due diligence even if they haven't. Once it's been published, it's been through so many different eyes, and people have passed it on so far and said, "This is acceptable, this is accurate," so, by the time it reaches the reader, a lot of the time, if they don't have any other points of reference, they'll take that as truth. Having something to kind of steer writers in the right direction so they think about those things would be really helpful.

K: Can we talk about your fiction story "Tracks" in *The New Quarterly*? This is the only fiction piece of yours that I've read. Have you written other fiction?

A: I've written a few things. It's something that takes me longer to write—it's more of a process than writing my non-fiction.

K: In "Tracks", obviously, I trust you and the authenticity of the voice. I assume the protagonist, Emily, embodies what I imagine you're familiar with in your lived experience, even though it's fiction. Can you speak to how you approached writing difference in this piece? Like, you write male characters, though the point of view is still a woman. Can you speak to how you approach writing difference, and did you have any hesitations as you were crafting the story about what you shared in this piece?

A: Well, I think that it's kind of weird for me when I'm writing fiction, because it usually starts with an idea or an image or something along those lines, and as I go further into it, I figure out who the characters are and what they've been through. The nexus for that story was actually, believe it or not, a tragedy that involved a professional wrestler who had been, the night he was supposed to show up on the show, found dead in his house. He had killed his wife and his kids. There were a lot of problems with his brain as a result of numerous concussions. Before the wrestling event knew that he'd killed his family, all they knew was that he was dead. So they had a kind of tribute to him that night, and people were mourning and everything, but then once they had found out what had happened, it was like they didn't know how to situate everything.

I remember thinking, "What would you do if someone you knew did something that was unspeakable and you didn't understand it? How would you approach that situation?" The whole idea of the title too wasn't just to reference the actual train tracks in the piece, but also the way that you look for tracks that led to this outcome. So, the character of Emily is very much trying to sift through her memories and look for signs that she could have prevented this, or that she should have seen it coming, and kind of torturing herself around that.

In terms of writing difference, I think for me what's most important is thinking of your character as a person. You know, a person isn't perfect. Like when I started writing the piece, I didn't know that Emily was having an emotional affair with the husband, but that's something that I figured out as I was going through the piece and getting to know her character. It was a process of trying to figure out what this looks like, what this person would remember, what this person would feel bad about or feel angry about. There are moments where she's angry. There are moments where she's sad. There are little moments of joy where she's a little bit happy, but it's tinged with sadness because of the tragedy that's kind of in the background.

I made a very conscious decision not to reveal what had happened until closer to the end, just because I feel like when you hear that someone has done something like that, you automatically have certain assumptions that you bring to the person. I wanted to really establish relationships and characters without having that kind of stigma hanging over them, so that you get to know the character, get to know the situations, before you know the tragedy that bookends everything. And I think that was me thinking, "What do people think about this, about someone in this situation?"

K: Yes.

A: Taking aside the fact that it's about an Indigenous woman, you know, anyone who's in that situation is going to be looked at in a specific way, especially a mother. I was very conscious of how people would look at her and judge her. Knowing this information was going to taint everything, I wanted to hold off, because I wanted there to be this knowledge of people mourning her, and that she was someone worth mourning.

K: Did you consider the impact of your writing on different communities?

A: I don't know exactly why, but [laughter] there is more of a pull for me towards stories that are really difficult and stories that are really tragic. I knew that in Indigenous communities, specifically Six Nations where that story is set, there's a lot of tragedy playing out, very regularly. There are suicides, drug overdoses and stuff like that, and there are some people I know who go to funerals very regularly for family members, to the point where it seems like it just never ends. There doesn't seem to be a moment of peace where they're not mourning someone.

And so I was trying to be very conscious of that while I was writing it. It was important for me to make the reader feel a sense of loss the way that Emily felt a sense of loss, the way a community would feel a sense of loss—making a character who felt real, and felt vulnerable and was strong sometimes too, you know, someone that wasn't just a flat character. I wanted that, because those are the types of women that I know. Those are the types of women who I wanted to go behind these headlines, where we don't really see more than the tragedy. So I wanted to kind of look at what this would be like in very close quarters with this one particular character.

Intergenerational trauma was something that I was mindful of when I was writing it as well. Emily's dad went to residential schools and also died when she was young. I think these kinds of things all have an impact. I wanted to show that trauma in a real way as opposed to just talking about it, showing how it plays out. Even though I was writing about something that was very sad and very tragic, I also wanted you to feel for her as a character, not just as whatever you would see in a news story. I wanted you to feel the emotions that she would feel. And I wanted people from my community to read it and think, "I know who this person is. I feel her loss, and I feel the complexity of the situation." Because these situations can be very complex. Just looking at something and simplifying it and saying, "That was a bad person. That was a bad mother," or "What was wrong with her? She was crazy." All these things aren't helpful. I wanted to contextualize someone in a very specific way that made them realistic, made them feel human, made them feel like they were worthy of empathy and worthy of being mourned.

K: Yes, some of that depth was beautifully written through the boundary created around April Hopkins as the reporter for *The Star*. I felt that this was a really important element. Because there was an understanding of the reporter's efforts to be balanced, but also, clearly, her intrusiveness, and then the clear boundary around her role, and then onward with the story.

A: Yeah.

K: I think that would build trust in the reader for sure. As you said before, having a voice in this whole process is just much more possible nowadays, but it hasn't always been like that. And, it still isn't always, because at times an audience will only pay attention to a very narrow stream of information. But yeah, that was a great scene.

A: Oh, thank you.

K: Will you continue to write fiction? You spend most of your time writing non-fiction.

A: Non-fiction just comes to me easier, so I can write it faster. With fiction I feel like, even if you're basing it in the real world, you're starting with nothing. I like to really think about who the characters are, what situation feels realistic to them, where they're going to start, where they're going to end, and how I want the story to unfold. There are so many moving parts that it takes much longer for me. I am still working on fiction, but it just takes a long time for me to feel like something is complete and ready [laughter]. When I'm working with creative non-fiction I already have all of the pieces. It's just a matter of assembling them.

K: Do you think that fiction still has an important responsibility, then, in terms of accuracy and authenticity, its reach and the part it plays in dynamics of power and influence?

A: I think that it does, especially in specific communities. The ways that we get stereotyped really are kind of reflected in various forms of media, whether it's TV, movies, books, whatever. There's something about those representations. When you don't have any other way of knowing whether those representations are accurate or not, you're just going to assume they're accurate. And so, if someone hasn't done their due diligence and they just kind of write whatever they think is accurate and then unknowingly reinforce stereotypes, for example, then that can feel to someone who doesn't know anything other than stereotypes, accurate or authentic. That is, someone who knows that those are stereotypes will read it and say, "That's not actually—that's not it at all" [laughter]. But someone who is uninformed might think that stereotype is authentic because it rings true for them, it feels familiar, even if it's not real [laughter].

K: Like a rumour that you've heard so often that it begins to sound true to you.

A: Yes.

K: Do you have any suggestions about how to write difference well?

A: Well, I think that the first thing writers really should do, which, I think—I wish that more writers did this—is ask themselves why they're telling this story, and why they want to tell this story, what they want to bring to it. You have to be honest with yourself. Just because something is a cool idea doesn't necessarily mean that you're going to do it justice.

Everyone likes to think they're the best writer or they're the one for the job or the story chose them. But, that's not accurate. A story isn't going to choose you—you choose to tell the story. You choose to sit down and write it and edit it, go through all these hours and hours of work. That's something that you're choosing to do. You do have the option of choosing not to invest all of your time and energy into something if it's maybe not the best fit. If, for example, I wanted to write a piece set in South Africa during apartheid. I've never been to South Africa. What I know is what I've read, which isn't a lot. Then why am I wanting to write about South Africa and apartheid?

K: Yeah.

A: Is there something in particular that to me is interesting in terms of how it's similar to situations of Indigenous people in Canada? Or is that going to be what I bring to it? Or, is it going to be something else? There are all these questions that you have to ask yourself. Just saying, "I want to write it," isn't necessarily a good enough answer.

If you're only writing it because you want to write it, and not because it's something you want to get right, then I also feel you're not going to write very good fiction. There's this idea that, just because you can do something you should do it, and I don't think that's true. You really need to be self-aware to write good fiction, and that means knowing what your motives are in writing.

If I wanted to write about South Africa and apartheid, how would I go about doing that? Well, reading about it is one thing. Going to South

Africa to talk to people who had been through it would be something else—developing relationships with those communities so that I can understand, because reading something in a book is not going to be the same as going to those actual places and talking to those people. Even if you're just doing an interview with them, that's not going to be the same as developing relationships with people, where they trust you and can be vulnerable with you and you can see the complexity of their situation in a way that you wouldn't if you were just reading an article about it.

Those are the layers of depth that, I think, if you're writing any fiction, you should be aiming for, but especially if you're writing about a community that's not your own. In a sense, you're taking their stories. So, I think that you need to honour them by doing it right, giving back to that community by trying to accurately reflect what their experience is. Or, as much as you can, making it something that when they read it they'll feel represented. They'll feel like you did a good job, not that you just came in, took the story and then left. Kind of like a miner—you just come in, mine it and then go.

K: Right.

A: The thing that people don't think about is that, when you're not a part of a community, that's kind of a luxury, in a way, because if you do wrong by that community, you can just go.

K: Yeah, there's no risk. There are no stakes.

A: Yeah, exactly. You could just leave, and you've already gotten the story. You've written it. It's in the world. You don't have to listen to them. If you don't want to talk smack on social media, you can block them, make your account private, shut those people out. If you're from a community and you're writing about that community, you can't do that.

K: Right. Big difference.

A: If you're going to do that, you have to be willing to hear other people and lessen the chance that they're going to react that way by doing the best job that you possibly can to represent them. It's good to have sensitivity readers, but I feel like if you're doing a really good job of creating community with whatever group you want to write about, you shouldn't need sensitivity readers by the end. You should have already created those relationships and understood the situations and specific kinds of struggles and things that people go through, so that you can put that in your story in a complex and respectful way. By the time you're done, if you do have sensitivity readers, there's not going to be an issue.

I think that's what people don't understand. They're like, "Well why do I have to do all that work to write something?" If you don't want to do all that work, then why are you writing it?

K: And why are you a writer, because honestly, this is the hardest work I've ever had to do [laughter]! There's so much work that goes into every sentence.

A: If you're researching something, say, for example, you want to write a story about a scientist, a neurologist. You would do a lot of research. You would talk to neurologists. You would go into all of these things. And I don't understand why people can understand that, but they can't understand why that would be the case also for other areas of difference, like race or disability or gender. You know, these are things that you also don't have access to—the knowledge that would have come from that lived experience. So, you should be going and doing the research for that, the same way you would be doing research for any other subject.

K: So, if we do it well, is that enough? There seems to be a kind of spectrum of respect, where even if you do it well there's still some tension around, "Do you have the right to do it at all?"

A: That's always going to be a personal question. I can't answer for any particular person or particular situation. I think that's why it comes back down to, "Why do you want to write it?" If you're really aware of all of these things, and you come to a realization that you care so much about writing this well, and you care so much about this community and giving them a platform, in a sense, then, you know, that's great. But I do think, personally, that this comes from community mindedness. It comes from being in community.

If you're going to write this and write it well, I also think that you need to maintain the relationships that you've created as a result of doing that research and trying to figure out how to help them in certain senses. It shouldn't just be, "Okay, I've done what I've needed to do, now I'm going to get out of here forever." I understand that this is a lot to ask of people, and at the end of the day, it comes down to what you're comfortable with. If you're comfortable with going in, getting the story and then leaving, then that's what you're comfortable with. But that also means that if people criticize you for it, then you should know you're going to have to deal with that. And if you don't want to deal with it, then you have to go to bed at night and be okay with what you did. And if you're not okay with that, then you have to think about why. Why aren't you okay with it? What could you have done differently? And bring that with you to the next project.

I don't think that there's a perfect way to do things. Everyone is going to make mistakes, but you have to be humble when you're writing about a community that's not yours, and open to criticism, because that's ultimately going to make you a better writer.

It's the same way that we get our work critiqued and then edited, and we revise and come back stronger. I don't see why that's a problem for cultural elements, you know? Or, writing difference. It should be something similar. If I'm not doing it the best way possible, if it can be improved, I would want it to be improved. And if that means that it takes longer, then it takes longer. And if it means that I'm writing and I know I'm going to come back to this community and I've developed relationships with these people and they have problems with it later, I'm going to listen to them. I might say, "I did my best when I wrote this, but it's come to my attention that there are certain parts of the book that aren't the best." No matter how many people you talk to, it's never going to be representative of the entire group.

K: Right, there's diversity within every group.

A: Yeah. You could have ninety percent of people enjoying how you wrote about something and still have ten percent of people who read it from that community who didn't like it, and that's okay. Not everybody has to like your work; not everybody has to agree with it. But I think it's important to listen to their perspective and see what their opinions are on your work and not say anything back right away [laughter]. I think everyone has a tendency to immediately defend themselves. Just listen. And then get mad in your head, and then think about it over the next little while, and see if there was something there. And, maybe, you just take that with you to your next project.

Everyone's going to make mistakes. Everyone makes mistakes even when they're writing about their own culture, or their own situations. I think that just writing with care and open mindedness and being humble is important.

K: You said earlier that we really need to ask ourselves why we're writing something. If a writer's answer to that question is, "I'm writing it because it's fun, this is a craft and I'm really good at this and it's entertaining"—is there any place for that?

A: People are going to do whatever they're going to do [laughter]. If they're going to get published, they're going to get published. But I think that, to me, that's very naive thinking. People who think that way lack a certain self-awareness that I feel always comes across in writing.

The best writers, to me, are often those who are very thoughtful about their role in the world and their responsibility as writers. And there are those types of people who always think about their rights as writers: "I have a right to write this. I have a right to freedom of speech. I have a right to imagine whatever I want and publish whatever I want." Fine. That's fine. But you have a responsibility as well. And if you're choosing to write about this, that means you're also choosing to take on the responsibility that comes with portraying a community that's not yours, and, like I said before, you can choose to ignore that, but the reality is that we're living in a world where people can speak back to these representations in a way that they couldn't before.

To some people who aren't used to being criticized, criticism feels like censorship, but the reality is that their work has been published. That's the opposite of censorship. People who are asking you to do a good job in your writing, that's a form of criticism, saying that you didn't portray this accurately—"This is a very shallow depiction of a Black woman," or "This was a very shallow depiction of a trans person," or "This is not how this is. This is gross, the way you focused on this as opposed to that. It didn't feel authentic to me, as someone who has that lived experience."

Because it's all based on identity. People seem to measure it differently than if you were to criticize plot or character, or any of these things. For some reason that's legitimate, a legitimate sort of criticism. But criticizing your portrayal of difference is not. And I think that comes from a very privileged place, where someone has never had to think about that before. It's also careless in a way.

So, if you do have those ideas, fine, but that means people are going to criticize your portrayals, and they have every right to do that. So, if you don't like it, then maybe you should have done a better job when you were writing it.

K: Right. And chances are that criticism just isn't going to impact them anyway. But, hopefully it will broaden awareness in whoever is paying attention.

A: Yes. No one is going to stop that person from doing whatever they're going to do. Those types of people have written pretty much all of the books [laughter]. They continue to get published. There's no barometer for "How well did you do?" at the moment.

K: That brings up the broader context of publishing and audience and marketplace. There's so much in this network and the processes involved, such as hiring practices and publication choices. That kind of change can take a while. Have you noticed a change in the last few years?

A: On the business end of things it's been very slow changing. Who are the publicists? Who are the editors? Who are the people who are hiring? Who are the people at the top who are in charge of publishing? Who are the people who are in charge of advertising? Designing? All of these things are part of what goes into publishing.

By and large, the people who are doing most of those jobs are straight people, White people. I think a lot of women actually work in publishing, so I don't want to say necessarily just men, but very much cis people. Usually able-bodied people, people who are neurotypical. They hold a particular view where they might not have that much access.

I'm not talking about someone who's wilfully ignorant. Sometimes you don't have access to being around certain communities. Say you came from a small town where it was mostly White. There are things that very much colour your view of the world, and not all of it is necessarily your fault. But you also have to be aware of that and the fact that if you've never been, for example, around lesbians, but you're reading a work that's portraying a lesbian protagonist who has a lot of friends in the lesbian community, you might not be the best person to assess how accurate that is as a depiction.

You can read it, and assess it based on craft level, on character, but it would be good to have someone who has more experience than you to ask, "Is this on the up and up?" or "Is this offensive?" Because being able to say, to admit, that you don't know something—a lot of people are scared to do that—but I don't think that's a bad thing. That's evidence that you're self aware, that you're willing to acknowledge your limitations and ask for help.

I do think that in the past couple of years people have become more aware that authors who are coming from different viewpoints and different identity axes are creating in ways that are different. For example, if you're an Indigenous woman, you're writing in a way that's totally different about topics like sex or gender or going out dancing or stuff like that. You're writing about that in different ways than a White woman would. Or someone who's trans will have different ways of thinking about things and creating than someone who's cis.

I think that there's more openness than there has been before to people from different viewpoints, and there's a hunger for stories told by different people who have different perspectives and different approaches to craft.

In | Appropriate

I read so many books by Indigenous authors last year. That was a conscious thing. I wanted to read a lot of work by Indigenous writers, and it was all so different. The idea that just because all of the writers can be identified as Indigenous doesn't mean that their stories are going to be the same or that they're going to use the same structures or that they're going to have the same prose style or the same kinds of characters. It's silly. You know, you read Billy-Ray Belcourt's poetry and how different it is to Katherena Vermette's poetry or to Arielle Twist's poetry. There are differences, and the fact that publishers are starting to recognize that is great.

There does need to be more space for different people on the business end of things as well, because just like in writing, someone who's had different lived experience can bring something new that people who don't have that experience couldn't necessarily see. That's also the same in all other aspects of publishing. So things like editing or design and stuff like that—these are things that other perspectives would probably bring richness and uniqueness to as well. But, I think, for the most part, that it's going in the right direction. It's slow moving, but there are more people from different perspectives getting published. I'm hoping that means there's going to be more people on the business side of publishing that are going to be diverse as well.

K: Where is this leading us, do you think? What is the take-away as this equity becomes more embedded and deeper?

A: Well, I think that some people—and I understand this because I get scared to write about my own community [laughter]—might feel some anxiety. But when you're worried about what the response is going to be, that usually means you're going to put more care into making sure it's done well. All of this pushes people to creating better, richer work, more complex work, work that goes beyond stereotypes or clichés. Asking these questions leads towards better work in general.

K: Right.

A: I don't want to say that it's going to be easy, but nothing about writing is easy. You need to be very aware of how you fit into this and what you want your legacy to be, really. At the end of the day, even if only a few people read your book and it's not lauded with a ton of commercial success, if someone comes to you and says, "You wrote in a way that I felt in my bones. I felt so connected to it, and it really gave voice to an experience that I haven't really been able to articulate. I really appreciate that you did that. It made me feel validated," that kind of a response is success as a writer.

To me that's the best response you could hope for. And anyone who isn't hoping for that kind of response from their writing makes me question why they're writing. Why wouldn't you want someone to say, "Oh my god, you wrote this so well that it felt exactly like an experience I had," or "I can't believe that you wrote this. It feels so good to be able to read this." These are the kinds of responses that you can't necessarily measure in numbers. It's not going to be reflected in an award or tons of fame or fortune. It's writing. It's probably never going to be that profitable. But there's a reward there that you wouldn't have if you weren't doing good work.

K: Yeah. It drives towards connection and meaningful communities, and it's not so much about profit or short-term, superficial benefits.

A: When you do write something good, people who've actually experienced it are like, "Yes, this is it. This is how I felt." That does lead to better work. And sometimes that means more success, and sometimes that means getting other recognition, like awards or whatever. Like I was just thinking of David Chariandy's *Brother*. Even though David's never been through that exact experience, he portrayed it in such a way that you felt so much emotion. You cared about the community, and you cared about the brother who died, and David had a lot of success with that book as well. I just think that people want to read those kinds of stories that feel authentic. Authentic in terms of feeling human as opposed to feeling wooden like a stereotype.

K: Do you think that readers consume fiction differently than creative non-fiction?

A: Oh, absolutely. I think the whole point of fiction is to weave a world where it's almost like you don't see the mechanics at play, the craft at play. When you're reading a really good novel, you get swept away in it, and at a certain point you're not thinking, "Oh, how is the plot progressing?" or "Why would they pick this kind of structure?" or "How did they craft this character?" That kind of stuff all falls away when you're reading really good fiction. And that's the whole point—to make the craft almost invisible, even though it's very time-consumingly created. If you're reading good fiction, you're not necessarily going to stop every few seconds and ask, "Is this actually realistic? What does this mean in a socio-political context?" You know what I mean?

K: Yes.

A: Those things aren't going to happen in the same way as when you read creative non-fiction. A lot of the time, even the knowledge that this is something real gives you a different lens through which to read it and think how it relates to the real world as we know it. Does this challenge some of my views of this particular experience or does this feel real? Is this something I've experienced? The knowledge that it's real turns a certain switch in your mind where you're going to be more critical than you would be in reading fiction.

K: What I'm getting from that is that we're just more conscious when we're reading creative non-fiction, but that fiction kind of goes straight into our subconscious. We just kind of absorb it without boundaries.

A: Yeah, absolutely. That's been my experience of reading fiction versus creative non-fiction. I'm sure there are all sorts of different experiences of reading it, but that's what happens for me.

K: From that perspective, it almost seems that there's a greater responsibility to be mindful of the context in fiction writing than in creative non-fiction writing.

A: Yes, because people are going to absorb it without even necessarily stopping to think, "Is this a stereotype?" And when you're writing about a different community, and then someone comes from that community, they're wanting to have an immersive experience. But when there's those little things like stereotypes peeking out or racist language that's used in a problematic way and not as part of the story, those things pull someone out of it, where all of a sudden they're like, "Hey, I was just here to read this."

And that's where, as a fiction writer, I think you fail—if someone is reading that, and then they say, "Okay, this doesn't make sense" or "Okay, this is obviously not written by someone who's from this community, or who's lived this experience." You can tell. So, that's the kind of thing you don't want to create in your fiction. And if you're wanting to be a good writer, then that means you have to do your due diligence.

K: Is there anything that we haven't talked about that you'd like to? Is there anything we haven't touched on that you think important to include?

A: I think that maybe I just want to stress that this issue is scary, because the scariest thing is the possibility of people saying, "No. No, you shouldn't write this. No, this shouldn't be something you write, this isn't your community." And, realistically, if that is the worst thing that can happen, then it's not really that bad [laughter].

And people forget that. They don't really think about what the worst case scenario is for them. Worst case scenario—people don't like the way that you've portrayed them. They tell you this. You feel bad about it, and you get angry about it, but then you move on with your life. That's really not that big in the scheme of things. Whereas, for example, if you wrote something and it encouraged people to have a really negative view of this community, and, as a result of that, they voted in an election against the interests of that community—these are things that create real world implications. Or, that have real world implications that I think a lot of writers don't think about when they consider their role. What are readers going to take away from this? If they write a trans woman as a villain, are readers going to think, "Oh yes, trans women are awful, and I don't want anything to do with them, and I'm going to make sure they don't have the same rights as me." These are the kinds of things that writers sometimes don't think about because they're so in their heads.

But you do have to think about the wider implications of your work and what a reader is going to take away from it. And if the worst thing that's going to happen if you publish that story is that trans women are going to say, "This is transphobic. It's going to hurt our actual material lives. This is a terrible climate to be publishing something like this in," you're going to be mad. You're going to feel bad about it, but it's not going to affect you at the end of the day. You're still going to get your money for whatever you've written, and you can move on with your life. Whereas that's going to have material impact on their lives that they can't just walk away from. And it's the same thing if you're asking, "Can I write a trans story?" and someone says, "Well, you treat trans people really badly, and this whole interaction has made me feel really uncomfortable," then I'm going to say you probably shouldn't be writing about trans people.

If I had a story I was going to write, but someone told me I shouldn't write it, I mean, I wouldn't like hearing that, but maybe they're saving me from writing a really terrible thing where I would have had a lot of negative feedback.

At the end of the day, we're writers. We don't just have one idea. There's a whole world of ideas around us. If one thing doesn't stick, or maybe if you write a whole novel and you're like, "This isn't working," and you put it away, there are lots of times in our lives where we've written a story and we haven't published it, or it wasn't working so we've put it away. So, if the worst thing is that someone tells you, "No, you shouldn't write that. You probably aren't the one who should write that," that's not that big of a deal. But I feel like people who aren't used to hearing, "No," or who don't think about their responsibilities, that scares them a lot.

And I get that, but there will be other ideas. There will be other things you can write. And even if someone says, "No," you could still write that story, it's not censorship. But then, you've already got that answer from someone, so you really shouldn't be surprised if it offends people and they voice that displeasure. You really shouldn't be surprised.

K: As you were describing that, I had this thought of a scientist whose science is then used to build weapons. And then, what's the role of that scientist? What do you do? It's out there, and then you have a lot of regret, maybe, if you have any feelings about it at all.

A: I guess it would depend on the situation. There are people who live to regret things they've done.

K: Then you apologize and you make amends.

A: Yeah, or you try to make amends to the people however you can, like if it means you say, "Wow, I feel really bad about this. I'm going to try to make sure that this book isn't published anymore, not in print anymore." Those are decisions that you can make or not make, depending. That's a thing I think a lot of people forget about too: often the people who voice displeasure don't have a lot of choice in the matter. They're just telling you their opinions, and there's not a lot that they can do about it other than just tell you their opinion. It's up to you what you do with those opinions. If you decide not to do anything or if you decide to do something, those are your decisions.

That person criticizing you doesn't have the power to do much else other than criticize you. Yes, that feels bad, but that's all that it is. As opposed to you hearing it and then saying, "I don't care. I'm just going to keep getting invited out to speak about these issues, even though I'm not from this community, even though I wrote a problematic thing. I'm going to keep going out and doing speaking events." Well then, if people come and show up, protest at your event or confront you in a Q & A session, then these are consequences of those choices. Even if you don't accept them, they're just going to happen. At this point you really should be expecting them.

Arif Anwar

March 8, 2019

Arif Anwar is an author, professor, and international development professional and technology expert. His first novel, The Storm *was critically acclaimed by the* New York Times *and published in multiple languages. Arif's work has appeared in* The Daily Beast, Vice Magazine, Electric Literature, Dhaka Tribune *and* The Daily Star. *He has also authored and co-authored a number of academic works. Arif has worked for BRAC, the world's largest NGO. Based in Bangladesh, BRAC works in issues of poverty alleviation, including micro-credit, education, public health and agriculture. Currently, Arif is working on his second novel and a short story collection, while working as an instructor at The University of Toronto and Adjunct Professor at Notre Dame De Namur University in California. He lives in Toronto.*

K: In your novel, *The Storm*, your characters are of British, Burmese, Japanese, Indian, Bangladeshi and American descent, if we're looking at ethnicity, but there are also differences in time period and gender. And the setting is in a horrific disaster, so the emotionality around the event is complex. What's the risk in setting a novel in the context of such a horrific disaster?

A: I can tell you some sort of concrete real world risks in terms of the book being out there. When the book came out in the States, a really large retail book chain—I won't name who they are—essentially said they didn't want to buy any copies of the book because, "Books based on disasters don't sell well." Then the reviews started hitting, and they were positive, and then this book store chain grudgingly said something like, "Okay, I guess we'll buy a hundred copies," and then it went up from there.

I think the risk of setting the novel in a disaster is that it might be perceived as being exploitative. And, you know, your intention isn't, "I want to write about this big disaster, and that will make me rich and famous," that sort of thing. But the reason I set the linchpin of the novel as being the 1970 storm was that, even in Bangladesh's own history, because the liberation war of 1971 followed so quickly after the storm in 1970, there actually was a synergistic relationship between the two events—the liberation war followed so quickly that our own knowledge of the storm of 1970 and its place in our history books has faded somewhat and has been relegated as secondary to the 1971 liberation war.

Not only is this probably the greatest natural disaster of the twentieth century, if not of all time, but barely anyone outside of Bangladesh has even heard of it. Even in Bangladesh our recollection of it is vague, and it's only ever discussed within the context of the 1971 liberation war. So my intention with the book was really to say, "Hey, this event that happened, it was very formative for the new nation. We should really look at it. We shouldn't just forget that so many people died in a matter of hours." And we don't really talk about it anymore. I thought our attention needed to refocus on that event—Bangladeshi attention and international attention.

K: With that intention in mind then, it seems that historical accuracy, even though it's fiction, would have been a really important thing for you.

A: To an extent. I've always believed that in historical fiction the story line shouldn't shape itself strictly to the shape of historical events in a way that constrains the story. I mean, there are limits to this—I can't say that World War Two started in 1940 instead of 1938 because it suits my story—but I did take some liberties with historical events. The epicentre of the Bhola Cyclone, hit in Bhola, which is still the coast of Bangladesh, but it was a little bit farther to the east. I set my story in Chittagong, which is a little farther to the west. The dates match up. And actually, in my novel it's never explicitly said that it's the Bhola Cyclone, but it's inspired by it. And I wanted to look at the stories of people's lives who it might have been caught up in its path.

If I can mention an historical event to the extent that it gets the reader interested in researching more about it, then my job is done. Nowadays we all have cell phones, and we can look things up in five seconds. And people can get way more detail than I can ever give them, and it becomes tedious to read something, unless it's an historical non-fiction book, in extreme detail. So my job is to give the outline of an event and the overview of an event, and hopefully get the readers interested in it.

K: This brings us also to the idea of the responsibility of fiction authors. Where does that lie in terms of representing difference? You've mentioned that the creativity of the story has a role, so we don't want to be too rigid. But where does our responsibility lie? What is the difference in the consumption of fiction as opposed to other forms of writing?

A: I think the simplest difference is that we primarily read fiction as a form of diversion and to entertain ourselves and in some ways, perhaps, to step into the shoes of someone we would never otherwise be able to step into. There's not the expectation that fiction will be rigorously fact checked. Or that it will be held up as a citation of actual events or as research material. That said, I do think it's actually easier to lie through non-fiction and to mislead through non-fiction than it is through fiction, because I think you can always marshal facts and statistics to shape a narrative through non-fiction in a way that's very difficult to detect. But the insincere, agenda-ridden fiction book—people will sniff something wrong with it right away. It's very hard to fake, in fiction. It's very hard to have an agenda. Readers see through it really quickly. So, in many ways, I think fiction is a more effective vehicle for truth than non-fiction.

K: I once went to a writing workshop with Lisa Moore, and she related how she'd once written a character who was unfaithful to his partner, and then all of her friends started looking at her husband differently. She actually had to say, "I wasn't writing about my husband." What can be said about the consumption of fiction and its impact on an audience in terms of their thoughts and perceptions about the author's life?

A: I think that it's very difficult not to do that, because it's very difficult for writers to look outside of their own environments and experiences when writing fiction. Of course, it doesn't mean that Lisa Moore's husband actually cheated, but what was the inciting incident that would have her envisioning a scenario where she would contemplate writing about it? As writers it's almost impossible for us to write about anything that hasn't been coloured by incidents in our own lives or by people we've met—aspects of our own lives. I do think every character I write is an aspect of me or is a version of me, with perhaps one of the characteristics exaggerated to an unrecognizable extent. Or a character is a way to explore a solution or a pathway not taken in life. It's normal for readers to make that assumption, but that doesn't make it true.

K: So, then, how do you approach writing such diversity in your work? How do you attempt to find authenticity in those voices? Again it was British, Burmese, Japanese, Bangladeshi, American...

A: Well, a funny thing happened. A British website had a review of my novel a couple of months after it came out, and it was actually a very complementary review. But, at the end of it, the reviewer said, "I don't know about the British characters in the novel. They seem sort of stereotypical to me." I laughed and thought, "This is great," because brown people have been complaining about British writers writing stereotypically for so long, and now we've managed to turn the tables. So, all is well with the world. I think if we take being perfectly accurate and authentic and true to a certain culture or ethnicity to the logical extreme, then we can never write about anyone but ourselves. And I really don't want to live in that sort of a world.

I do think that writers have to give themselves the permission to do that, and they have to be prepared to be criticized for it, because no matter what, they probably won't capture an accurate picture, no matter how hard they try, no matter how much empathy they approach the subjects with. I tried to read as much as possible about the characters that I wrote about. I read diaries, journals, books, history books. At some point, you start to picture yourself in those situations, from those perspectives, in those scenarios, and you start to get a sense of that world.

For the Japanese soldier, I read very long books about the Japanese invasion of Burma. I read the actual journal entries of Tokkotai or Kamikaze pilots who were about to go into war, and these were young men really in the prime of their lives who were suddenly faced with their own mortality. Not just their mortality, but the fact that they would have to kill themselves. And, when that happens, a lot of the externalities of race or a culture or a country fall away, and you're stripped to your human core. And that's what I was looking for with every culture that I wrote about. It was about that human core. What makes us human.

K: What influence do you think fiction writing has on social dynamics in the real world? You admire Tolkien and Stephen King, Atwood and Mistry. Do you think their novels can have an influence?

A: Yeah, yeah, I do. It's a medium of mass market consumption. It might be easier to talk someone into reading something saying, "It's just a story," than it would be to say to someone," Read this, you'll learn something." It's a way for us to imbibe certain things about the world that we wouldn't otherwise be willing to imbibe. Monica Ali wrote that book called *Brick Lane* in the early 2000's, and it was about this Bangladeshi community in London's East End. And for good or bad, whether accurate or not, the inner workings of that community, were laid bare to a much broader worldwide audience.

I wonder how much exposure that community would have gotten—about the inherent inequalities of that community, their struggles, their challenges—how much the world would have taken an interest in that topic, if she had done a doctoral dissertation on that community instead of writing it as fiction. So, I think the role fiction might have is that of finding a wider audience for a particular community or situation that wouldn't otherwise be found, because it's being repressed or isn't in the mainstream.

K: Do you think there's a difference in the reception of a story if it's from a widely published author who's won a lot of prizes versus a new voice?

A: Definitely. I think you have that built-in cachet when a story is from an established author, versus a new voice. And not only just a new voice, but a new voice that has had no previous connections to the writing community, like mine. I hadn't published a single thing, a single piece of creative writing before *The Storm*. I didn't have an MFA. I didn't really know anyone in the writing community. I didn't know any publishers. I didn't know any literary journal editors. I didn't know anyone.

K: So, how did it happen?

A: You know, as they say, a little knowledge can be a dangerous thing. I just said, "I'm going to write a novel." I wrote an unwieldy, bad one. Then I did a hasty second draft, and I sent it out to a bunch of agents and started dreaming (delusionally) that I was going to become a famous author. And, obviously, that's not how it works.

The rejections started piling up and whatnot, but thankfully this one wonderful agent in New York City, Ayesha Pande, she really liked it, and she gave me a chance. We got together, and then there was like a year and a half of just incredible amounts of rewriting before we sent the book out into the wider publishing world—to publishers in Canada and the United States, and lo and behold, they liked it too. Then I had to rewrite it again to make it better.

There are some new authors (and bless them for this, because they were astute enough to plan their careers this way and I didn't) who have been writing for a long time, who have been to writer's retreats and have grants and scholarships, and they could get the blurbs from the big famous authors that could help them create this sort of pre-release hype that I honestly didn't know anything about. And if I had planned my writing career better that way, maybe I would have come out with that sort of attention, but I didn't. So, maybe now I have a bit more of a foothold in the writing world. Maybe the next novel, I don't know, maybe it will have a broader reception.

K: Now, your next novel—I think you told me it's between the border of India, Nepal, and also in Ireland and Tanzania.

A: Yeah, very good!

K: I'm assuming you're doing lots of research.

A: Yeah.

K: Now, here's a tricky question. You said you'd hate to see us not give ourselves permission to write difference because it's the craft, but given that there's limited platform, and that there are people who have a larger presence than others, do you feel that there's a social or moral component to broadening that platform for newer voices who can speak more authentically to lived experience?

A: As in because I'm writing about certain communities, it's perhaps depriving someone from that community of speaking?

K: Yes.

A: Yeah, yeah, I do think so. I'm careful to consider the repercussions about the choices I make about the communities I speak about. When I wrote about a Japanese character, it's not like I'm the first person ever to write about a Japanese character, or like there aren't Japanese authors on the worldwide stage. It's not like the British authors are struggling when I wrote about a British character, and I really robbed them of their voice in the community.

So, yeah, I don't think you can divorce yourself from that and just say, "I'm going to write." I wouldn't necessarily attempt to write a novel with a Nepali character and say, "This is an authentic Nepali novel," when I do know a friend of mine who's from Nepal, and she writes about those sort of things. A character might still be from Nepal, but it might be incidental to the story yet integral to the plot. I would be careful not to frame or market a story in such a way that gives the impression that I'm authentically speaking for a community. But again, for me, I'm always looking for that human core, rather than the externalities of the visible minority status, or how they're visibly a minority or from this community or that community.

K: When you had that review, the very positive one from the British reviewer, which also said it felt as though the British characters were stereotypical, how did that make you feel as a writer?

A: I think I received it with equanimity, because I expected criticism. As I've said before, you have to let writers write about the people they want to write about, but the writers themselves have to be willing and ready to be subjected to critique and criticism for making those choices. I don't appreciate it when that criticism aims to shut down a publication or platform or stop someone from writing altogether, which occasionally happens in the young adult literature world. But I do think that writers have to approach these characters with great understanding, knowledge and, most of all, empathy. And they should still prepare themselves to be critiqued for it, because that just comes with the territory.

K: How did you prepare yourself for those critiques? Has it worked?

A: I probably didn't [laughter]. I don't think I've received a lot. Honestly, that was the only review like that, and I think I read one other review on Goodreads where they said something about how a Japanese person might feel about it. I just told myself, "That's going to come with the territory." I'm still glad I stepped into the shoes of this person and tried to bring their voice into the story, this greater, connected tale. And, I've no regrets, honestly.

K: You mentioned the culture of own voices in young adult fiction. If you could wave a magic wand and shift that a little bit, what would you suggest might help it move forward in a healthy direction?

A: I think it links back to your original question about the responsibility on the part of writers. I do think right now the issue is that there simply isn't a level platform for writers of all backgrounds. That's why some people tend to be very vocal when they feel that this already unequal platform it's getting even more unequal, when mainstream writers, or White writers, write about other ethnicities or communities.

We have to keep expanding the opportunities and platforms and acceptability of writers of colour, writers from non-mainstream communities, LGBTQ+ communities, etcetera. And it seems to me to be that it has shifted significantly in that favour, maybe not completely, but there has been a significant shift, just looking at the awards and recognition that these writers are getting. I find it really concerning when a writer is told, "You can't write about this or that, about this person or that person." In the literary world, that's just not appealing to me.

K: What's at stake here?

A: What's at stake here is that we all get locked into our own echo chambers, and that can happen just as much in the fiction world as it can happen in the non-fiction news media world. If I only get my own perspective on my own culture, on my own race, that might keep me locked in a state of arrested development. That's not going to be ultimately helpful. We need scrutiny. We need external perspectives on ourselves. That's the only way we can grow.

K: Did that process happen with you as you worked with your editors and your publisher?

A: I was very fortunate in that one of my editors and both of my co-agents were of South Asian background. I didn't have to explain a lot of stuff to them that happens in the book. They were like, "Yeah, I get it, I get it." Those who were involved in an editorial capacity who were not of South Asian background, they might have a question about a few things, and I'd say, "Yeah, that's because of whatever. That's just how it's done." And they'd be very open to it. But, I was fortunate to have that sort of understanding and support. We were all working from the same page, literally.

K: Is there anything that we haven't covered that you'd like to talk about?

A: The last thing I can say is that, from what I've observed, human tendency is to want to read about people like ourselves, and we reject the new and the strange. Fiction really is the opportunity to welcome the new and strange into our lives. I hope that it keeps the current trajectory that it has, in that lots of new voices are coming into the picture.

K: Yeah, we didn't talk at all about money, and how that impacts things. Well, I guess you did, when you talked a little about the big bookstore chain that was very aware of the marketplace and didn't want to buy your book. But it's a huge investment to write a fictional piece. I remember reading that Alice Munro said she spent an average of six weeks per short story—that's all the time she had when her kids were younger, but a novel—that's a huge investment of time and energy.

A: It is. And I think even the writers who get paid million dollar contracts—if you consider the hours they've put into that project, not just sitting down and writing, but it's been occupying their thought cycles for maybe ten years—it's not that egregious. And you know, I would love for my novel to be a bestseller and for it to make more money and to get a huge contract only in the sense that it would just give me more time to do what I love, which is to write books and short stories. It would be a means to an end, rather than an end in itself.

Michael Crummey

April 24, 2019.

Michael Crummey was born in Buchans, Newfoundland. He grew up there and in Wabush, Labrador. He has written six works of fiction, Flesh and Blood, River Thieves, The Wreckage, Galore, Sweetland, *and* The Innocents. *He lives in St. John's, Newfoundland.*

K: I listened to your Henry Kreisel Lecture on CBC's *Ideas*. In that lecture about misrepresentation of Newfoundland and its culture in the novel, *The Bird Artist*, you had said that you "felt alternately furious and demoralized and insulted" by the way the book was written. Have you spoken with the author—Howard Norman?

M: No, I haven't.

K: Do you think an author has an obligation, after the fact, to address the impact of their work?

M: I think everybody makes their own decisions on where the lines are, and the lines will be different for everybody. I have no idea if Norman would have written the book any differently if he had a notion that it might impact locals the way it has. He may have just thought, "Well, I don't really care," and that his only responsibility is to the story he wants to tell. Knowing that it upset me, for one, may make no difference to him, I don't know.

A writer has the right to do whatever they want, and readers have a right to respond as they feel, and then there's a dance between those two things. Sometimes a writer participates in the dance, and sometimes the writer just turns their back on it. As far as I'm concerned, they absolutely have the right to do that, but it does mean they're an arsehole if they do.

Part of it, for me, is a moral thing—it's about trying to be a good person in the world. And that's a different thing, not always but often, than trying to be a good writer. People may see those as completely different things. I can't. I'm not able to make that separation.

K: I'm curious about how that informs your work. Can I read a quote to you? This is from Claire Tacon, interviewed in *Queen's Mob Teahouse*. She said this about writing her novel, *In Search of the Perfect Singing Flamingo*—

> *In writing characters that were further from my experience, I felt like I had to meet three requirements. One, I had to know what I was talking about. This book involved a lot of research in many areas[...]. Two, I wanted to be accountable to the communities I was representing. Three, I need to look at how writers from within those communities have been ignored.*

Do you resonate with any of these things?

M: Yes, to a certain extent. When I'm working on a book, if I'm writing about things I'm not familiar with, or that are outside of my own experience, I do whatever I can to learn as much as I can. And I also do whatever I can to minimize my chances of getting things wrong. In my second novel, *The Wreckage*, I had a Japanese Canadian character who plays a pretty pivotal role in the book.

K: Yeah, a prisoner of war guard, right? A very cruel prisoner of war guard.

M: Yes, that's right. And that was based on a real character. What made me interested in him was the sense that here was somebody who was positioned as "the Other", who was being extremely brutal in his treatment of these Canadians, and the reason he was so brutal was because he had grown up in Canada where he'd been made to feel like "the Other"—where he'd been made to feel like an outsider. I was perfectly comfortable with that dynamic because it was based on a real situation. But then the challenge for me as a writer is, "How do I create that character in a way that feels real to a reader. And, more specifically, how do I write that character in a way that feels authentic to a Japanese or a Japanese Canadian reader?"

When I started doing the research for that particular part of the book, every book I picked up about Japanese culture started by saying,

"Unless you've been born and raised in the Japanese culture, you will never understand all the nuances of Japanese culture."

K: Wow, that must have felt daunting.

M: Yes, absolutely, it was terrifying. So, one of the things that I tried to do was to make his part of the book as small as possible. Basically just to minimize the opportunities I had to screw it up. And I have no idea, actually, how I did.

K: You've had no feedback?

M: I haven't had any feedback from that particular community at all.

K: Do you remember reading Annie Proulx's *The Shipping News*? She visited Newfoundland. I realize she has Canadian roots, but do you feel like she captured it well and accurately?

M: The published version of my lecture, "Most of What Follows is True", is much longer, and I do talk about Annie Proulx quite a bit. As I pointed out in the written essay, a lot of people in Newfoundland really hated that book.

I don't think that was at all to do with how it was written. My sense of it is that it was written from lived experience. Her presentation in terms of the place, the character of the people, and the description of the climate and the landscape and that sort of thing, I thought, was bang on. And I really like the book. I think it's a great book. What most people were upset about was the book's depiction of sexual deviance, and in particular, the abuse of children as a defining aspect of the culture of the place.

And as I say in the essay, she was writing it around the time that the big scandal at Mount Cashel Orphanage was breaking. For decades the priests and brothers who had been running this orphanage in St. John's had been abusing the boys who lived there, and everybody knew it. The police knew it, the politicians knew it, and they just kept sweeping it under the carpet. When it finally broke, it was a huge scandal here. And it was the first place in the world where the Catholic sex scandals became public.

For a while, a lot of people elsewhere dismissed it as something specific to this place and people here, as opposed to being part of the culture of the Catholic Church. We've since seen what that is and how it operates. But I think Annie Proulx's presentation of that part of the novel was deeply coloured by that scandal. A lot of people here just didn't appreciate that, at all. And it's so over the top, how it's presented. It almost reads as satire. So I'm not quite sure what to make of what she was going for there. But outside of that one issue, I feel like she really got the place in a way that seems completely opposite to what *The Bird Artist* does. My sense of *The Bird Artist* is that it was a book written by somebody who had a map of Newfoundland, and that was their only knowledge of the place.

K: Yes, and that's astounding to me, because it was also nominated for a book award. So, the people who nominate these things, do they share a role in this? A responsibility?

M: Well, I don't know. It was the National Book Award in the States, so the people who are nominating for the award—they probably knew less about Newfoundland than he did and just took him at face value.

I just heard from a woman who had me down in South Carolina to do an event. She wrote to say that when she read *The Bird Artist* twenty years ago, she just assumed that it was a fair presentation of the place. And I'm sure that, like her, the people who gave out the award had no way of knowing that it wasn't. Even if they did, they might have said that's irrelevant to the quality of this as a piece of writing.

K: That brings us to this idea of what's at stake here. And you covered this in your lecture as well—whether something in fiction is perceived as real, and sometimes it's perceived as more real because people don't have their filters on. It's consumed very innocently and naively.

In 2017 in *The Walrus* there was an article responding to the cultural appropriation issues around Indigenous appropriation in Canada. The author, Robert Jago, references the Sasquatch phenomenon in that way. He describes what's at stake, from his perspective, in this cultural appropriation climate, that Sasq'ets and Dzunukwa are some of the original stories in some Indigenous cultures where the North American idea of Sasquatch or Big Foot came from. But what's consumed more by Indigenous children at the moment is the Hollywood version portrayed in *Harry and the Hendersons*. They know that better than they know their own original story that founded the fictional character. And this has serious cultural implications for their community. So I'm wondering, then, what's at stake? And maybe we can circle back to Annie Proulx and examine that because it actually happened. If half of the community in Newfoundland didn't like it, what was at stake? What were the consequence of that?

M: Part of the whole issue of appropriation is power dynamic, in terms of what voice do people have in the world. When Annie Proulx published *The Shipping News*, part of people's response to it was defensiveness about Newfoundland being portrayed by an outsider, because there was a feeling that Newfoundland hadn't had the opportunity to portray itself. I think that a lot of the appropriation animus is driven by communities who feel like their own voice isn't being heard. And for someone else to be given a platform to present something that doesn't belong to them, when the community hasn't been given an equal or larger platform, is harmful.

And I definitely felt that then in Newfoundland. That was a time when there was almost no way for a Newfoundland writer to get published by a big house in Canada. The sense was that no one outside of Newfoundland wanted to hear a story about Newfoundland. That was the feeling among the larger publishers. So there was a sense, at the time, of actively being marginalized by the gatekeepers, and then here's an American who came to Newfoundland to go canoeing, bought a house up on the northern peninsula, and then writes a book about the place. And this is what the world sees of us, through the lens of someone from the "outside". And I think there's a very similar dynamic in Indigenous communities.

This is certainly true of the dynamic in the early days of the feminist movement, in the early days of the gay rights movement, that sense of a community saying, "We haven't been given the opportunity to tell our stories, and for someone else to do it instead is harmful to us."

K: So, given that reality—we can look back now on *The Shipping News* and see a little bit of the unfolding pattern to where we are—you have Ed Riche, Michael Winter, Janet McNaughton, Ramona Dearing, Lisa Moore, Wayne Johnston, yourself. Did it actually open the doors in some way?

M: Absolutely. I think it absolutely did, because publishing is a faddish business. *The Shipping News* not only gave the lie to this notion that nobody outside of Newfoundland would want to read a book about Newfoundland, but it actually created a market for people who thought, "Oh, here's another book about Newfoundland. Okay, I really liked the last one I read." So, we went from a situation where someone like Wayne Johnston had been publishing with McClelland and Stewart, but his novels were only published in soft cover, and he was considered and marketed as a regional writer. We went from that to his book, *The Colony of Unrequited Dreams,* being published as a lead title by big houses in Canada, the US, the UK, in Germany. And then Toronto publishers and agents were flying to St. John's to try and find the next big Newfoundland writer. It absolutely had a positive effect for Newfoundland writers. And because there's a sense now that Newfoundlanders are out in the world telling our stories and that people are learning about Newfoundland through our own writers, people are a lot less defensive about it.

K: How long did that take?

M: It's a gradual process. People still come to books written about Newfoundland by outsiders with an eye of, "Let's see what they got wrong." I still feel that way. It's because it's a complicated, specific culture, and it's really hard to get it right if you're not immersed in it. But I think there's less offence now that people's defensiveness is just about people not doing the work to know the place enough, as opposed to people feeling, "We're diminished by it," when they didn't get it right.

I think with *The Bird Artist*, part of my fury was at just how actively disinterested the guy was. Just as an example, Buchans, which is my hometown, is very close to Red Indian Lake, which was the last sort of refuge that the Beothuk had. So that's why he picked it as the birthplace for the main character's father. But I don't think he looked at any maps set in the time that he was writing about. I think he got a tourist map or something. Because Buchans wasn't on the old maps—it didn't exist back then. That's just lazy writing. It's disrespectful to the world at large, let alone the place he's writing about. And I think that kind of disrespect is going to be met with anger and frustration regardless of where the story is set or what it's about.

K: So, you were saying earlier that you respect and recognize that everyone has their freedom to make that choice—to write something lazily, or irresponsibly—and at the same time, that also invites feedback. You had mentioned in another interview, "Two faces of the Rock" in *Quill and Quire*, "The thought of sitting in a room with people I knew well and giving them my stuff and hearing what they had to say about it, I'd rather have forks stuck in my eyes" [laughter].

You admitted that getting critiques from trusted friends has now become one of the favourite parts of the writing process. How did that become the favourite part for you?

M: I guess partly just getting over a congenital shyness that I've had my entire life. And also recognizing how useful that process is. And that took a while. I started doing it just because I knew I needed to, but then I started seeing how much it improved what I was writing. It's one of the places where a book seems to take quantum leaps.

So much of writing a book is just sitting at a desk and banging your head against it for hours on end and not seeing a lot happening. But there are different parts of the process where it feels like something magical is happening, and that point where I've taken a book as far as I can, and then I'm giving it to other people and getting their feedback—that's a place where I can often make small changes that really open the book up in a way that I hadn't expected. It's also a place where I'm spared a public humiliation, you know, where someone finds something in time for me to fix it. My wife is a wildlife biologist, and she's often picking out things in the books and saying, "That just isn't right." That's a really helpful thing.

> K: In *Quill & Quire*, Ken Babstock said, in his review of *River Thieves*—

> *The household's barely formulated hostilities and passions are mirrored and refracted through any number of cultural groups forced to share an unforgiving landscape: English, French, Irish, Mi'qmaq, Beothuk, St. John's 'quality,' the dirt poor of the outports, and the British Navy all collide and are each consumed by the riptides of history.*

> So, when you were in the process of writing *River Thieves*, it's through the point of view of a settler—he unfolds the debt of obligation of the Beothuk. How did you approach your research for this work? Would you approach it the same way today?

M: I basically just tried to find whatever I could to get my hands on, everything I could find that was written about the Beothuk. I mean, there's Ingeborg Marshall's *A History and Ethnography of the Beothuk,* which is the seminal work about the archaeology and history of the Beothuk. And then there's a book called *The Beothuk, or Red Indian,* which is actually a compendium of all the writings about the Beothuk by settlers that this guy could find around the turn of the twentieth century, which was incredibly useful, because it was how people saw the Beothuk at the time. So, I was trying to get a sense of how much we know about them and how much we know about what happened to them, and also trying to get a sense of how they were seen at the time through a settler lens. I didn't want to write a book that was anachronistic in terms of how people interacted with or how they talked about or how they saw the Beothuk. And there were a couple of reviews where the reviewer felt like some of the characters had attitudes that were twentieth century attitudes, and that's absolutely false—there were no attitudes expressed by any of the characters in that book that weren't expressed in those papers that I found. Even the sense that the place belonged to the Beothuk because the Beothuk were there before the Europeans arrived—that was expressed publicly by some people fairly high up in the administration of the colony, which was a surprise to me, and obviously to some reviewers as well.

Those were the two main things I was looking for. And then also, I knew nothing about the time itself. I didn't know how settlers dressed, what kind of houses they lived in, or what they ate. My plan was to do all this research and to have a clear sense of those things and then start writing the book, and of course, I started, stupidly, writing the book almost immediately after reading Buchan's journal of the trip down the Exploits River [laughter]. I wouldn't do that again. That was a mistake, and it made the writing of the book not a lot of fun. If I were writing the book now, the book would be different, because we know things we didn't know then, and questions have been raised about some of the things that people thought, even from twenty years ago. So, yes, I think the book would be different.

K: I've heard in an interview that you just love poetry, that it's very nourishing for you to write poetry, but that fiction is kind of a slog, sometimes.

M: Yeah.

K: In your essay about poetry in *The New Quarterly* it says:

And I'm still after that as a reader, the place where meaning shimmers like a heat-haze over the world's everyday presence; seeming, at once, to rise from the details of our lives and to exist beyond them; to almost and nearly say who we are, and why. Which seems to be as much as the world is willing to offer by way of explanation.

M: Right. And when meaning is co-constructed by an author and a reader.

K: Where does our responsibility lie? Surely there's just so much that's beyond our control in terms of interpretation—how do we do this well?

M: I think part of what makes the whole appropriation discussion so difficult and so messy is that when something is well written it feels like the real world. It feels like reality. And it doesn't have to be true to the real world to feel like that. I think that's why people are so protective of the places and people they come from, because it can feel like an assault. To have somebody from the outside present a picture that feels real to the world at large but is so obviously misbegotten. I totally understand why there's so much anger about it and why writers need to be mindful of the world they're trying to portray. How to do it well? If I had an answer for that, I'm sure I'd be richer than I am.

Every writer has to find their comfort zone and has to decide what risks they're willing to take with that. Every reader will draw their line somewhere different in terms of what's acceptable and what isn't. And I don't know if there's any way to make it clearer. That messy sort of two-sided Venn diagram is as good as it gets.

The main thing is—and partly it's an education thing—for writers to realize when they're outside. I remember hearing an American writer, John Updike I think, talking about how he'd written a novel about a Black woman, about "becoming" a Black woman to inhabit that voice and experience, and about how that's the gift of a writer's imagination. And the arrogance of that, it seems to me, is laughable.

The gift of really good writers is to be able to give the illusion that they're inside the head of these characters. But not to know that there's a difference is automatically setting yourself up for failure. To not even recognize you would have blind spots in that situation is ludicrous. So part of it is to recognize when you're standing outside the thing that you're writing about, to be clear about how much you don't and maybe can't know, and to find a way to work around that.

There's a mystery writer I once heard being interviewed, and the interviewer was just shocked by how much this person knew about so many arcane subjects. The mystery writer said, "Well, for example, if I'm writing a scene in which a character is picking a lock, I don't have to know how to pick a lock. I need to know enough about picking a lock to make the reader think that the character knows how to pick a lock." I think part of the job, when writing outside of your own experience, is to be able to find yourself inside the door just enough, to open that door just wide enough to give a picture to a reader that feels true, even to a reader who lives within that experience.

That, obviously, can't involve knowing that culture completely. If you're born outside of a culture, you'll never know it completely. What it involves is knowing enough to give a picture that feels authentic to someone from within. That's a really difficult thing, and even when you do all of your work, you may not get it right. That's true even when I'm writing about Newfoundland. There have been so many times that I've gotten things wrong in what I've written.

K: And what's at stake? What are the consequences of that?

M: Well, for me, it's mostly just public ridicule. And they're small things, usually, something like whether there are honeybees in Newfoundland or whether codfish have scales (they don't).

K: Does that interrupt your artistic fervour, trying to be so careful—or, does it drive you to poetry?

M: Part of the challenge, and part of the thrill of it too, is trying to get as far inside as you can, and to know as much as you can—to be as true to the place as you possibly can be. So, it's intimidating, but writing should be, because if you're not intimidated by what you're trying to write, and if you're not being pushed into the places that frighten you, then you're probably not going to write a good book. You're just going to be repeating yourself. So that kind of challenge for me is actually invigorating.

K: Yeah, you had said in an interview when you were a Writer's Trust Fellow in 2015 that in being a writer the rewards are few and far between. Your advice was—

> *Gird up your loins, it's going to be a long haul. And whatever it is about this work that does something for you, personally, that's the only reason, ever, to write.*

Do you believe this is where all good writing comes from? And, do you think everyone writes for that reason?

M: I think that most writers do, just because there are almost no other rewards. If you're not doing it because you have to do it, then you wouldn't. That's certainly not true for absolutely everybody. For me, at this point in my life, there's an economic side to it as well. I'm writing partly because that's how I make my living. But that was never in my head when I started out, and was so far off as something that even seemed remotely possible. That would never have kept me going.

I do think there are people who would write for money who are capable of writing really great things. But that's a rare instance. I feel like ninety-nine point nine per cent of the people who are out there slogging away at it are doing it out of some inner compulsion, and that some kind of personal satisfaction is really the only thing you can count on. Everything else outside of that is just gravy.

K: Annie Proulx, when she was asked for advice for novice writers, said,

> *Don't be afraid to underpin your work with large themes. But be aware that you have a responsibility to the time you live in. A writer is an interpreter of the world, whether in small compass or great.*

She said, "Find your own way and read omnivorously." What role does reading play for you?

M: Well, I think they're inextricably linked, reading and writing. I wouldn't be a writer if I wasn't a reader. The desire to write came from my love of reading. All through my life, I've found writers who have made me want to be a better writer, or made me want to write in a different way, or made me see the world differently enough that I wanted to write down whatever that new thing is that I'm seeing. I don't think it's possible to carry on being a writer if you don't also carry on reading. Those are two sides of the same coin, as far as I can tell.

K: How do you choose what you read?

M: It's completely haphazard. A lot of books are recommended. Sometimes it's just what's on sale at the bookstore. It feels like it's completely random. And I used to worry that I was somehow not going about it in a way that was logical. But the older I get, the more I realize that what we end up reading in some ways is completely random anyway, regardless of how rigorous we are in setting up some kind of system. The books that get published and find their way into our hands—there are so many accidents. There's so much chance that leads to those books being in the world at all, let alone in your hands, that now I just take whatever comes my way. Because that does feel like how the world operates—that chance and randomness are really at the heart of everything we are to a certain extent. This idea allows for a sense of some kind of magic happening in the world.

I'd been avoiding reading Gabriel Garcia Marquez most of my life, for a lot of reasons, one of which is that I don't like reading long books, because I'm a very lazy person [laughter], but I was on a book tour for my second novel, and I was getting on a plane, and I needed a book, and *100 Years of Solitude* was on for half price because the cover was damaged. I thought, "Okay, well, everybody talks about it, so I'll try this book," and reading that novel and then moving on to all of his other books, that was one of the biggest discoveries I've made as an adult reader, if not the biggest. It's had a huge impact on everything I've written since. And, you know, that book was there at that moment, at that bookstore, with a ripped cover, and if not for that, my writing life might be completely different.

K: Is there anything else along the lines of this topic that comes to your heart or mind that you'd like to share?

M: I'm just thinking now, about some of the stuff I've said, and I think I do want to add something, and this goes back to the question of what's at stake.

In | Appropriate

You were talking about how Indigenous kids now are more familiar with the Hollywood version of some of their own stories, that sort of thing. And I think, in that particular instance, where a community, a cultural community is at risk, the stakes are way higher.

Even here in Newfoundland, there's definitely a marginalization that went on. But the culture itself was not at risk of being erased by other versions of who we are. It was more of an annoyance, more of a personal infuriation to see it misrepresented out in the world. Whereas, I think, in Indigenous communities, there's a sense that they are at risk of disappearing or being seriously diminished as cultural groups. And that's one part of the cultural genocide that's gone on for hundreds of years. And I think that's also part of the reason why the appropriation discussion is so fraught in those communities.

My sense is that for a lot of Indigenous peoples, they feel like they're fighting for their lives. And I also think that's part of the reason why any writer who isn't from those communities who's writing about them needs to be extra careful and aware of the dangers of misrepresenting those communities. When I was writing *River Thieves*, I didn't want to ever try to guess at what they thought or how they saw the world, because there's no one around now to say how they saw the world. And, to me, that felt like one more awful thing that could be done to the Beothuk. Misrepresenting Indigenous communities, whether deliberately or not, is one more thing being done to them, in a long, long, long, list of things that have been done to them already.

Ian Williams

May 20, 2019

*Ian Williams was born in Trinidad and moved to Canada as a child. He is the author of two works of fiction—*Not Anyone's Anything *and* Reproduction, *which won the 2019 Scotiabank Giller Prize. Williams holds a PhD in English from the University of Toronto and teaches poetry in the Creative Writing program at the University of British Columbia.*

K: Have you had experience in conversation, as an author, with this topic of cultural appropriation or the respectful writing of difference recently? It seems to be a hot topic in our neck of the woods. I'm wondering if you've been engaged in conversations about it?

I: Yeah. At the University of British Columbia I teach poetry. The debate is really charged in the genres of fiction and non-fiction. When we hear these conversations about appropriation, they center around taking someone's story, around authority, authenticity, and privilege. In poetry, occasionally you'll hear, "Taking my voice," but, for some reason, that's not the same as taking someone's story.

K: I noticed in your book, in *Not Anyone's Anything*, there's such a range of characterizations—you cover music and math and different genders and different ages and different cultures and ethnicities. It's really all over the map. Did the idea of potentially crossing acceptable boundaries—in taking stories or voices—enter your thinking as part of the process?

I: I wrote *Not Anyone's Anything* in 2011, and the appropriation debate really shifted after that. When would be the peak? I guess, the issue has always been a part of non-fiction, like hoaxes and things like that, people who fake their stories and whatnot. But the debate on appropriation really heated up in Canada, maybe with the Hal Niedzviecki issue [where Hal wrote a piece in *Write* magazine calling for an "appropriation prize"]. Before that, there was a kind of courtesy or common etiquette around respectful treatment of other people's identity positions, but there wasn't a law. Now I sense like we're moving towards a law, rather than an etiquette. For the stories in *Not Anyone's Anything*, I felt very free, and I still feel very free to write those stories. I think intent matters to some degree. That is, it was never my intention to be the authoritative, representative of female experience, or of the Korean experience.

Writing the very first story in the book, the title story, with Soo and Goran, meant writing from experiences very different from my own. I'm not Serbian. I'm not female. I'm not Korean. I'm not any of those things. I studied Korean; I took a couple of years of Korean language courses. I tried to get as close as possible to the inside of what the world of those characters might be. And where my labour stopped, that's where my imagination had to start. I think the problem arises when people don't do the labour. They don't make any effort toward understanding a culture, how a culture thinks, how they use language, what their foods are, their practices, the soft unspoken customs of culture. Instead, they just go straight to imagination.

One has to do one's work in advance. I think I did my work, to the best of my resources at the time.

K: In doing the work, research obviously plays a huge role, and we all do it differently. Are there any specific approaches that you found, or that you would recommend to your students?

I: Speaking to fellow writers, I think an embodied research is much better than book research. There's a time to go to the library—that's where you start off. I'm reading about Muslim eschatology right now, and what do I know about that? I'm going to start with a book, so that when I have that embodied experience, I go there with some degree of preparation. I don't go there ignorant and bumbling, asking for forgiveness, when there's basic internet research or book research that I could do. But the core research is really embodied practice.

For example, with the last story in *Not Anyone's Anything*, I had a colleague who has property up in New Hampshire, and so I went up there, and I chopped wood and used a chainsaw and did all these sort of lumberjack type things that I would never normally do. That's what it means to embody something—to go out into the world and actually face the hardship and difficulty of it. That's one way to get more sympathetically involved with your characters.

K: What's at stake? What are the boundaries? When might you say it's inappropriate? Even if you have dived into personal experience and embodied practice, is there a time when it's not appropriate to then write about it?

I: Oh, for sure, for sure. No amount of research can get you right to the soul of somebody else. We devalue people when we assume that we can know them fully. Even in the most intimate relationships, we strive our whole lives to get closer and closer, but we never quite hit the core. It's like an asymptote in mathematics; we never quite hit that axis. Especially in cases of trauma, in cases of people's personal and deep suffering, in cases of their accumulation of habitual discrimination, those things that accrue and sort of form tumours inside of us—those things are hard to represent. And to do it very casually is to dishonour that person and that group's experience. So, I could not, say, write about a genocide that is presently active that hasn't touched me or my family, or something like that. I can't guess at somebody's else's pain like that. No. It's a disservice to them.

K: Let's just hypothetically imagine that this happens. That someone in innocence, perhaps, or in ignorance, steps over that boundary in the name of writing fiction. What's at stake?

I: The surface of what's at stake is usually their reputation, their credibility, their respect or ethos as a writer. Those are the things we see played out on Twitter. But beyond the personal stakes lie larger social problems—the sense that in trying to help you've in fact reinforced the problem if you're in a dominant position. Let's presume you're a White writer who's writing about Black experience or Indigenous experience. If it's done badly, and if you've really screwed it up, there's this reinscription of the patterns of dominance and inferiority. So, sometimes it's just better to stay silent on things as writers. We're all into free expression and experimentation and all of that, but culture teaches us the reverse of that too. There's blank space for a reason, and there are oblique ways of approaching things. Sometimes the skill is not in language but in silence.

K: It takes discipline to recognize and let a piece go if we really want to write it and then realize we might be crossing an important boundary. What about the greater community within publishing, like the marketplace, the audience, the publisher, the editor? What roles and responsibilities do they have?

I: There are definitely stories that we should give up, but depending on one's relationship or orientation to the story, it's okay. If you're a journalist, and you're covering some charged situation, that's legit. You're bringing our attention to something. You're a conduit for this other story. If your intention is to silence other voices and to profit from their story by taking the storyteller's place instead of making the space available for them, that's not okay. There's a difference there.

As for editors and publishers and the marketplace, I feel like right now we're in a great moment of Indigenous revival. The industry, the marketplace, has really tried its best to bring voices to the surface that haven't been heard for a long time. But there are still forces within the structure of publishing where the same kind of patterns emerge. So, for instance, the star system emerges. You won't have a broad range of Indigenous voices. You'll have a few stars, a handful of stars, and then the other voices are still kind of excluded there. You see this pattern with a number of historically marginalized groups.

K: Yeah.

I: In the Black community we joke that Canada can only handle like three to five Black writers at a time [laughter], and you could probably name them, right? Like who are the Black writers in Canada? And I feel like the same sort of thing is replicating itself with Indigeneity. We've got a handful of writers and names that we recognize. However, when you think of the abundance of white Writers, you can keep spouting off names. They're countless. So, there still seems to be an unspoken sense of quota within publishing.

K: How have you navigated that quota culture?

I: The quota issue plays out slightly differently for writers in the academic world. I've got a public-facing professional role as an author, then I've got this other work that I do within the university as a professor. It's not entirely public. They're both work, but I do important work with students of colour, the rare ones that pass through my classroom, who are navigating institutional spaces professional codes. I'm trying to get them to feel comfortable and believe that they belong in these spaces. And that's work that's really invisible.

Students go forward, and they write their work, but they need a little bit of protection and a little bit more attention. I try to develop a kind of resilience in students—I can see their faces right now. It's a little heartbreaking. The ones who kind of show up and sit in your office, and they're not quite sure they know what they need, but they need you.

I think this millennial generation is different from my own. They're more courageous and bolder and all of that, but there's still a kind of vulnerability in them that really needs bolstering. They've got the fire and the courage, and they believe in something. That's not a clear and direct answer to what you're asking

K: No, that's great, and I appreciate the work that you're doing. I'm glad that you're in Canada again.

I: I'm happy to be here, believe me.

K: If you could make recommendations or suggestions, either to fellow professors or to those emerging student writers, what would you share?

I: I think we could avoid the issue of appropriation if we oriented ourselves appropriately to other people's stories. So, for instance, the issue of anti-Black racism can be written about from Black authors, the Black perspective, but whiteness has a complicity, has a major part—the defining part, in fact—in racism. But White people don't write about racism. So, for a White person (and this has become increasingly common in the last couple of years or so) to write about their whiteness and to write about their interactions and what racism looks like, that kind of stuff, there's enough work there to do. There's really rich material there to explore without trying to take the voice of a Black author or a person of colour. Believe it or not, I would say to a White writer who wants to write about race, you've got a story. And if you want to enter this really charged landscape, you've got a position and a place already. You have always been part of this landscape. Because you inhabit it, because it is home to you, it seems dull, but, in fact, you have a really important role in explorations of race. Maybe do that writing, from the position of whiteness, first.

K: Ian, it was such a pleasure to meet you at the Festival of Literary Diversity, and I really enjoyed reading *Not Anyone's Anything*. It was very poetic. Your short stories had so many interesting visual and structural elements to them—there was just so much that I loved. Are there other fictional pieces that you'd like to talk about, a little bit?

I: My last novel is *Reproduction*—that's the one I was talking about and read from at the Festival of Literary Diversity.

In | Appropriate

Reproduction is about a Black woman and a White man who meet and have a biracial child, and their interactions across racial lines and gender lines sort of populate the novel for the next forty years. She's also poor, and the White German man is rich, so you've got this clashing of race and this clashing of economic status and this clashing of privilege, because he inherits money as well.

So, what does that complicated world look like in the following generation where these inequities don't even out? You don't get half of your dad's wealth and half of your mom's poverty. You get your mom's blackness and your mom's poverty. I'm speaking about ideas for that book, but in fact, the characters do more than meditate on their states; they go about their business and live their lives. But those foundational inequities are always beneath their efforts. There's this energy and this kind of weather beneath it all the time.

In terms of structure, I'm really keen on that. There's a prevailing sense that the Black imagination is primarily only concerned with stories of blackness, with stories in blackness, rather than with technical stuff and form and all of that. In fact, some of us have really engineering-type minds and are actually really innovative formally. Think of Black musicians. Black rappers get a lot of flack for their content, but in fact, they're so fresh with language, compared to pop songs.

I'm pretty big into expanding what books can do, what poetry can do, and what novels can do. If I were White, I think some of the spotlight that gets shone on my blackness—sixty percent of that would get moved toward all the technical stuff I'm trying to do. I think I need to do both in my position.

K: How are you researching? Is this close to your personal experience? How did you do the embodied practice part of your research?

I: In *Reproduction*? I didn't go to any extremes, you know, get a business degree or anything like that. The book actually started with idea and voice. It's funny, with respect to blackness, as a Black man I don't need that same kind of research apparatus as I do for writing about a Korean woman. And whiteness, for better or for worse, because of its own positioning in the culture, has become a kind of default, standard language. You can't appropriate the standard. You can't appropriate whiteness. That's some of the consequences of grabbing power. You've erased your uniqueness. You've forced everyone to accept that as the standard. Yeah, so we'll take it, and we'll keep our own as well.

K: You had mentioned that it's like a sixty/forty split if people are going to be analyzing your writing about race and ethnicity, but that you feel that that's okay because, given your position, you have a responsibility. That kind of commitment to social dynamic and power structures—do you feel like writers in general have that awareness?

I: We're not all socially minded. I mean, these days, there's a lot of politically driven writing, which doesn't always make for great writing. We don't always turn to writing for an ethical compass. Sometimes we just need some light reading or entertainment or what have you. I'm not very heavy handed. I think my project is really to show the more nuanced and subtle dimensions of how race operates.

There are a lot of books that are explicitly, overtly about racial interactions and about power hierarchies. I think the work I'm most interested in, and the one that's best suited to my temperament, is work that's smaller in scale and a little bit more intimate (in the scale of story, not structure)—intimate and oftentimes, domestic. And, personal. Not large sweeping political systems, but really just, "How does a Black woman get through her life?" One day at a time, just one scene at a time. That's the kind of stuff that I'm given to.

K: Don't you think that inescapable? It's a powerful way of reflecting those larger social dynamics. For example, when I was in Portland, I had taken a lot of work with me, but I was so exhausted each evening that I couldn't do it, so I just started to put my head up and see what was around me.

I saw this play called *The Revolutionists* by Lauren Balderson—it was fantastic. She created a composite character from the Caribbean and positioned her alongside three women who lived in France during the French Revolution who were all executed in 1793. It was a satire, really well done. It was challenging. I was really impressed with that writing and was lucky to be there.

Powell's Bookstore was fabulous too. They had a book signing—a creative non-fiction memoir called *Proud* by Ibtihaj Muhammad, a US Olympic Team Fencer who wore her hijab at The Olympics. I wasn't able to go, just given the timing of it, but I was so excited—"It's happening right here, right now!" When I mentioned it to other people at the seminar, they had never heard of her. She represented their country, she had an op-ed on CNN about the controversy around wearing her hijab, and I was so surprised that none of the people I spoke with even knew who she was, let alone that she had written a book about it.

I: Yeah, so where's our attention then, right? If it's not on these things, clearly there are other things that we deem important. I think that actually speaks to the sense that these kinds of conversations about race are happening elsewhere, in the sense that it doesn't touch or impact our lives. So you had, what, three days in Portland? And some pretty significant opportunities to engage in and see these things play out, right? To see race play out. We don't have to go to Portland. In Toronto, in Guelph, in Vancouver, wherever, you just step out the door—racialized or not, if your eyes are open—you'll see the discrepancies in how people are treated and received in the world. It's just everywhere. It's an issue of whether people's eyes are open, whether they're blind or not to what is happening.

K: How do you see your role as a writer in this landscape?

I: I think my place is really inside a book. There's a seed germinating right now, and I think I'll know in the next five years what the next phase or next step is for me. But right now, I don't have the skills or the courage to kind of pursue it. But I know it's there, and it's nagging me, and eventually I'll yield and give in to it. But for right now my role is inside of books. It's not on twitter. It's not calling people out. It's not shaming. There are some writers who are just excellent at very immediate and public mobilization. They get people behind them, but that's not for me,. That's not my place.

And I think it's a bit of an illusion to make authors feel like they have to be a conscience or a voice, and an immediate one. A lot of us are much more reflective in nature and slower in pace. Ponderous. And we don't parse issues into a few characters and dole them out. We actually have to sit and expose the complexity of a problem, and that's the kind of writer that I am. Not super public and immediate and angry and righteous. I'm not a prophetic figure, calling down fire from heaven. I'm just very quietly and steadily, reliably and thoughtfully, doing my work.

Angie Abdou

July 18, 2019

Angie Abdou holds a PhD in Creative Writing from University of Calgary and has published seven books. Her first novel, The Bone Cage, *was a finalist for Canada Reads 2011. Her most recent novel,* In Case I Go, *was a finalist for the 2017 Banff Mountain Book Award in the fiction and poetry category. Angie's newest book is a memoir called,* Home Ice: Reflections of a Reluctant Hockey Mom. *Angie Abdou is an Associate Professor of Creative Writing at Athabasca University.*

K: Considering the topic of this book, writing difference with respect, can you share why you wanted to be part of this project?

A: Because we're at a point in history when we're trying to approach writing (particularly writing about race) differently, for very good reasons. The controversy I found myself in with *In Case I Go* means that I should have something to contribute to that discussion. It's something I spend a lot of time thinking about—"How can we approaching writing and research and representation differently, how can we be respectful, how can we change in the ways we need to change, but also not be so bound by rules that we lose creativity or lose our own voice or lose the ability to empathize with others and imagine ourselves into the existence of others?" There aren't any clear answers as far as I can tell right now. I think people have to be unafraid of exploring these issues in order to come to those answers. So I'm happy that people like you are taking on this project.

Part of me thought, "Well, I don't want to be part of that because I might say the wrong thing unintentionally, and I might offend someone, and I might draw negative attention to myself again and find myself in a controversy I don't want to be in, so maybe I should just silence myself." But part of me felt like I really admire what you're doing, and if there's anything from my experience that can help you find a way to some of those answers, then I want to be a part of that.

K: You mentioned the idea of trying to find a sweet spot between following boundaries and limits that safeguard respect and also allowing ourselves the freedom of imagination. That's one of the trickier spots in this conversation, and why we wanted to focus, in this project, on fiction writing. It's different from writing creative non-fiction, poetry and academic writing. One of the things you mentioned in your interview with Kat McNichol in *Dreamer's Magazine* online is that when you transitioned from academic writing into fiction writing it was exciting to be able to explore the realm of anything-can-happen in fiction. You qualified that by saying, "As long as I can make the reader believe it." I'm curious about this idea of belief. What are the social implications of fostering belief in fictitious narratives, and where's the writer's responsibility in that?

A: I don't mean, "Believe it," because they know it's made up. My son was quite young when this controversy erupted around my novel, and he said to me, "They know you made it up in your head, right?" I laughed, because his comment lightened that sense of pressure I had. Of course, we also have to accept responsibility for the things we make up in our head and put out into the world. I'm not asking anyone to believe that the events in my fiction actually happened. What I mean by belief is that the readers are willing to give themselves over to the story and invest in it emotionally as it's going on, that nothing pulls them out of the story and makes them think it could never happen. They're willing to give themselves over to the story and immerse themselves in it.

K: Good fiction does that, right? Are there any social implications to that kind of engagement?

A: Yes. It's something that I hadn't thought of in a particularly conscious way until the follow up to the *Quill & Quire* essay that I wrote. Despite not having thought in a conscious way about my social obligations, my fiction *In Case I Go* and my fiction leading up to it has mostly had a social justice bent. My social intentions for the novel were good. I guess the thought now is not just what stories we're telling or what intentions we have, but who is telling it. So one of the questions at the centre of the controversy was, "Do I, as a White woman, have any right to be telling a story that involves Indigenous characters?"

When I set out to write *In Case I Go*... well I don't think about these kinds of things when I begin to write a novel. But as I was actually into the writing and had a better sense of what the story would be, then thoughts of how much right I had and what role I should take as a non-Indigenous woman did occur to me, of course. My answer at the time was that I wasn't trying to tell the Indigenous story. I was telling the story of these non-Indigenous characters who were trying to find a way forward from the mistakes of their ancestors. So, that is my story, but my story overlaps—our stories overlap so much. I don't know that anyone can write a full, complex novel by pretending that our stories don't overlap.

There was an early draft of *In Case I Go* that had nothing from the point of view of Mary, the Indigenous girl, and then I had silenced her, so, you know, it's very tricky. Do I go into her point of view? Am I appropriating voice? If I don't, then am I silencing her? This is where I start to wonder if we're at a point where novels just don't work. How can anyone write a novel in 2019 in Canada and not talk about the horrible genocide of Indigenous peoples? It would be like wearing blinkers and ignoring the biggest problem in this country, which is essentially what my novel ended up being about—the genocide of Indigenous peoples and the exploitation of our natural world and how this next generation is going to move forward from these catastrophes.

As an artist I find myself compelled to address the big issues. If I can't do that, if I have to put on blinkers and pretend those issues don't exist, isn't that true White privilege? Now, I have to come to terms with what White privilege means when I'm trying to grapple with those problems, when I present my art to the world as a White woman, as a Syrian, Canadian, Scottish woman.

K: Yes, it's so complex. It seems that one of the things you've learned in your experience—and please forgive me and correct me if I'm wrong—is that active consultative process throughout the writing. A draft was accepted by your publisher, and it was in a conversation with your publisher that you decided it would be helpful to gain some insight from those who are more familiar with the culture. That led to meeting Natasha, and that led to meeting with the Ktunaxa Elders, and that led to many more things and many significant revisions. Is that a process that you're including in your next projects as well?

A: It'll be a while before I'll try to write a novel again. It's going to take me time to process this experience, to consider what I've learned and how to apply it to my approach to fiction writing. I just published a book about myself. It's about me and my son and my family in our world, and now I'm working on a follow up, on my daughter's story, and I'm choosing to write memoir very deliberately, because it's going to take me a while to figure out what I have worth saying in fiction and what the rules are.

I don't have any regrets about the consultation process. I formed great relationships with Ktunaxa women and with some Elders, all of whom I admire immensely. The changes that they suggested made *In Case I Go* a much better book. I also read Gregory Younging's work. My editor went to workshops with Gregory Younging, and we did everything that he suggested. That didn't stop my novel from receiving quite intense criticism. So I'm still trying to figure out what that all means. But so far the criticism hasn't been directed at the novel. The reviews of the novel have been good. The criticism has been directed at my *Quill & Quire* article about the consultative process. I can see why.

Initial responses to my article were good. Many writers, Indigenous and not, held my process up as an example of someone trying to consult in new ways. That reaction turned when a Ktunaxa writer said that I had lied. He wrote an article in *Quill & Quire* arguing that I was like companies who pretend to get consent from Indigenous peoples and then rob them of their natural resources. That essay was the catalyst for the online controversy, and then a Jonathan Kay essay came out in response, and controversy really exploded.

What I really wouldn't want to happen is to have the way my experience has been portrayed in the media deter writers from consulting with Indigenous peoples when writing about Indigenous characters or Indigenous history. I can see how someone might read about my experience and say, "Look at the lengths she went to and how hard she tried to consult and be respectful, and look what happened to her." I wouldn't want that to happen, because there's a very big difference between what happened in real life and what happened on social media.

In social media I was skewered and degraded and dragged through the coals. In real life, that wasn't my experience. My relationship with the cultural liaison remains intact. My relationship with Anna Hudson, a Ktunaxa woman whom I met because she had blurbed the book, is very strong. So, while I watched myself being called a racist on social media,

I was spending time in Ktunaxa territory on reserve land with people who supported me and supported my book. There were two stories going on, and I had to remind myself of my physical, local reality versus my online reality, because it doesn't feel very good to be at the bottom of an internet pile on. I had to remind myself that I did try my best, that I had good intentions, even if I made some mistakes. The people in my feet-on-the-ground life—those relationships are intact.

K: Did they comment at all on the internet pile up?

A: Some did, and some didn't. The Ktunaxa people involved—well, it's a small community. There are Ktunaxa familial relationships that are, of course, much stronger than my relationships with Ktunaxa people. While some people might comment to me privately—or enter into civil discussions with me about the issues and the controversy—I don't expect the same people to comment publicly and complicate their relationships with family members.

K: You mentioned in an interview that Richard Wagamese was a great inspiration to you and that this is your response to the truth and reconciliation process.

A: I was in the middle of writing the novel when I attended a festival on Denman Island with Richard. When I began the novel, I thought I would write a story based on my own house, which is in a neighbourhood that is on the site of unmarked graves. I intended the book to be a ghost story, inspired by genre fiction like that of Andrew Pyper, but as I proceeded the story moved in the direction of my other fiction—more focused on social justice and issues that trouble me. The project grew out of my control, which is usually a good sign.

At that festival, Richard said something like, "I scare you White people. You don't know how to respond to me. You feel so bad, and you don't know how to fix things." He said, "You don't have to fix things. All you have to do is say, 'Yes, yes this happened,' and then we figure out steps forward." When he said that, I thought, "Oh, that's what I'm writing. I'm writing my 'yes', and my personal family's steps forward."

After that controversy, I was in Kelowna where my cousin Frank Busch lives. He's a Cree-Lakota writer, and we were there with his kids who are very Indigenous looking and my kids who are very White looking, and they were playing together, and we were having this big family thing at my aunt's, who is half Syrian and half Lakota. And I thought, "You know what? Because Frank helped me a lot in the early stages of my book, and we got a lot closer because of this consultation process. Maybe this novel was a kind of reconciliation at the family level, at that feet-on-the-ground level." I wrote this novel from that place. Maybe social media—that world we as writers feel obliged to exist in—is just too big for me to control (in terms of what people think of me and how people represent me and how people respond to what they think I did). Instead, I need to focus smaller on what I can control—the way the novel offered some truth and reconciliation at the family level, and I have to focus on that as an important success.

K: You said that in *In Case I Go* you try to get out of your head and into your heart, letting go of control to a greater extent than you have before and that you're happy with that process. And I think it was Kat who asked you if it was part historical fiction and part ghost story and what inspired you, and your response in that article started with, "This book proved impossible to control—the more I tried to reign it in, the less it came alive." I'm interested in this idea of control from a writer's perspective, from the perspective of craft and writing fiction. What replaces this notion of control for you, in writing fiction?

A: As back story, I'll tell you that I was going to write something that was more genre fiction, because I liked Stephen King when I was a kid, and I had this great setting where I live that would work for a ghost story. I had this idea of following an outline and a more generic formula. Not that genre writers do that anyways, but I had it in my head that it would be easy. I think I have it in my head that there's an easy way to write a novel [laughter], and it's never yet happened. As I attempted to write that horror novel, I was so stiff, and it just wasn't coming to life.

Then I was speaking at a Writers' Guild conference in Regina, and Michael Helm spoke about this idea of writing into the dark and letting go. He said that by writing into the dark, and just seeing what comes out onto the page, you access a part of your mind that you would never otherwise access, and you realize you knew things that you never realized you knew. I was getting so excited as he was talking about this mysterious process, because it was what I loved about writing that just wasn't happening this time. So, I just started doing that. I'm not writing to please anybody else. I'm not writing to gain fame and fortune. I'm not writing with the idea of filling some kind of generic mold. I'm just going to follow that creative impulse.

On the days when writing is energetic, sometimes what comes out of the pen is very surprising. Later, once the imagined material is all down on paper, I can figure out what to do with it. More than ever, with this novel, I had sections that I thought, "Where on earth did that come from? Where do those stories come from?" A lot of writers, when they talk about their process, talk about that kind of channelling, that kind of true and deep empathy that comes from writing —this radical empathy.

Of course, if the story comes out on the page and someone says, "That doesn't work, and that's not what the experience is like," then you do more research. That's why I'm having trouble writing fiction now. We now have so much emphasis on consultation, and we're told we should be writing our own stories and not other people's stories. After my own controversy, I feel hesitant to trust that empathetic instinct that belongs to a novelist. That kind of hesitation can freeze creativity.

K: You talk about the act of radical empathy in creating these fictional stories. Is this a learnable skill? Can we get better at it? Or, is it just an innate sensitivity?

A: That's a good question, I've never been asked that before. As a mother, I always go to my kids as examples. My son, who I think is a little writer, is so empathetic. Sometimes it's a hard way to live. Some people are born more empathetic, and they tend to be creative, artistic people. Hopefully everyone can learn empathy—the world will be a better place then—and that's a role of novels. If you can't imagine yourself into other people's worlds on your own, a novel can help you imagine yourself into other people's existences, and reading can become an act of empathy.

K: As an educator, do you have strategies you employ to help people develop habits or skills around becoming more empathetic?

A: If I'm reading a student's work, and a character is coming across as hollow or stereotypical, I will have that student try to write from that character's point of view. I might ask them to interview people like the character to try to bring the character to life and create a more complex and fully realized portrait. Even when we're writing from the outside and not engaging in the point of view of that character, it's important to have rich and complex depictions.

K: You mentioned that Richard Wagamese gave you advice that made you reflect on what you were doing. Do you feel that his perspective reflected the general perspective that you've come across in Indigenous communities? Or, was it too superficial? Would you hear that advice differently now?

A: He's a wonderful man, and I'm very disappointed that I never got the chance to share my novel with him. He was so influential. He died before *In Case I Go* came out. His partner, Yvette, read it and was happy about the dedication, so that meant a lot to me. Richard's advice was given while looking out on an audience of White, well-intentioned, left-leaning people, and he could see how the enormity of the mistakes that have been made in this country and how the enormity of the oppression can be so paralyzing. We can think, "How can we fix it? It's not fixable. I can't do anything." The enormity can be so paralyzing that people don't want to face the mistakes, the injustice, the oppression, or they think they can't do anything, so they do nothing.

His advice to face it and say, "Yes, this happened. Let's all acknowledge that this happened. Once we do that, we can all figure out little steps forward," is good advice. So, no, I don't think it was superficial. It was more of, "Let's start here, because we have to start somewhere." He offered a very real solution to a very big problem. How can we start finding a way forward?

Do I think it's the general belief? No, it's impossible to generalize. Twitter gives this idea of there being a general opinion because people group together, and the discussion ends up being very adversarial—people group up around two far-flung sides of an issue. That's what happens on social media. I don't think any argument indicative of what's going on in the real world. Every person has a very specific opinion, if they bother to think about whatever issue it is. There are a wide range of complex responses, because we're talking about incredibly complex problems. There's no general, "This is what Indigenous writers think," or "This is what activists think," or "This is what White people think."

K: You were very candid in your process of truthtelling and learning by recognizing that you might have had a myriad of motivations for writing the personal essay in *Quill & Quire*—promoting the book and defending the book and protecting your work was important to you as it launched. You also mentioned a spiritual community who told you, "Hey, you misrepresented us." If we have all of these rules, and we're worried about representation of every community, where does that leave us?

A: Oh, I should show you that letter from the spiritual community—it was the last straw. I was like, okay, forget it, I'm done. I should frame the letter and put it on my wall.

K: It has paralyzed you—you're not ready to launch yourself into writing another novel. How do we protect ourselves as writers? How do we continue to do our work?

A: Some people who are non-Indigenous are writing books with Indigenous themes and characters—they're just not talking about it, right? They're not drawing any attention to what they're doing. They put their work into the world, and there seems to be no problem. I really drew attention to myself with that essay. If I hadn't have, maybe the response to the book would have been fine. I mean, the book had been out for a while, and there was no anger or no controversy. So, maybe if I hadn't written about my consultation. I have that curse of being both an author and an academic, so I want to talk about process and about what we're doing and what we're learning.

K: How do we keep a healthy perspective while we're doing these things? You seem very aware that social media is dichotomous in nature, is extreme, is also fleeting. Yet, psychologically, it's hard to keep that in perspective in light of the great value the work has in reconciliation with your family, for example, which is so profound that I would think it might encourage you to do more.

A: The thing about social media, and what was so unpleasant about the controversy, is that I'm fifty years old, and I've worked really hard, and I try to be a kind, generous person, and I'm concerned with social justice issues. People in my life like me, some of them [laughter]. So, to see this non-stop stream of hate directed at me, and to read what people who don't even know me were saying, I had to close my social media accounts to stay sane. I would say to my husband, "Can you see if people are still talking about me?" I'd watch him scroll through, reading all this hatred directed at me, on and on and on. When I talk about that time now, I'll say, "Oh, I wasn't suicidal," and my husband will say, "Really? Weren't you?" I don't think I was, but I did keep saying, "I'm dying, I'm dying." This idea of who I was and who I'd always been was being replaced by this other "Angie Abdou" who was racist and a liar, and I had no control over that.

I'm not saying I don't make mistakes. Anyone who knows me will tell you I make all kinds of mistakes. I do things too fast. I don't always stop and think as much as I should. I get ahead of myself, and I do dumb things. But, I'm not a monster. And this Angie Abdou on social media was a monster. Who would ever write a novel or express an opinion if this is what can happen so fast?

Social media has a huge effect—on our psyche, on our professional lives, on how communities perceive us—and there's a point where I couldn't control any of that. Nothing I could say was going to turn the hatred around. Nothing that I could do was going to turn the online attack around until it had run its course.

K: As I'm listening to you, I'm remembering that last time I was in South Africa. I was actively researching, so my visit was different than previous visits. I started writing about my family history. I was recording interviews, I was taking a lot of video and photos and taking a ton of notes, and I was just paying attention differently.

A: That's one of the things I love about writing: you do pay attention differently.

K: I was at a small museum, and I was speaking with the woman who curated the museum. She was the last living descendant of the family who had started this clothing factory in a community that once thrived and is now under gentrification in Johannesburg. I remember leaving that interview with the same feeling. She was very polite and courteous, but at the same time the reality was that I represented, to her, a lot that is wrong with South Africa. Because I had poked that reality, I became the recipient of all that vitriol. I tried not to take it personally, but it did have a strong impact on me. I just became super aware of my relationship within the web of power dynamics she was sharing.

A: And that's what makes it hard to write. I think you hit on something there—that we become a representative of something. We enter tricky territory when people become representatives of something, rather than complex and flawed human beings who are trying their best, hopefully?

K: Yes, and at the same time, this also makes me think, "Wow—if we use that frame or insight now to think how for hundreds of years this is exactly what colonial culture has done to marginalize and dehumanize people. This is what they've had to endure, this is where it's coming from." And then for me to experience it for two hours, and two years since then, really that's very little in comparison. Do you know what I mean?

A: One hundred percent, I know what you mean.

K: I try not to take it personally, because there's the reality of the privilege of my life. But then, to get over the guilt and think, "Okay, is there anything of value that I might do now, as a writer, and still enjoy the writing process? Is there a place for that, and if so, what is that place? And how do I exist in this context without compartmentalizing or ignoring it, and what is my responsibility?"

A: I'd like to go back to what you mentioned—that I had competing motivations for writing that personal essay. One was truly that I had been through this consultation process, and I had learned a lot and wanted to share that process, because people are trying to figure out how we can write Indigenous characters more respectfully. The other, of course, was that I have a book to sell. I definitely jump both feet into the promotional process of the writing. I always have. I was definitely happy that *Quill & Quire* was willing to feature me, which would hopefully lead to people talking my book and maybe even going out and buying my book—I had that motivation as well.

In retrospect, I can see how the two motivations got twisted and how the mixed motivation could make people cringe. I mean, I could see if I were an Indigenous writer I might think, "Who does this chick think she is, talking about how great she is that she went through this consultation process. Like, good for her. Give her a medal." I can one hundred percent understand reacting that way. That's what I talked about in my tendency to do things too fast, to be racing in without thinking through all the potential connotations.

In the *Quill & Quire* article, I protected the one story that is most important to me, about Alfred Joseph. The Chief had shared a story about a woman he knew who had the ability to talk to the old people, and when he shared the story, both Natasha and I got goosebumps, because that similar story had been in my book. He said, "Obviously this novel is a gift." I didn't put that in the personal essay, because it's so special. I didn't use it to sell myself. I saved it.

I think I should have let that impulse spread, and I should have done that in the whole essay about the consultation process—that, no, this is not something that should be shared when I'm trying to sell my book. That's the one thing, in retrospect, that I would have done differently. That's hard for me, because I like the promotion part of it. I like getting out there and talking about what I did and the process I went through and saying, "Hey guys, pay attention to me." I like it. It's not one of my more admirable qualities, but I do. I can see the error of my ways there, for sure.

K: Given this idea that the novel is dead if we're over-vigilant about representation, how would you say we can best tap into the life of a novel?

A: First, when I said the novel is dead, the way the journalist structured the article made it look like I said that in response to the controversy with the Ktunaxa. But, in fact, I blurted it out after I got that response from the East Kootenay spiritual community. So I think that's an important detail, because it's been quoted as if I said it in response to the Ktunaxa controversy, and I didn't. I was like, "Okay, now these White people on the East Kootenay around a fire circle also say I can't represent anyone." I represented the retreat from the perspective of a young boy who saw it for the first time and didn't understand it, so it wasn't meant to be an accurate representation—it was a little bit satirical.

I thought, "Okay, so I can't write from the point of view of someone who doesn't understand something?" For that reason, I thought, the novel is dead. If I can only write things that will please the people who are being written about, if I can only write from the point of view of a White middle class, middle-aged woman, then there's no room to explore other voices. That's what a novel does. A novel is about imagining yourself through many ways of existing, capturing the complexity of life which I don't think has ever been as complex as it is right now. If I can't allow myself to imagine myself into other ways of being, I can't write a novel. It's no coincidence that my two books since then have been memoirs.

K: Do you think it's different when the other that we're trying to represent in our fiction is from an Indigenous background versus any other kind of difference? Ability, gender, age, for example.

A: Perhaps, and that's why I want to make it very clear in that my saying the novel is dead is not in response to Indigenous community but in response to the East Kootenay community's letter to me. It does matter who we're writing about. It's so important to be as respectful as humanly possible with Indigenous people, given our history in this country, and given that we're in the process of trying to find our way to reconcile. Even that word may create problems, but we're trying to find a way forward. It's not possible to make amends, but a way forward. So yes, care and consultation in writing about Indigenous characters is important.

K: In terms of finding a way forward, we've talked about the truth part. In the ninety-four recommendations from the Truth and Reconciliation Commission's report, much points towards the United Nations Declaration of Indigenous Rights. Do you think, as an educator, if we're writing or trying to write about Indigenous matters in fictional work, that there might be some value in taking that document, in actually looking at it and talking about it and thinking about the implications in our work and in our relationship building?

A: Yes, I do. I don't teach literature any more. I teach creative writing courses. I know people who are teaching Canadian Literature courses who are moving their courses in that direction, and that's important. You're right, that should be incorporated into the creative writing curriculum as well.

K: I've never been part of a formal program that does that. But it seems obvious to me that it needs to be a step. We need to learn how to do that and have more opportunities to think about it in spaces where we can talk about it, consider it, and think about what it means.

A: Yes, I agree.

K: Are there any other tips you might have for fiction writers to elevate their writing or their awareness of how the socio-cultural context in Canada might be relevant to their work?

A: It's important to ask yourself why you're the person to tell this story. To make sure you consult with relevant groups. Once you've done the best that you can do and written a book that you can stand behind, you put it out there and stand behind it.

Someone said to me, "They're treating you like you're a politician, not a creative, artistic person. They're holding you to the standard of a politician." While I understand where that comment is coming from, we're in new times, and everything is politically loaded, and it's important for artists to absorb what that means and account for it too. At the same time, we can't be so scared of saying anything that we write nothing at all. At some point writers have to realize that they've done the best they can, and they put the book out and stand behind it.

And criticism is not censorship. Criticism might spark conversations in which I might learn, as a writer, that I could have done something differently, and I grow as a writer, and then I do my next project. That's how it works. We're flawed human beings. Our artistic output is also going to be flawed. We're also evolving human beings, and hopefully our artistic products will also be evolving. So I don't ever want to be inhibited by doing or saying the wrong thing. That's what I'm working on now. It's harder than it sounds.

And I love what Rosanna Dearchild said, I come back to that a lot—that we don't have to kick people out of the circle—we just make the circle bigger. Hopefully, in Canada, we're making the circle bigger and bigger, and we have more voices and more people represented and wonderful diversity. I hope that doesn't mean I'm not allowed to write anymore, and I hope there's still room for me, the Syrian, Scottish, Austrian writer [laughter].

K: This is an important insight. I wonder what has made the circle bigger? What works in making the circle bigger? Is it only the writer's responsibility? There's a whole system around this work.

A: Oh yeah, who's the media covering? Who are the festivals inviting? What books are getting reviewed? All of it. So that's a place to start, to make the circle bigger, but then we have to figure out what that means in practical terms. We're really at the beginning of massive change. We keep doing our best and posing the questions—there are so many answers that we don't have yet. It's true that Canadian literature has gotten much more diverse, quickly, and that's a resounding success, thanks to people like Jael Richardson and the Festival of Literary Diversity.

K: Thank you for this conversation. I've come to the end of my questions.

A: It's been so nice talking to you. Sometimes I think through talking, and you've had great questions and comments. Through every great conversation I have like this, and they're rare, I understand what happened a little bit better. One day, maybe, I'll understand most of it.

Jæl Richardson

August 5, 2019

Jael Richardson is the author of The Stone Thrower: A Daughter's Lesson, a Father's Life, *and a novel entitled* Gutter Child. *Richardson is a book columnist and guest host on CBC's Q. She holds an MFA in Creative Writing from the University of Guelph and lives in Brampton, Ontario where she founded and serves as the Artistic Director for the Festival of Literary Diversity (FOLD).*

K: What do we need to know, as writers, about the topic of writing diversity at the moment in Canada?

J: A lot of people talk about the topic of appropriation in relation to what people should or shouldn't write. For me, that's a really tricky space to go into—to prescribe who should write what and who shouldn't. For me, the big issue with cultural appropriation is the economics of it. It's about who is making money off of whom. I think it's really exciting that people are interested in diverse stories, that they're interested in seeing diverse characters in books, but cultural appropriation in the past has created economic disparity. It has meant, for example, that White male authors have grown their writing careers and grown their business as writers by writing about other people and have been seen as the experts about other peoples' lives. And we have multiple problems from that. We have people with misunderstandings about what certain communities are like, what they're about, who they are. We also have an underrepresentation of stories by people who have actually lived those experiences.

Economically, we have an underrepresentation of writers of colour and writers from marginalized communities who can actually make a living off their work. And I know there's a lot of things that complicate the "make a living off your book" statement, but certainly, because we've historically been satisfied with stories about the Black community and the Indigenous community that are written by White authors, and because people are more likely to buy a book if it's written by someone they've heard of before, there's this economy that continuously feeds established writers who are appropriating and makes it difficult for writers who are writing from an own voice perspective.

When people turn to me and say, "Shouldn't I be able to write whatever I want to write?" my answer is, "Yes, but should publishers publish it? Should schools buy it? Should students be studying it?" That's the part that I'm much more invested in, because, yeah, you should write what comes to you, and I can't necessarily judge anyone for that, but I can certainly question whether we're doing the industry justice by continuing to support stories by people who maybe have no business writing that story but are profiting from it financially without having lived it themselves.

When I was in high school, I loved reading. I sort of wanted to write a book, but I never really pictured myself doing it. All of the writers I read in high school—all of them—were White. That has an impact on a writer and a person, when they never see someone who looks like them.

I can think of many careers I thought of myself in. I could be a professional athlete, a track star, because I saw FloJo. And I thought I could be an actor, because I saw people who kind of looked like me do a thing that I thought I could do, and I could imagine that. It wasn't until my second year of university when I met a Black woman who had written a play that I thought I could write plays, or stories—that I could be a writer.

You know, university isn't something that everybody can do. When I look back and I think, "What if I hadn't been able to afford that? Would I have found financiers? Would I have realized that I could be a writer? Would I have found Lawrence Hill and Dionne Brand, both of whom I was introduced to in my university career?" And now as a writer, I go into those classrooms, and I see the looks on the faces, particularly of young women of colour. I see what it looks like to them when they see me, and I know that they see something that suddenly becomes possible.

That experience works in two ways, making a difference in the lives of Black students (Black girls in particular) when I go into schools, and

I also see the way my presence changes the way the White students see me. It becomes a situation where their perspective shifts as well. So, for me, appropriation is also about who we see when we look at the back jacket of the book, and what we've imagined to be possible.

K: You have a novel coming out—what's it about?

J: My first novel is called *Gutter Child*. It's about what it might look like to grow up in a world that's designed for your failure. The world is a country where the rules are actually set up to make life particularly difficult for people of colour, and I was really interested on a personal level with what kinds of choices you make when the laws are designed against you. So it's about a bunch of young people, and it centres around one young woman who has to make a series of choices when her life takes a particular turn.

K: In relation to our topic of writing difference with respect, we're both women of colour, and our identities are so multivarious, and we have intersections of privilege and oppression throughout our history and ancestry. Do you feel like you were writing from your own experience even though it's fiction?

J: There are lots of challenges with the thought of appropriation as I'm writing the story. I'm very interested in what it looks like when you don't have privilege or access. As a person of colour, I've lived a very privileged life, and so I'm looking at what might be similar to what my grandmother and my father might have experienced in their lives. There's a certain way that this approach is both appropriating and not appropriating. It's a way of digging into your past and unearthing what your family lived through, but also of talking about an experience and a perspective on a life that you never had. I've never had no options. I've never had no money. I've never lived in a community that was even a little bit impoverished. As the main character is navigating these experiences, I felt very much like, "Do I know what I'm talking about? Is this something that I'm making assumptions about?" There's all those kinds of questions going on in my head.

I also had a really tricky moment when I was creating the back story. What happened? How did they get there? What was tricky about that is that I don't (personally) really have a backstory. As a Black woman, from an American perspective, when you talk about your actual roots, when you talk about the place you were born and the country you're actually from, I don't feel that I have a distinct or clear backstory. If you think of it as a continuous line, it was one that was kind of broken and then reset in another place.

If I had been from a country like Ghana, for example, I think I would have dipped deep into Ghanaian culture, and I would have researched it, or I would have known it from having my grandparents or my parents telling me. I would have been able to pull from those kinds of traditions. But I don't have that. And so, when I was writing a backstory I had to try to figure out how to write a backstory for these characters when I don't have one to pull from myself. I sort of dipped into a number of different places, and that felt like appropriation in a way—it felt like stealing from places that weren't mine, but then I was like, "That's the world that I've been given, a broken history, which, when I write a story, I have to put together from somewhere."

I don't think that people would see that as appropriation at all. I don't think people are saying that if you make a backstory for a character that it has to be rooted in your specific experiences, but it certainly was the place where I would have started. When I didn't have that, I automatically had to default to these other places. People might argue that this process makes you more creative. You're thinking more, making things up. It's the beauty of writing fiction. But I would have actually liked to be able to speak to my place of origin. I would have liked to call to attention and celebrate my ancestors.

K: How did you go about doing that in a way that felt respectful and authentic and also in service to the art?

J: I don't know if I feel like I was respectful or authentic. I mean, I think authentic for sure is a struggle, because it's not a real place. It's an imagined world where you can really make anything up. I could base it on Irish traditions. I don't have to base it on anything. That's the thing with fiction: you really can and probably should, on some level, write anything. But you have to be really thoughtful. For me, I just had to realize that the story of this character was really important. It's something that's really close to me. It means a lot to me. I've lived this personally, in a way—a lot of the trauma that I feel comes along with being a Black American. I haven't lived in poverty, but I certainly feel it. I feel the anxiety of it in a way that makes me have to mine it.

I know the reason I wrote *Gutter Child* is because I went back to the community where my dad was from, and I didn't know that life at all. I felt deeply guilty about that and deeply troubled by that. I think writing *Gutter Child* and mining that experience of what it's like to grow up with little choice and little power is a way for me of coping and asking questions and coming to terms with who I am. I think that this is part of being respectful and being thoughtful—coming at it from a place of genuine curiosity, without assumptions, and trying to figure out the answer to these questions. What do you do when the world is stacked against you? What choices do you have, and what's the likely outcome, and is that good or bad?

K: It sounds like it requires some genuine humility and a desire to understand. You've had readers, I'm sure, along the way—did you try to have readers who have more lived experience with what you were writing about?

J: I did. One woman in particular, because the main character is a single mom, well, she (spoiler alert!) becomes a single mom. There are multiple reasons why I asked this particular woman to read it. There were a number of things she brought to the table that I was very concerned about. What it is like, the struggle of being a single mom? And also, I don't think until that point there had been a woman of colour who had read it.

My biggest fear is always that someone from the Black community will read it and be like, "You don't know what you're talking about. You don't know anything about dreadlocks. You don't know anything about xyz." So I did try to get those perspectives early in the process, not as much as I would have liked. I have to figure out, to be honest, how to get a better sense of community in the writing process, so that there are more eyes on it before it comes out. I've got a great agent. I trust her a lot. I've got a great editor. I trust her a lot as well. They both happen to be White women, so sometimes I worry that things have been missed, not because they're bad people, but because they haven't lived certain experiences and in many ways I haven't either, so it's that—it's making sure you're doing your best to solve hard problems before the book comes out, hoping it goes okay.

K: You talked about the economics of it. I'm wondering how many people would think of writing as a viable career.

J: I don't think most people do. I think there is a small percentage of people who will say, yes, they're making a living from writing, and it comes in seasons. They have a really big book, and they win an award, so for a year or two it's good. But most of them know that it's not, generally, sustainable in the long-term. At some point they're probably going to teach at a university or a college, or they're going to generate income from another source.

There's also another aspect. There are some names that are most recognizable, and a lot of them tend to be names that are easier to pronounce. There's the economics around the sale of a book that's impacted by race, identity, by things that make it more difficult for a large community of people who are readers to remember or know. So it's a tricky thing, the economics, because we're not just talking about making enough money off of each individual book. It's also about that writer's representation at literary festivals, that writer's ability to stay in the minds of people. When I do the CBC Radio show, and I recommend a book, can the audience remember the name just by hearing it, or is it something they're likely to forget or misspell or not know, which decreases the chance of them putting it on their Goodreads or buying it later? There's all kinds of things, economically, that a writer has to be aware of.

K: Let's say somebody writes a great story. It's fiction, it's important, it's relevant, it's really well-written. Percentage-wise, what do you think the chances are that it will be picked up in the stream of literary flow in Canada?

J: Oh, really low. There are so many books that come out all the time. And there are so many factors that go into whether a book picks up momentum or just sort of puffs up and disappears. I think of this past fall, where I watched a number of books really closely, and I thought a couple of them might be nominated for the Giller (they weren't), and as a result they sort of faded from memory in a lot of ways. It wasn't just the Giller, it was the Writer's Trust and a series of things didn't happen for them, or didn't work out. And they have statistics on these things, like if you win the Giller how much of a percentage your sales go up, if you're on the shortlist for the Giller versus the longlist. There are some that don't make any difference—the longlist doesn't usually impact sales in a significant way. But there are a lot of factors.

The reality is, and I know this going into my second book in a way that I didn't know going into the first, that it's very unlikely for a book —even if it's well-written—to do enormously well without some kind of help, without some sort of award or channel like Canada Reads. That's what makes it so tricky. There are ten books that are really going to get that extra bump. Amongst those ten books, not all of them are easy to read or great, if I'm being honest, and so the ones that are great and easy to read do really well, and the rest do okay. The other books, good or bad, tend to just disappear.

K: In terms of motivation for writing, then [laughter]?

J: Why do I do this [laughter]?

K: What motivated you to write *Gutter Child*, beyond personal identity formation and learning more about your family history? Do you think your writing can make a difference, and if so, what difference do you think it can make, if people read your book?

J: Yeah, multiple times in the process of writing *Gutter Child* I thought about just not finishing it. If it's not going to win awards, and it's not going to sell a lot, which is a very high probability, why do it? I don't know any writer who doesn't ask themselves that at least once or twice, or maybe every day. And the truth is, at one point I stopped writing, and I thought this is a dumb idea. I'm not going to write it. And then I realized that I couldn't actually stop.

The way I describe it, I actually remember what it was like to have contractions when I was having my son. I was having contractions, and I got really tired in the middle of contractions, and the midwife was like, "Stop for a bit if you want," and I was like, "Okay, I'm going to take a rest." She said, "Yeah, just rest." Then the next contraction came, and I was like, "How do I rest? I can't rest! My body is saying, 'Push! Get this thing out!'" It felt like that with writing *Gutter Child*. I wanted to not do it. I wanted to quit. I wanted to walk away. But my brain and my body were like, "Get this thing out!" So my new motivation on the second half of working on it was get it out, get it done. Get it done and make it the best possible book I could make it in the process, but just get it out and don't care about all the other stuff. So, there's that part of it.

On the other side of it, when I started writing the book, I built the Festival of Literary Diversity for myself, in a way. People were like, "Oh, it's so great. You're so thoughtful and generous." Yeah, but in some ways it was just super selfish. It's something to keep me in the industry, to keep me front of mind, to help understand the industry better, and when I arrive with this book, it will be very different than when I arrived with *Stone Thrower*. And even if *Stone Thrower* turns out to be a better book, I will probably sell more copies of *Gutter Child* on sheer logistics alone. So that's why I keep doing it—my body is making me, and because I've sort of set myself up to do this thing, and, at the very least, I need to finish this book.

K: When I read *Gutter Child*, what is it that you hope I'll understand better?

J: That's a great question, because I was actually interviewing (not to name drop, and it always feels like I'm name-dropping when I say this one), but I was interviewing Colson Whitehead the other day, and he, of course, won the Pulitzer Prize for *Underground Railroad*. And I remember a specific line. He said that a novel can't change the world. I was like, "Huh. Do I believe that?" But then I think he was just being realistic in that you don't give someone a novel and they read it and the whole world changes. It just doesn't work like that. Even if everybody read the same novel, it probably wouldn't change the way the world actually runs. But, the process of writing a novel and the process of reading a novel does change people. It does change individuals. We ended up leaving the conversation and saying that a single novel isn't going to change the world, but a single novel can change a person. And a person can change the world.

Think about the impact of Obama, for example—a singular person, whose life decisions monumentally changed the world. There have been others like him who have done similarly great work. And he will tell you—these are the books that have changed my life and contributed to my life's experience.

My hope is that, when people read *Gutter Child*, they think about their world, and they think about the rules and the laws and the way their nation is set up, and they ask themselves what they're doing about it, about the people who are forgotten or overlooked. Eden Robinson said recently at an event that when she writes a book she writes for a single person. She doesn't think about all readers. She thinks about one person, like a cousin, and it's very specific. And this may sound egocentric, though I think a lot of writers do this for their debut novels, but for me, I'm writing to myself—to the teenager I was and the books I read when I was a teenager.

I'm so hard on myself and so disappointed with the teenager that I was. I'm so disappointed with what I didn't know. I can blame the system, and I can blame all these different people, but I'm just disappointed that I didn't know more and do more. I'm disappointed that when the Rwandan genocide was happening I was totally oblivious to what was going on. Massive numbers of people were dying, people who looked like me, who, frankly, could have been my ancestors. So I wanted to write a book that called attention to these things, that made people think, "Wait, wait, wait, is this something that happened in history? Did this happen in real life?" I really want people to ask questions about what they see around them.

K: We all have these choices to make every moment of our lives, and every choice, I believe, has a resonance, an impact, a consequence. If something inspires us to act, say a novel like *Gutter Child*, how do we channel that energy? What guiding principles help you, as a reader, to channel that kind of energy in a way that you feel will do the greatest good? Do you have any guiding principles?

J: I would describe myself as a very spiritual person. I really believe that I write from an inspired place, that when I'm not writing from an inspired place it's really just not good. So I try to tap into that responsibility, that role. I'm the storyteller. I'm the writer. This is my job, my duty. I try and give that weight to it.

I remember Richard Wagamese speak about starting at his desk each morning and thanking The Creator for the gift of writing, before writing. I try and remember that. My Creator created me with a purpose to do this thing, so that's an important guiding principle, because along the way of making a lot of decisions about the book, you really have to trust in something bigger than you.

I'll give you an example as it relates to *Gutter Child*. It's not that I've finished it. Well, I have finished it, but the ending is always a thing—and so the big question for the ending has been how to end it and a question of hope. How do you give the reader hope? Are you responsible for giving the reader hope? It's a question I'm asking, because I literally haven't yet figured out what my response to that is. I think that early on in the process I knew that you could make one of three endings: you could make an ending that was sort of like doomsday, where life is terrible; you could make an ending that was really happy and good and hopeful; or you could do something that was more what I would call realistic, where there's both a sense of hope and despair for a character or for the community.

I think with a dystopia I'm not interested in doomsday, but I'm also not interested in an overly happy or hopeful moment. I'm interested in something that's much closer to reality, because I believe this kind of ending forces people to think. If you give people more hopeful and happy, they close the book, and they don't think. I recently read a book that I would say is a dystopia with a realistic ending, and it messed me up! I was so angry. I couldn't stop thinking about it. That's probably my inspiration. That's probably what I'm going for—really getting people to think about it.

K: I feel like art for social change often has that intention, of creating a desire in the audience to think deeply and rise to action. It's a difficult goal when our attention is in such demand by many distractions, entertainments and diverse calls to action. We live in an aggressively materialistic marketing world that demands so much of us so much of the time. How are we meant to find our voice within that, just as a person?

J: I think, honestly when I first started, I would have wanted *Gutter Child* to have an impact, to inspire a collective action. I think I set out with that kind of large, ambitious intention. And then I kind of realized, no, I'm really just interested in this one character, in particular, making a series of choices. I'm not sure that her choices can have that kind of collective movement. I think I can see different ways the story could have been told that maybe would have made a larger political statement, but really I'm just interested in why people make this choice in this situation. Why, in this moment, do people do this? What would happen if they did this? Those were my questions. And so, for me, it helped me to realize that I'm not trying to change scope. I'm just trying to figure something out.

I'll be shocked to hear that people have finished reading the book, to be honest. That's what my mentality is. I'll be shocked if people read the whole thing. And it will be very overwhelming to me, because it's just a bunch of questions that I had to resolve, and I made stuff up and hopefully it's okay. In relation to that other book and what it prompted in me, I think what it did and what was relevant to *Gutter Child* is that when you grow up in difficult life situations—in low income communities, in abusive relationships, for example—I know this is going to sound super dismal, but the odds are not great that you will live a peaceful, sane adult life. The more serious it is, the lower the probability.

So when we read books and we read characters in difficult situations, we want them to overcome, and we want them to conquer, and we want things to turn out great for them. But the reality is, it often doesn't. I'm not sure it does us any good to continue to sell these narratives that say, "If you work really hard you can go from a low-income community to a wealthy home living situation. If you grow up in the foster system, you can still grow up to become President or Prime Minister or, you know, a lawyer." I'm not sure that's beneficial.

I've had foster kids. Our foster kids don't have a lot of money. They don't come from a lot of money, and they have really bad habits from not having people to look out for them, and they're in the Children's Aid system or have crossed paths with the system. What I learned recently was that three percent of kids who grow up in the system live lives above the poverty line. We're not talking about wealth. We're talking about the poverty line. When I'm thinking about this book, and I'm thinking about exploring this idea of poverty and class and systemic racism, I'm not sure it does any good for me to leave people feeling really hopeful about the world, because it makes us lazy, and it's not realistic to sell these very unusual stories.

My dad's story is unusual. He grew up in a low-income community. He had three kids, all raised middle-class, doesn't drink. There are no signs of trouble in my dad's life from having a very troubled childhood—alcoholic father, abusive stepfather, you know? People often look at my dad's story and say, "This is so great, it gives us hope"—and it does, and it's good, but the reality is that the system that these kids are growing up in is not working. If we continue to tell stories like my dad's and say, "You can just be like him," we're setting people up for failure, and as a society we have to be paying attention to what's real—not what's hopeful, but what's real.

In terms of tying it back to where we started, and looking at appropriation and telling a story that's not my own, that's really what I wanted to explore, look at and invest in. I see it too often—you see it in the news, in the media—people touting these rags to riches, lovely hopeful stories, and I'm seeing more and more. But these aren't just rare examples, like one in every four kids. These are really, really rare circumstances. What happened to all those other kids who grew up in that same neighbourhood, in those same communities, and didn't have a champion or a special talent or someone who got them out?

K: Given that we will all get a different look at reality that might inform our choices and motivations to be part of social change, what role, if any, does fiction play in that journey?

J: I almost exclusively read fiction. For the Festival of Literary Diversity I also read non-fiction, and for CBC's radio show *Q* I have to read non-fiction. But I love fiction. I love fiction that works close to the truth. Whether it's historical fiction or whatever, just call it fiction and I'm in, generally. I think it's because I love writing, and I find that with fiction people make more choices in their writing. I think when you're writing non-fiction, a large majority of writers follow a fairly standard structure. First person or third person, is it linear or is it jumping back and forth, is it essays—there are a couple of choices you make, but most non-fiction writers don't make as many of those creative choices as a fiction writer will in terms of like, "Who's the central character? How is it unravelled? In what style?" There's all sorts of things that happen in fiction that I love.

Actually, in my memoir, I did make a lot of choices, and I think I got really creative with how it was told, which made it infinitely more fun for me, and so I'll read non-fiction that does a little bit of that. But I just love the way we get to play with fiction, and the freedom of it. The fact that we can literally make any choice.

You know Colson Whitehead's recent book is based on a true story, but he took that story and unpacked it and did a whole bunch of things to it that he wanted to do. So, for me, the added value is that I learned about a place I didn't know about, learned about history. I can go back, and I can read more about the initial place, the school that he based the book on, but I can also read his book and be like, "I wonder why he made that choice? I wonder why he picked that character? I wonder where that story came from?" When I interviewed him, I could have asked him a hundred questions simply about choices. Why did it start here? Literally, choice is a fascinating one for me, and that's what I love about fiction, because you learn something about the author as you read, and you learn something about the world that they're writing about too.

K: Do you think in today's climate, in Canada, that it's more important who the author is than what they've written?

J: It's an interesting question, because I think that people buy books on the basis of who an author is versus what the book is about, but people are moving to a point where they'd actually like to read it based on what they're writing about. I'm not sure we always know, as an industry, how to market that, how to sell that.

At the Festival of Literary Diversity we've made a significant and concentrated choice to sell sessions and programs less on an author's name and more on the conversation. For example, in 2019, our opening session was called, "Rage Becomes Her". The year before was called, "From Boys to Men". We did two sessions back-to-back opening year: one was more centralized on how we raise boys, and the other was about what women can do in this particular climate. We sold those events largely on the basis of the conversation and the topic, rather than saying, "Hey come see Rachel Giese or Vivek Shraya."

The reality is, it's hit or miss whether somebody's going to recognize an author's name or know what their book is about. It's really exciting to be able to just say, "Let's get together and talk about women's rage; let's talk about how we raise boys." We get a lot of atypical literary festival people as a result of that. I think that marketing based on themes and topics is a better strategy. If I were a marketing person at a publishing house, I'd be looking at the topic of a book and finding hashtags that were relevant to that theme and really working that conversation into news stories and things like that.

Farzana Doctor

August 28, 2019

Farzana Doctor was born in Zambia to expatriate parents from India, immigrating to Canada with her family in the early 1970's. She has written four works of fiction, Stealing Nasreen, Six Metres of Pavement, All Inclusive, *and* Seven. *She works as a Registered Social Worker in a private psychotherapy practice. She lives in Toronto, Ontario.*

K: Do you remember that moment when Hal Niedzviecki resigned from the Writer's Union of Canada publication?

F: Yes, I serve on the Equity Task Force for The Writers' Union. When all of that happened, we got active. We were really upset and angry because this Equity Task Force had been around for a few years, and the focus had been on making The Writers' Union a more equitable place. The problem with the Union—it's had a lot of amazing successes—but there just hadn't been enough representation of racialized folks, Indigenous folks, people with disabilities, and on and on. The Task Force was set up to work to try to change that. There had been waves of this kind of work before us. Each decade there has been a group of people working on it for a period of time and then for whatever reason stopping (probably burnout).

We had been in the midst of some really good work, pushing, pushing, having some success, and then Hal wrote his editorial in a way that was particularly heinous given that it was an issue of *WRITE* magazine that was focused on Indigenous writing. We got very active in that moment. I contacted one of the writers from the magazine—they were going to be responding to this—asking if there was anything they needed, anything they particularly wanted us to know. We made a statement with a number of demands, and those demands got taken up at the Annual General Meeting, which happened not long after that.

I actually feel like that was such a powerful inciting moment for the Union, because all of our demands were agreed to by the membership, by the National Council, and have been slowly worked on since then. It was a powerful, stressful moment that took place over the course of two days, and we were constantly online with each other, drafting this set of demands [laughter]—yeah, we got close. So, I do remember. It's still so fresh.

K: In retrospect, do you feel like it was the best response?

F: I think the Equity Task Force felt that we had done our best. We had acted very quickly, and as volunteers. I think that the membership took up the demands well, that they made the right decision, knowing that this was a crisis moment for the Union and that things had to change really quickly. Many, many people who supported us were threatening to leave at that point, so there would have been a mass exodus of Union membership if change hadn't happened.

K: Since then do you feel like there's been a cultural shift?

F: In the very slow way that large organizations work, yes. There's that metaphor that it takes a long time for a ship to turn. There have been a few key things that have happened that I see as really quite positive. They hired Charles C. Smith, who did a wonderful needs assessment and wrote a report. The result of that was that an Equity Coordinator has been hired.

In terms of the larger cultural shift, I think it will take time. The Union is a microcosm of the larger society, of the larger publishing world, which is still very much White and male dominated. There's still lots of work to do, but there has been good work done. It needs to keep happening, of course.

K: It sounds like a lot of the heavy-lifting is undertaken by people from these marginalized communities. Do you find that that's still, generally, the case?

F: The Equity Task Force has been mostly comprised of racialized folks and some terrific White allies who have been taking on a lot of leadership. I can't comment on what's happening with the two thousand people in the membership. I can't really comment on what's happening with staff. I'm simply not in touch with how the culture in those groups has shifted. But I think, generally, this is what happens. It's predominantly women, and predominantly racialized women, who end up taking up the cause and doing the work.

K: Can we talk about your writing? I understand you're working on the final edits of your novel. Can you share some of the ways you approach writing about difference in your work?

F: Yes, this is my fourth book. It's called *Seven*. It will be out in Fall 2020. As for writing about difference, certainly it's more comfortable for me to write from the perspective of a South Asian person. In all of my novels, at least one character has been from the community that I'm from, which is the Dawoodi Bohra community. That's always the most comfortable positioning for me, of course, because I can feel very comfortable with representing that world. Now, there will always be people who feel that it's not being represented well, but I feel very grounded in writing from that position.

As I've continued to write, I've been thinking that my books can't always be about my own community. You need to have other characters, other stories. For example, with my second novel, *Six Metres of Pavement*, I was very interested in the experience of the Portuguese widows in my neighbourhood. But I was seeing them very much as an outsider. I didn't even have Portuguese friends. I had three main characters in that book, and I wanted to have one of those characters be a Portuguese widow.

I really had to work very hard at doing some of my own research. I read articles, and I had a couple of beta readers who were from the Portuguese Canadian community who could correct things—things like, "Make sure she puts that red wine back in the fridge, because that's how we drink it." Details like, "Yes, I think that emotional experience really does work because of the things I saw happening with my grandmother." So, both the deeper observations as well as the more superficial details, because you don't want to misrepresent a community. You don't want to have all of your biases coming in there. You don't want it to be all about stereotypes. That's very important to me.

So, I was nervous after that book came out. I was so relieved when a fifty year old Portuguese Canadian widow who is a neighbour of mine said, "Whoa, you captured it." It was like, "Thank God, because doing a good job is really important." I don't know, there could be a whole lot of other disgruntled readers out there, but I didn't hear from them.

And then, with my third novel, *All Inclusive*, I wanted to base it at an all-inclusive resort in Mexico. There are a few secondary characters who are co-workers of my main character, and three of them are Mexican.

So again, it was important to have a beta reader to be able to check the superficial stuff, correct some of the language, but also to tell me, "Yes, it seems like you didn't have stereotypes here, and where you did, there was a variety of perspectives on that." So I think beta readers are a big part of my writing experience in terms of getting things right.

With my fourth novel, *Seven*, pretty much all of my characters are Dawoodi Bohra—I don't know why that happened. Some minor characters are White American. I don't get beta readers for writing the characters from the dominant culture identities because I feel, as a racialized woman, I'm pretty well-versed in White people's stuff. I did get a couple of beta readers to look at some of the Dawoodi Bohra references, because the way I'm situated in a community is different from some of my characters who are orthodox. Again, I just wanted to make sure I got details right.

K: You had mentioned that we really can't control the responses—that there might be people who feel that they have not been represented well, even though you are situated within your community. Have you had any negative feedback? And, if so, how did you respond to that?

F: In *Six Metres of Pavement* I wrote a character named Ismail, who's been living in Canada for a long time. He's a non-religious guy, a "bad-Muslim", you know? He's let go of a lot of his cultural and religious upbringing. One person read that and said, "It doesn't seem like he's a Bohra guy. I would have thought he was from this other community, so I don't think you wrote a Bohra character there." I thought about it, and I thought about my reasoning for why I made him who he was, and I thought, "Well, I know people who call themselves Bohra and are like that too." So, I thought maybe that's the reader's bias. But it gave me pause—it always gives me pause, because it's a critique. Criticism is hard.

Another example: I was doing a reading from the first novel, and a South Asian woman came up after the reading and said, "You're pronouncing Fatima wrong," and I thought, "That's so interesting." It's upsetting when people say these things. I figure she was probably triggered, because BIPOC people's names are always mispronounced. I know as a diasporic first gen kid, I have had my name mispronounced many times. And I've even pronounced it differently over the years, depending on what context I've been in.

And the comment I'm going to make now is probably about larger criticism. Do you know how Brené Brown quotes Theodore Roosevelt about "the man who is actually in the arena"? Like her, unless you're in the arena, I'm probably not going to take your criticisms too seriously. If people aren't being vulnerable in the way that you're being vulnerable, then it's very easy for them to walk up to you at a reading and tell you that you're mis pronouncing the name of your character, who you've been living with for years.

K: How did you respond to this woman?

F: At the time I was a little shocked, and I think I just said, "Oh, that's interesting—this is the way I've been thinking about her for years."

I think most of the difficult feedback hasn't come from the places where I was most afraid it might come. Even with the third novel I thought, "Are people going to think I was racist against Mexicans?" or when I wrote about the Air India bombing in the third novel, and I thought, "Are there going to be people who are family members of the people who died who are going to say that I exploited this story and be really angry with me?" The things I'm afraid of are the things I never get.

It's the critique from my own communities, actually, that I get more of, as I mentioned earlier. Another example: I was told, "You represented that queer experience in a way that's not realistic" and I think, "Well, it's realistic for my character. It's realistic for things I've seen in the world. Maybe it's not your experience, though." It's more the insider stuff where I've been getting the critiques, not the outsider stuff, which is so interesting. Maybe because I work really hard at the outsider stuff.

K: Have you read things where you've felt offended by the representation of a particular character or community in fiction?

F: Yeah, I've seen mistakes. It's often with secondary characters. You know, they have a Muslim secondary character named Krishna, and I think to myself, "You just needed to ask someone. You just needed to google this and do a little work—google "Muslim names" [laughter]. And I think, "How did this slip through?"

K: And it wasn't intentional, perhaps for comedic effect?

F: No it wasn't. It makes me think they're thinking, "You and this character don't really matter. I'm just dappling in a little colour because I'm supposed to be writing diversity." Yeah, so I have encountered that.

K: What's at risk there? What's the response when you read something careless like that?

F: I think, "This is careless, and this isn't skilled writing."

K: Are there any other consequences, do you think, when something like that is published?

F: Potentially. It offers misinformation. It doesn't deepen anybody's understanding of the character. We've been told that the person is Indian, but they're just reading White with the wrong name, so I guess it reinforces things that shouldn't be reinforced, like "We're all the same." Or, maybe it reinforces a kind of gaze, that the white gaze is the important gaze, and we don't need to look more deeply. Whereas when I've read books about experiences that I didn't know anything about, about marginalized identities that I hardly knew anything about and needed a lot of education around, I just have this deep dive and empathic response and deep learning. That's what we need in fiction.

K: Yes, and I think there are many and varied reasons for authors to write fiction. We also chose to focus this project on fiction writing and not on creative non-fiction, poetry or journalistic or academic writing. What do you think is the role of fiction in social change?

F: I agree with you that there are lots of reasons why people will write fiction. Like Ani DiFranco said, "Every tool is a weapon if you hold it right." So fiction can be a tool. It should be a tool for change. It becomes a weapon if you hold it right. It's a way for us to communicate ideas and teach empathy and learn empathy and explore ideas about being human, and that can be in a political sense, but it can also be in the very personal sense of, like, maybe we're writing about grief. That's going to touch somebody and help somebody deepen their own understanding and their own healing around grief. It can make us deeper, better human beings.

I do think that when we're writing about marginalized identities we have a role in not maintaining the status quo. So, I would say to a writer, "Don't bother writing those marginalized identities if you're just going to maintain the status quo. Just write your own community then." But—there's a but—sometimes you'll see, maybe it's fear, maybe it's White writers not wanting to appropriate, and their whole book will be only White characters. If you're going to do that, if there's a good reason for you to only write White people, I want them to somehow signal through the writing why they're doing that. Why are there only White people in this story? Why are there only dominant people in this story? Why have you forgotten everybody else? Why have you erased everybody else? Maybe there's a good reason. Maybe it matters. Maybe you're writing about some small Ontario town that only has White people and you have to stay true to the setting. But you can signal, and this might happen in the editing or revision stage, you can signal why that's happening, why everyone else is erased from the story. If you don't do that, there's a risk, I think, of just erasing.

K: Does fiction have a responsibility to mirror the way society is?

F: To an extent, yes—it depends on your genre of fiction, right? You're not going to mirror it if you're writing science fiction or speculative fiction, because you're writing about a different sort of future. But I think we have this opportunity as writers to provide a piece of art that helps the reader to think more deeply about life and society. You don't have to be didactic, and you don't have to match the percentage of characters to your community's demographics, but let's show the world in which we live. My world includes all kinds of people.

K: When we're thinking about these things, in your experience, do you find that it interferes with the artistic process?

F: It can, because the first ugly drafts need to be free and careless, so I would say do your examination of whether you've been oppressive in the revision stage. Otherwise, we can get a little stopped up and stuck.

Where I get stuck the most is when I worry about misrepresenting my own communities. I can have these moments of thinking, "What's she going to say?" I'm naming a character, and this person has the same name—"What's she going to say? How are they going to feel? Everyone's going to be mad at me," and so on. So you have to let that go and just know that you'll fix those things a little bit later, if there are mistakes.

I can give you an example. I recently had the great experience of reading Dorothy Palmer's new memoir called *Falling for Myself*. It was fantastic to read it. While I've done some education around ableism, there's always room for much more. I read her book when I was in my last round of revisions a couple of weeks back, and it helped me to notice some of the scenes differently. I looked at language and descriptions of some of my older secondary characters, and asked questions like, "Why did I represent that character in that way? Was that detail ageist? Ableist? Or was that a helpful thing to include?" Palmer's list of words to exclude got me thinking about alternatives to the word "crazy", for example.

I'm still thinking about it. The promotional back cover copy went out a while ago, and I need to ask my publisher to help me change some of the language that describes the character deciding that she must "take a stand". I learned from Dorothy's book that "taking a stand" is a particularly ableist way of writing. What I really want to say, and I haven't figured out how to say it in a short way, is "take a position" or something like that. So, yeah, the revision stage is the place for thinking about these things.

K: Have you found your editors and the publishing team around your work to be supportive and helpful with this aspect of the process?

F: Yes. As I was doing my revisions, I wrote a note to Shannon Whibbs, my editor, letting her know I was thinking about these issues. She was helpful in giving me perspectives, editing changes, and also leaving some things alone that were probably okay but I wasn't sure about.

K: Does the market play a role in your process? Do you think about selling books?

F: Yes, I do. I do think about selling books. With each new book I've worked on things like how does this book become more of a page turner? What makes this book more commercial? Some of that does help the craft—tightens up the work, for example—and I like the idea of making work more commercial if it fits the work, because it means more readers will read the book and take in the messages I want to share.

At the same time (this is a complicated question) you can decide as a writer how much of this is going to impact your own writing, because we don't have control over the publishing industry. We're just one piece of it. We have influence, like in the example I shared of bringing the issue of checking my ableist language with my editor.

And, we know it's not a very diverse industry, still. What that means is that books are judged by whatever dominant biases are in people's heads about what's an important book, what's a saleable book. I think it's very easy for the mainstream to pick up a book that's all about White people and feel that it more closely relates to their experience. That's a saleability thing. Deeper readers will work harder and be interested in more diverse stories.

We're seeing some positive, hopeful things happening. For example, we're seeing some more racialized people, more Indigenous people, winning awards. I'm so happy about that. That means their books are being read much more. It's that ship that's turning very slowly, inching towards something better.

K: I wonder, from your perspective, do you see the impact of decisions related to the Indigenous community differently than those made about other marginalized communities? I'm asking because the socio-political context for Indigenous peoples is different, say, than for migrating populations, for example.

F: I think that perhaps, especially amongst politicized people, there has been a deeper awareness of the Truth and Reconciliation report. I don't know that it's had a big impact on the broader Canadian population. For me, it impacted how I deliberately chose which authors to read, realizing that I'd only read a few books by Indigenous authors before then. It was a good way to spotlight—like, "Oh, crap! I could do more here." So maybe for some people that has highlighted something, and that's good. It's only a small gesture towards the larger corrections that need to happen, but it's good.

K: I think my question (in my head) is more to do with the potential impact of misrepresentation on the Indigenous communities than on the rest of us.

F: Yeah, I could see that. I came to Canada as a baby, and my family is in India. There's a rich publishing industry in India that addresses Indian stories and lives. So, we don't have the same experience of being appropriated and misrepresented. Even in the last twenty or thirty years there have been amazing Indo-Canadian writers bringing out stories without (or little?) appropriation. Sure, there's probably a body of racist narratives out there, but we have a wide range of writing that's mainstream and available, in India and here. So maybe that's where it's different.

People like me who are first generation have had to write our own and different stories compared to what exists in India or what was written by previous generations. And the second and third generations will have to write their own stories because they're differently impacted by the immigration story.

K: In fiction, do you feel that there's still a strong place for the novel?

F: I think so. Novels offer a deep dive into a story, and there's nothing like that experience of getting lost in a story. I think it's still one of the more popular forms.

K: Is there anything else about the topic about writing difference with respect that you'd like to add?

F: Alicia Elliott wrote in one of her essays in her recent book, *A Mind Spread Out on the Ground*, about writing with love. When writing difference, it's important to go beyond respect to love. I think that makes a lot of sense. And often we do love our characters. Maybe we do need to work harder on that with our secondary characters who we might have included to represent difference. But, I think that's where we have to go. We have to think about how this character will be read. If my character was out in the world, and she heard me talking about her in this way, would she know I was talking about her with love?

The other thing I wanted to talk about, and this question has come up at Q & A's quite a bit, are tips. Writers always want tips on how to avoid cultural appropriation. I always say, get a couple of beta readers, question your own biases, do your work in understanding the marginalized identity. The other tip is to maybe work with a co-writer if you don't share your primary character's marginalized identity (an idea I learned from Jael Richardson) and otherwise make those characters secondary.

So far those tips have worked out okay for me. I haven't yet exhausted the desire to write South Asian characters as my primary characters. But I wonder, will I one day? I hope I have a lot of novels in me, so what are my options? If I wanted to write, for example, an Indigenous woman, or a Black youth, or even a White disabled character, or... or... or... someone who's different from me. Do they always have to be my secondary character? And what does that mean?

I've been working on a young adult novel as a kind of experiment, and I have three primary characters: one who could look a lot like me when I was her age, one is a Lebanese teacher, and one is a White girl. I'm not worried about writing the South Asian character, not worried about the white girl, but I'm asking myself, "Can I write this Lebanese character?" I'm trying it out, and I'm going to see what it's like. Perhaps it helps that this first foray into a dominant character (who's not White and not from my own marginalized experience) is someone from my partner's community. Because of this relationship, I have quite a bit of access to socio-politcal-cultural information.

K: Would you say you're approaching that with love?

F: Yes.

K: In practical terms, what does that mean for you?

F: I'm really trying to be inside her world, her context, and to be building empathy for how she makes her decisions. I'm also making her imperfect. She's going to make mistakes and be challenged, otherwise she's no good as a character. But maybe writing with love means writing her as fully as I possibly can, with lots of quirks and not flat. And asking my partner questions like, "If she were to do this, and her family reacted in this way, what would that be like? What might be the repercussions?" Trying not to make her a stereotype but just a deep person who I love—I love her. I love all kinds of imaginary people [laughter].

So yeah, it's about being very self-reflective about what I'm up to with her, and I do see it as risky, so I'm being extra careful. And my partner's revisions are going to probably take more space and time than the South Asian one who is not so different from me at sixteen.

K: If the audience is perhaps younger for a young adult novel, do you feel a heightened sense of responsibility?

F: Not really because of that. It's more that it's my first time writing YA, and I think about the young adult novels I've read and where things stop—like, where does a romantic scene go? How far would it go? I'm thinking more about what's age appropriate. How would a young person think about this? How might I have thought about this at sixteen compared to the way a forty-eight year old would think about the same issue?

K: Given the context in Canada in 2019 for the literary fiction community, are there any things you wish the readers in our country would know about what it's like to create these stories and characters?

F: I would like readers to think deeply about which books they decide to buy and which ones they don't. Yes, please read everything. But, are you reading everything? Who are you not reading and why? Why do you think the book that's next to the book that you're buying might not be as good or as important a story? How many books have you read by Indigenous writers? People of colour? Disabled writers? And so on, and so on. I'm a slow reader, so I pluck away at this very gently.

Even more so, I would say to publishers, why do you say this story is more saleable than this story? When you decide to turn down a manuscript—you love the manuscript, you think it's great, you like the writing, but it's just not for you—this is the feedback a lot of marginalized writers get—"Great writing, great author, it's just not for me." Why? Because that's the subjectivity that we need to be looking at very carefully. As readers, as publishers, as writers—everybody. Why do we say that this book is more valid? I would like us all to be just a little bit more thoughtful about that subjectivity.

Waubgeshig Rice

September 4, 2019

Waubgeshig Rice is an author and journalist from Wasauksing First Nation on Georgian Bay. His first short story collection, Midnight Sweatlodge, *was inspired by his experiences growing up in an Anishinaabe community, and won an Independent Publishers Book Award in 2012. His debut novel,* Legacy, *followed in 2014. A French translation of* Legacy *was published in 2017. His latest novel,* Moon of the Crusted Snow, *was released in 2018 and became a national bestseller. He has worked extensively as a journalist since graduating from Ryerson University's journalism program in 2002, most recently as the host of* Up North, *CBC Radio's afternoon show for northern Ontario. He currently lives in Sudbury, Ontario with his wife and son.*

K: Do you feel there's value in reading fictional characters that are different from you?

W: Oh yeah, I think so. From a young age it was important for me to understand perspectives and experiences that were outside of my own world. I think that was a limited scope back when I was a teenager, when I was first getting into literature. There was very little diversity in mainstream literature back then. But still, I think it was a way for me to understand that this is how you learn about other perspectives and other cultures. By the time I moved to Toronto for university, I became more exposed to those diverse voices, which have really helped me to understand the dynamic city around me and some of the communities that comprised it. I mean, the best way to learn about another culture or another person's experience is to do it first hand and to actually spend time with them in person. Outside of that though, you can really get into some deep context and really enjoy some rich descriptions and experiences in literary fiction and in books. So, yeah, it's always been important for me to try to learn about other people through fiction. It's crucial for other Canadians to do that as well.

K: Do you find a difference in reading about those perspectives through fiction versus non-fiction?

W: I think in fiction there's a little more detail that you can explore along with nuances about interpersonal relationships and everyday experiences that you may not necessarily get in non-fiction. And I think that's because the general format of non-fiction is, by and large, journalism. You get a lot of personal reflections, but I think there are some limitations in not really getting into some of those finer details that I mentioned, whether that's the taste of a meal, the sound of music, or the expression on a loved one's face, details that are maybe unique to that particular culture or community. Those are the things that I really latch onto in fiction. Of course, those things are possible in non-fiction, but I don't think they resonate as deeply as they do in fiction, because you have that opportunity to explore these things in a really creative and fun way. That's the basic difference that I see. I'd probably have to consider more examples to see if that hypothesis holds true, but that's the first thing that comes to mind.

K: In your writing, do you take risks and represent those who are vastly different from yourself?

W: Only in the sense that I want to be as true and genuine to my culture and community as possible, and that may not always necessarily be accepted in mainstream publishing or literature or the mainstream media around literature. I've been fortunate to work with publishers who wanted me to really get into what it means to be Anishinaabe and to convey some of those details and some of those nuances in a respectful and meaningful way to myself and to my community. So I think, maybe, on the publishing side, they may see that as taking risks, but for me it's about being true to myself and true to my own people.

And I think things are changing. Some of the things I've written about recently may not have been published twenty or thirty years ago. I guess, on a personal level, any risk you take is trying not to convey anybody else's personal details even though those influence and inform your writing, no matter what, whether it's consciously or subconsciously. So I definitely try to be careful around that. I don't want a reader to look at something as being someone's personal experience close to me, even though those different influences make up a lot of my writing these days. That's also about being careful and considerate to your own family and to your own community members and to your own culture. The risk is that you might draw back the curtain too much and reveal too much about things that are distinct about a culture that we hold dear to our hearts and amongst ourselves. Those are some of the things I have to consider as I'm writing.

K: Do you have insight into how to do that well, how to negotiate the boundary you just described?

W: I would say talk to older storytellers. Talk to the elders, whether they be storytellers or knowledge keepers. That's what I've always done. Even if it's just talking to my dad, who's a very spiritual person and an elder. I consult with him about what I should share, which cultural details about Anishinaabe culture I should share. Reading a lot too is really important. Checking out how other authors have portrayed certain elements of your culture and your background in literary form. First and foremost, I think it's about having a network of people around you who you can consult with if you have ideas and you're worried about taking risks or stepping over a sensitive blind. I would always recommend checking with a bunch of people, whether they be authors or elders or community leaders or even just your family. If you go it alone, that's where you're potentially going to make mistakes, because you don't have that feedback, and you don't know what's possible or how people might perceive things.

K: You're an accomplished author and journalist. Might you have, from your experience, any concrete examples to share of when representing difference in fiction was not done well, and the resulting consequences?

W: I'll speak about my personal experience. My first book is called *Midnight Sweatlodge*. It's a collection of short stories that are about the young Indigenous experience. I had originally written those short stories when I was much younger, and I had a chance to revise them when I was in my twenties. I wanted to put them in a collection that was bound together by some sort of narrative, and I had the idea of putting them all in a sweatlodge, having each of the storytellers in a ceremony, a sweat ceremony. So that's potentially a risk, because that's a really sacred ceremony in a lot of Indigenous cultures, and a lot of Indigenous people think that you shouldn't talk about those finer details with outsiders, because these are things which were kept hidden, that were protected in the face of colonialism, in the face of brutal measures that were meant to erase them.

So, fortunately, when I was working through this, my editor, Jordan Wheeler, who is a Cree author and television writer, really helped me accept my own limitations and the cultural limitations of conveying some of these things and doing them in a really sensitive and careful way. His advice was, "Don't write about anything that isn't already on the public record. Don't go into detail about anything that's not already out there and easily accessible, because that's when you start giving things away, and that's when you potentially make some of these things more vulnerable, and some of these ceremonies and experiences more vulnerable to others who may exploit them, if they're out there in the mainstream discourse. More so, online, because there's just so much about Indigenous culture that's available online nowadays."

That's the strategy that we came to. If I was going to write about a sweatlodge, I was going to write about more superficial things and not about the history or the ceremonial background. That made me feel really good about the whole process, because I know some people would have been reluctant to read about a sweatlodge in that sense, because this is something we should protect and uphold in a very sacred and righteous way.

So, what I did in the end was just talk about the physical sweatlodge itself and the people getting ready to be part of the ceremony. We didn't talk about the history of it or about the teachings that would happen in the sweatlodge. We didn't talk about the steps of the ceremony that can occur in a sweatlodge and some of the ceremonial objects that are part of that as well. That was sort of the consensus we came to, and that has really guided me since then. I won't write about anything that isn't already accessible. I did grow up with a lot of ceremonial knowledge. I have a lot of experience with different ceremonies, but those are things I'll never write about, just out of respect for my culture and community and the people who made huge sacrifices to protect these things.

K: If that window into some of the sacred elements of your culture were to be broadened and your culture were to be more exposed and vulnerable, what's the potential damage that would happen through that exploitation? What's at stake here?

W: I think there's a lot at stake, from a writer's personal perspective to a wider community perspective. It could compromise a writer's own career, the trust they have with their own community, or with another culture or Indigenous Nation. It's funny, I was just talking with someone close to me today about something they're dealing with in their line of work in terms of cultural sensitivity and, without giving too much away because it's a confidential matter, what they discovered was that someone relied almost solely on the internet for cultural knowledge and assembling cultural information, and a lot of it ended up being a mishmash and being wrong in the end.

I think a lot of non-Indigenous people disregard the diversity amongst Indigenous cultures and nations, and they eventually blend things altogether in a sort of pan-Indigenous way. So, a writer going deeper into more sacred elements of their culture and putting it out there runs the risk of melding everything together and not really teaching anyone anything specific about what those ceremonies are supposed to be.

And that harms cultures. It harms many different cultures, not just the one that's being exposed. Other cultures may be pinned with this particular element when it doesn't have anything to do with them whatsoever. I think an example of that is the smudging process, smudging with sweetgrass or sage as a ceremonial opening for a lot of things. A lot of non-Indigenous Canadians are familiar with that now. As a result of its widespread visibility, some non-Indigenous Canadians think that all Indigenous cultures do that, which is not true. Inuit in the north don't smudge. Some other cultures out west don't smudge with those medicines either. So, yeah, it could have widespread repercussions. If this is how people, in general, are learning about Indigenous cultures and experiences nowadays, we have to be careful about how much we peel back that curtain.

So, to get back to your original question, if a writer exposes some of these things and does damage to their culture and to the relationships that they have with the people in their community, it can take a long time to recover from that. There's a lot of work that needs to happen to rebuild that relationship. As mentioned, these are things that a lot of communities take very seriously. So, a lot more thought has to go into the front end before these things are shared on the back end.

K: You mentioned that you feel like things have shifted in the last thirty years or so. You also talked about working with your editor, and about how this was a very helpful collaboration. Can you speak a little bit about that system around your work, about the shifts that are happening and where you think they need to go?

W: When I talk about that shift in general, it's just about general awareness in Canada as a whole, how things have improved in terms of knowledge due to a lot of different initiatives and efforts. I'm forty years old now, and I compare things to when I was a boy, and it's almost like night and day. There's a greater awareness of history and culture. That said, there's still a long way to go. Racism still thrives, especially as it relates to Indigenous peoples in this country.

In terms of my experience with publishing specifically, as I mentioned, my first editor for my first novel was an Indigenous editor, and that was the best outcome for me and the best experience I could have had as an introduction to the publishing world. My second editor for that novel was not Indigenous, but she was very open and very receptive to my culture and didn't want to impose any of her notions or concepts of Indigenous culture onto the manuscript that I had written. She was mostly concerned with what could help with the text, to make sure the story was tighter all around, from a literary perspective. And that was my experience with my second novel as well, *Moon on the Crusted Snow*. It was with a different publisher. The first two books were with an Indigenous publisher, but my current one is not. Still, my editor for my current book was hugely respectful and very encouraging, to the point where I was maybe even surprised by some of the things that she would bring to me in terms of the editing process.

For example, it was important for me to include some Ojibway language in the manuscript. How I'd originally written it, the character spoke some Ojibway, and then they translated it right after. But, she said I didn't necessarily have to do that, and to make the reader do that work themselves. They could figure out what it meant in the context of the scene or setting. That really encouraged me. I was heartwarmed to have her tell me these things and believe in the Anishinaabe elements of the story themselves and not change them whatsoever. So, I know that not all Indigenous authors have had that positive of an experience in terms of publishing and working with editors, but for me it's been great. I think, at this point in my career, I've been able to establish myself as a viable voice (for lack of a better word) in the literary realm. Those are the things I'm always going to fight for from now on, because I've been enabled and empowered to do so.

K: In your opinion, if fiction writing is somehow dehumanizing to others, what do you think the writer's responsibility is to repair relationships or move forward from that?

W: Yeah, I think it's up to the writer first and foremost to repair that relationship or do that damage control. And the good thing is, nowadays—I can only speak from an Indigenous perspective, but I think it might be true for other marginalized cultures—people are so connected online and through social media that they can network and provide a cohesive voice in response to something that may be problematic. We hear often about the internet pile ons and cancel culture and what have you, and initially there might be these emotional reactions, but I think what you have to remember is that people react that way because they care about their culture, and they care about their community and how they're represented. So, I think that once we look beyond that initial emotional reaction, we have to look at the constructive ways that a community or a group of people that feels wronged are responding and helping the author right the ship.

And I see that those opportunities are there. I see people try to reach out in different ways, and I think it's incumbent on an author that may have done damage to accept that offer and to do that work. If not, how can they be trusted going forward, right? That's the essence of storytelling from my cultural perspective anyway. It's building trust and trying to create community and a good way forward by sharing truth. Those are strong elements in Anishinaabe culture that I think we should always try to uphold. An author may feel offended or may feel sensitive to being called out to these things, but they need to acknowledge that. If they're not writing their personal experiences but they're writing somebody else's, it's their duty to do right by those communities, and they should accept the feedback that comes from those communities.

K: All of this exists in a system. You mentioned the importance of storytelling and sharing truth. Is fiction truth?

W: I think it is, yeah. I think fiction is rearranging truth and presenting it in different ways, in creative ways. At the core of most pieces of fiction is someone's personal experience, or someone else's personal experience who is close to them. So I very much think it's truth. With *Moon of the Crusted Snow*, the characters aren't directly influenced by people in my life, but the scenarios are, and other things are. The best feedback I've received about the story is from Anishinaabe people who say, "I see my community in that. I see my loved ones in this story, and that is how things are where I'm from." So, that's truth, right? That's me sharing someone else's truth with them and with a lot of other people. So yeah, I would definitely agree with that.

K: Does fiction play a role in social change?

W: I think it can play a huge role in social change. It may not necessarily be the driving force, but it can open people's eyes and bring people together, depending on the experience and the historic moment. If you think of the current state of affairs, a lot of people bring up the fact that dystopian fiction of the last century is coming true now. These works of fiction are reference points to how bad things could get and how people are saying, "Okay, they're getting this bad now." So, I don't think these works of fiction are the catalyst themselves, but I think they can open people's eyes and provide crucial perspectives and maybe help people think a little more critically about their surroundings, because of those sorts of speculative hypotheses that can be presented in fiction.

In *Moon of the Crusted Snow* what I wanted to do was try to encourage people to think about their own surroundings and their place in this world and what they could do to make it a better place. And I think a lot of other authors would agree that this is what they'd like to do as well. So, again, it may not be the thing that prompts social change, but it can help equip people to think differently about their experiences and about the world they live in.

K: I received permission from the United Nations to include an appendix in this collection of the United Nations Declaration on the Rights of Indigenous Peoples. Can you speak about that document at all, and whether it has value in helping people to write fiction and to be sensitive?

W: I have to say that I haven't read it all the way through recently—I did when it was first presented ten or so years ago, or whenever it was. Yeah, I think it has huge value as a crucial reference point in terms of some of the Indigenous struggles around the world. I think if anybody is going to tell any story about an Indigenous culture or community, they should read that document in order to understand what some of these universal issues are. I think art can play an important role in bringing people together in terms of understanding the Indigenous struggle, or for non-Indigenous peoples to understand the colonial harms that have happened to Indigenous cultures around the world. So, to answer your question briefly, yeah, I do believe it should be an important reference point for people, for pretty much everybody in this world going forward.

K: In Canada, do you see any nuanced contrast in the responsibilities of a writer who is writing difference when it comes to Indigeneity as compared to writing other types of difference, such as gender, age, ability, or another marginalized ethnicity?

W: I would say that maybe the same best practices apply, such as spending time with the people who are not like you and getting to know their communities and experiences. I've felt the same about my own work in terms of including two-spirit characters or characters with disabilities. I don't know what those experiences are personally. I have family who know those realities well, but I need to consult with them. I need to ask them what's respectful to write about and how far I may go in sharing an experience like that. So, I think the best practices are the same in that you have to do that outreach and do that work, building that good relationship in order to tell that story in an effective and respectful way.

K: What insight might you have about building that good relationship in the kind of work that requires a writer to connect with many people for a short-term project? Do you find yourself keeping those relationships alive, and if so, how do you manage so many relationships?

W: That's a really good question. That's hard, especially as a journalist, because I meet new people every day, and I talk to new people every day. Social media definitely helps in terms of connecting with different people, but what I try to do is to go back to those people periodically and not necessarily have them as a one and done, because I would feel guilty if that's how I practiced my journalism. Talk to a person for an assignment and never talk to them again—I don't think that's respectful. It's incumbent upon me to do that follow up if someone has shared their story with me, if someone has shared a deeply personal experience with me, and I've shared it with thousands of other people, whether it be online, or on air, or in a book. I have to reciprocate in some way to give them more opportunities if they want them, or to provide whatever assistance that they may need, or to help with whatever they may be working on.

I try to do regular follow up with people I've talked to, and it's hard because I talk to a lot of people. There are some people who really stick with me, especially if they share something deeply personal. I want to make sure they feel comfortable doing that, whether it be in the moment or five months later. That's crucial for us, as storytellers, to do that, because we have the responsibility and privilege of sharing other people's stories.

K: Is there anything that we haven't talked about related to this topic that you'd like to share?

W: I think the only additional thing is that, whether it relates to journalism or literature, we're in a really good time right now, where people from the so-called margins are sharing their stories and becoming journalists and becoming authors and getting acclaim and recognition. I think it's the best time ever for diversity in those sectors, but it's crucial that we also get those people into management positions and into outreach and sales and marketing and editorial positions, so that they're not just the people on the front line. They need people like them within the structures of these institutions to advocate for them and to ensure that this isn't just a flash-in-the-pan kind of moment and that it's ingrained within the structure of these institutions themselves in order to make the future more welcoming for any person from any background to share their stories or their skills or their experiences in journalism or in literature. That's what I'd like to see. I'd like to see both media organizations and publishers take that a little bit more seriously and welcome people from diverse backgrounds for management, for executive positions and that kind of thing.

Eden Robinson

October 1, 2019

Eden Robinson was born in Kitamaat, British Columbia, where she still lives. She is a member of the Haisla and Heiltsuk First Nations. She is the author of several works of fiction – Traplines, Monkey Beach, Blood Sports, Son of a Trickster, *and* Trickster Drift. *She is also the author of a work of non-fiction,* Sasquatch at Home: Traditional Protocols & Modern Storytelling.

K: How do you approach writing difference in your fiction?

E: I'm Haisla and Heiltsuk. I grew up on my father's reserve. There were clear boundaries about what I could share from our culture and what I couldn't. There's a protocol. There are about thirty potlatching cultures from Alaska to Washington. It's very hierarchical. People prove their status through stories, songs, dances. Stories belong to individuals, families, clans or communities. If I want to use any of those stories, I need permission. I'd have to throw a feast. A potlatch is more formal. A feast would suffice. I could also gift the chiefs, but that would foster a reputation for being a cheap person, which is a lifelong reputation with social consequences. So when I started writing fiction, that's how I approached it.

So, we have three different levels of stories in my culture. To tell the more formal ones, like the ones involved in a potlatch where there are names, titles and ranks, these stories fall under Haisla copyright. I could ask permission and throw a feast. I stayed in the more informal range with Trickster stories—any stories that are told to children so they can learn our nuyum, so they will learn the handsome way of doing things. Those stories are meant to teach and are in the Haisla public domain, so I could use those ones. The casual stories—stories that a family tells about grandmother, like the time she and grandpa were driving to Rupert after a wedding, and she was tired of her girdle, and he threw it out the window, and it landed on a cop car.

So that was my background coming into fiction. When I was writing my first novel, because it was set in Kitamaat Village and involved Haisla characters, I made sure to consult with Elders. I consulted with Elders outside of my family, because the Haisla are three tribes amalgamated into one: the Henaaksiala, the Haisla and the Nalibila. They're all on one reserve, but we still have that ethnic tension. To use any of those stories I went to those Elders, and to use any of our stories I went to my Elders. There's not many Nalibila left, and I didn't use any of those stories in the book. I was very nervous about *Monkey Beach* when it came out, but mostly they were annoyed that I had an open-ended novel. They were angry about it because, "That's not the way you end a story."

K: That doesn't come with the same kind of social consequences though—is it more of a critique of your writing?

E: Yeah, everyone's annoyed by that, not just the Haisla [laughter].

K: Will they stay true to that in the movie?

E: Yeah, they've had to change the structure to fit into ninety minutes, so they ironed out a lot of the time leaps, so it's not as circular. It's still complicated for a film, but it's not as complicated as the book.

K: Did you need to seek permission for the movie rights to be granted?

E: Because the story was all within the public domain, it was more a matter of protocol, and the people involved in the movie took responsibility for that. Loretta Todd is a Métis Director, so she's used to dealing with protocols. There were still some moments of conflict, but we mostly just talked those out. With the TV series, Michelle Latimer was very conscious of how protocol could be different, talking directly to the Band Council and to the community. Also, in *Trickster*, I was doing my own spin on supernatural creatures that were within the public domain. I didn't want to venture anywhere into Potlatch territory. It was very time consuming for *Monkey Beach*, and it was a lot easier not to deal with that.

Now there are more Indigenous writers who are dealing with the same issues—it's not as novel as it used to be. It's something people have become more comfortable with. Now the Haisla know my work, so they just ask me—like, when people assume I'm speaking for the Haisla or Heiltsuk, they've asked me to step in and say I've been asked not to speak for them. I'm not an elected official. I'm not an ambassador or a diplomat. I'm a creative. That's my role in the community.

K: Where does that role sit in your community? What kind of power comes with being a creative?

E: There's no power that comes with being a novelist. They were more impressed with the television series and movie—I kept having to explain that I have nothing to do with casting [laughter].

K: It doesn't matter that you know me… [laughter].

E: Yeah, you send in your audition tape like everyone else. They know now that I have nothing to do with casting, so I'm not as impressive as I used to be [laughter].

K: You received the Writers' Trust Fellowship, and you've said that your earlier work focused on the horror of things, and that your community and culture is so much more complex than that. How did that fact inform your later writing?

E: I was always very Emo. In the core of my being is a little Emo-Goth girl [laughter]. That's not the worldview of the Haisla. That's not the worldview of the Heiltsuk. That's just where I'm coming from. Most people in the village know that's my particular quirk. They're kind of expecting that. *Trickster* is still dark, but I had more fun with it. I didn't take it as earnestly as I took *Monkey Beach*, for instance. In *Monkey Beach*, I didn't play around with that. There were some moments of humour, but it was mostly earnest. Whereas *Son of a Trickster* gets a little bizarre. As the series progresses, it just gets increasingly strange, and I really enjoyed that. It was a lot of fun. I've been lightening up. When I say, "lightening up", I mean for me—when people look for a slapstick novelist, it's a little disappointing, but it's "light-er", it's "Eden-light" [laughter].

K: A new genre: Eden-light fiction. I love it. My family's from South Africa, and we use humour to deal with trauma and intergenerational effects of traumatic histories—you have to.

E: If you take it all seriously, it's just going to kill you. You'll have a heart attack, mental health problems…

K: All of that happens anyway [laughter].

E: [laughter] But you can laugh about it.

K: Yeah. You talked about the complexity of your culture. I wonder if you feel a responsibility, then, to represent that complexity? And if that's something you think other fiction writers might not consider?

E: In the beginning of my career I did, because there were very few venues or opportunities to explain that we're not a monolith. We don't all think the same way. There are different shades to the culture. There are people who are more conservative, people who are more liberal. There are people who potlatch, people who don't. But now that there are a lot more Indigenous writers, that pressure has eased right off. It's like, we don't expect White writers to be ambassadors for the White race, why would we expect Indigenous authors to take on that role? That's a huge sea change. I used to think I should come out in a Deanna Troy uniform [laughter]. "Ambassador Eden is here to explain things to you" [laughter].

K: Not just here, but the supernatural world as well—I can explain every realm... [laughter]. When was the shift away from that idea for you? Was it after *Monkey Beach*? Was it just before *Son of a Trickster*?

E: It was after *Blood Sports*. I thought, "I'm just going to go back to my serial killers, because they don't care how I represent them [laughter]. Then for ten years... I have a lot of aging family members, so I started taking on more caregiving responsibility and caretaking, and then I went through menopause. It was all pretty consuming. I didn't do a lot of writing, but I did do a lot of listening [laughter]. In those ensuing years the new generation of Indigenous writers was coming out with some spectacular books. Some of the scholars that are coming out now, the thinkers, who are examining just what is expected of Indigenous writers and is that fair? How does that differ from other writers? They've started questioning these things. And that's made it a lot easier for me.

The thing that most bothered me was that you have to have positive role models and positive representation. That's fair. That's not the kind of story I was telling. I'm not here to uplift you. I'm not here to make redemption art. I'm here to tell a story about someone who's going through a very specific experience. The redemption arc is not going to work with this guy. Maybe in the long-term, but that's not where my artistic interest lies. So in this time and in this place I still get complaints about my lack of positive representation.

K: Who's complaining about that?

E: People who are expecting Indigenous fiction to be what they expect it to be. And mostly I ignore that, because that's not within my realm of interest. I'm not interested in that at all. I grew up with, surrounded by, people who had been through the residential school experience. They were second, third and fourth generation survivors, and they came with a certain amount of trauma, and it came out in their lives a certain way. And some people had different reactions. It did impact our communities. It's more out in the open now, but I don't want to sanitize that experience or clean it up for consumption. That's nothing that I'm interested in doing.

K: Thank you. My ancestors came from apartheid South Africa and slavery before that. I believe we can't. We have to be truthful.

In another interview you had mentioned that your father told stories, and I think your grandfather (about the Trickster), and it didn't evoke the kind of humour you had expected it to evoke, and that perhaps some of the context of the Trickster had been lost. You then set about sharing that context. How did it get lost?

E: Because they grew up in Brantford [laughter] instead of on the West Coast, they hadn't heard West Coast Trickster stories before. Their moms are Haisla/Heiltsuk, but their dads are Mohawk, so they grew up with more Mohawk stories than they did with Haisla/Heiltsuk stories. So, the Trickster stories are twisty—it takes a while to get to the point [laughter], and you're on a journey discovering all these supernatural creatures, and if you're not familiar with them, if you don't know Tsonoqua, how would you understand the humour? If you don't know his sister, Jwasins, there's no context anymore. The Mohawk stories are very different from the Haisla/Heiltsuk stories.

K: Do the Mohawk stories also carry stories about a humorous Trickster?

E: Their Trickster is very different from ours, and from the stories that I've heard, it's not an equivalent. They're operating with very different rules. They have very different protocol. Like, when I went to visit, there's kind of a settlement feast, more equivalent to one of our thank you suppers. It was their ten day, and I'd never been to a ten day. So, after the person passes, their family has a ten day sit, and then on that tenth day they have a feast, but the women don't serve, it's the men that serve. I wasn't used to that. You know, you have a basket, and the food is placed in the basket, and they go around. And so I didn't know any of the protocol, but they knew that, so they gave me a lot of leeway. And that's the same with the stories.

I could never tell the kind of stories I tell with Mohawk characters, because I don't know any of that. Or, I could, but it would take a lot of research, a lot of attending the ceremonies, being part of it, you know, figuring out the intricacies. Whereas it's all baked in with mine [laughter]. I grew up with that. I don't need to sift through the different levels of complexity and nuance for even the basic details.

So, with *Son of a Trickster*, I wanted to reflect that there are sixty different First Nations in British Columbia. They intermingle, marry into each other's communities. When you go into a different town, it's a different First Nation. I had a lot of characters who were from different First Nations in Kitamaat or surrounding Jared. I had to get sensitivity readers early in the process. I just said, "Okay, let's figure this out. I want to use this nation, this nation, this nation, this nation—is it appropriate? Who can I talk to? How do I explain this to them?" And some of them only wanted to read the sections, some of them wanted to read the whole book. But, you know, I couldn't have put those nations in without doing my background research.

K: You had mentioned that your reserve is a bringing together of three nations. Do you also have a clan system within those three nations?

E: Yes. For the main Haisla group there are four. They've been amalgamated down—there were two others, but the fish amalgamated with whale, and the raven amalgamated with the beaver, the eagle clan—there are two different eagle clans, one from Haisla, one from Henaaksiala, two different whale clans one from Haisla, one from Henaaksiala, and the protocols are slightly different, so there are always complaints—"They're not doing it right. This is the way we do it, and that's the way they do it." So when we're at their potlatch, we're going to do it their way. But there are more Haisla than there are Henaaksiala, so when it comes to the language groups, they have a slightly different accent. A lot of the language material is in the Haisla dialect, not the Henaaksiala dialect, so there's a lot of tension when you use Haisla. That's something that would be really challenging to broach. So I leave that to the cultural people [laughter].

I'm like, okay, I have no idea—if you have Haisla and Henaaksialla kids in the same school, and they're learning basic language, it's fine. But once you start getting into more complex ideas, that's when the dialect things come into play. The first linguists who came to Kitamaat Village, all their consultants were Henaaksialla, so the Haisla people were like, "You're saying it wrong" [laughter]. "That's not the way you pronounce the words," and they were like, "Well, we were the only ones who would consult with them." So unless you understood that there were three different dialects—now there's mostly just the two, but back then there were still three—how do you deal with that? Many would go with the dialect that had the most people.

K: What's the population?

E: In the village, eight hundred. In total, like fifteen hundred. So these are very small groups. And ours isn't even very complex compared to like the Secwepemc, who have seventeen different reserves with seventeen different dialects. It's quite an extensive territory. To go to the writers I've spoken to from there, they're having the same discussion. They're having the same concerns. Yeah, the poet says, "I'm really lucky, no one cares about poetry" [laughter].

K: This idea of enlisting the help of first readers—do you find that important process hinders your artistic output?

E: No, it usually adds depth. It usually adds more realism. It adds more detail that I would never have thought of myself. If I know I'm going to be using characters from other nations, I bring them into the process as early as I can, so that I can incorporate the different details that come out of that, and I leave space for it. If I try to do it too late in the process, then I find it's not as thorough. It comes off as sloppy. I've learned to do it as early as I can in the process, so that I have as much room to play as possible.

K: How is *Return of the Trickster* coming along? Is the story influenced by feedback from the first two novels in the trilogy?

E: I don't know if I'll ever do a trilogy again—it's a lot of pressure. There's so much backstory. There are so many unresolved plot threads. Making my way through the first draft I realized that I was just going to have to let some of them go or it was going to be a six hundred page novel just tying up all the loose ends. I was like, "Okay, what do I prioritize?" Over the winter I pulled out about a hundred pages. It wasn't working. It wasn't doing anything for the novel.

I think it's probably going to be another open-ended story [laughter]. But it won't be as bad as *Trickster Drift*. *Trickster Drift* left at a cliffhanger, and I won't leave it like that. It won't be as open-ended as *Monkey Beach*. But, I was force fed so many novels with obvious morals at school. They would always hammer you over the head with what you were supposed to learn from the story, and they would take a chapter to lecture you from what you should have learned from the book. I came away determined never to do any of that [laughter]. Instead of spoon feeding you, I'm just going to leave it wide open, so that you have a lot of freedom as a reader to interpret.

K: I felt uplifted by *Son of a Trickster*. I was admiring how the hope and beauty shone through the challenging parts of these characters and their circumstances. I remember taking that away from the read, and that was after I met you at the Festival of Literary Diversity, a while ago. All to say that even though you're not intending to share lessons, I totally took away learning.

E: If it comes from the characters, that's what I want. I don't want to impose my morals or any of that on the reader.

K: Is that possible?

E: Yes. When you're telling someone what to think, you're imposing your ideas of what the story's about. And I think, when you're a reader, you have a relationship with the book, and you're bringing your own experiences to it, so if you have to explain to the reader what your book was about in a wrap-up kind of chapter, well then, I don't think you've done your job. But I've had a lot of complaints that I don't explain enough, so I've stretched into territory that I'm not comfortable in. I'm like, "I guess I have to wrap up somehow" [laughter]. Maybe a little more than I've been doing. That's where my editor comes in. She tells me where there are holes, like, "It will feel more satisfying if you close this thread."

K: From reading difference, growing up, did you see yourself in books? Did you read difference?

E: I never saw myself in books. I never saw characters like me or like my community in books. And the characters that were supposed to be Indigenous were pan-Indigenous and didn't speak to anything in my reality. I was clear in my purpose—to put everyday characters I saw into Canadian literature. I wanted them to exist. I wanted them to be seen. For *Son of a Trickster*, I was less driven by that, because there are more writers, more Indigenous writers period. There are more people who speak to the Haisla experiences, so I'm not the only voice—all that responsibility isn't mine.

K: What was the result of that? By having this in the canon, did it shift things the way you had hoped?

E: Yes, well, I hope the consequences have been good. When I'm talking with cousins, and they say there were moments on the ferry when they had to sleep on the floor because they didn't have a stateroom, and someone said, "I never realized that I'd never read that before, and it was weird to read 'home' in a book."

K: Weird good?

E: Weird good. It was like, "Someone sees my home, and here it is, and other people are going to see it." So it's validating, if you've been an avid reader all your life, and you've never seen your home. Even people in northern British Columbia who weren't Indigenous, who'd had experiences like going fishing every weekend, would tell me they hadn't seen northern British Columbia in fiction that way. There's a lot more writing coming out of rural areas of Canada now, areas that haven't been explored as much. It's not Vancouver and Toronto-centric all the time, but there are some experiences that we just don't get to see.

K: In your writing, when you've written characters that you don't see in your everyday, those who are different than yourself, what has this practice brought to you, as a writer?

E: When you try to think yourself into that reality—like, "What would my life be like if I couldn't understand these social cues or if I didn't have this range of emotions and I saw the world in this way, what would that be like?" And then, "What would it be like to be that person's cousin [laughter]?" So anytime you're writing a novel, hopefully that exploration helps deepen your understanding of the world that you're writing. If you're not thinking about how your characters are going to change you as you write your way into their world, then you're probably writing superficially. Whatever world you're writing—if your writing isn't changing you, how deeply are you getting into that world?

That's not a goal for every writer. If you're writing something, and it's not meant to be terribly deep, then that's not a question you ask. But with every novel that I've written, I've had to sit and think about that particular world and that particular set of characters. I've asked questions, done the research, just sat and thought about how it's changed me. That's usually a sign that you've written something that you're going to be proud of.

K: How did writing psychopaths change you?

E: It taught me where not to go [laughter]—don't hitchhike! And just what level of psychopath we all have within ourselves—it's a part of us. It's a spectrum. It's not you either are or aren't. It's the same with sociopaths. There are certain aspects to our culture that have those elements in them, like factory farming—psychopathic. It's a very dark part of our society, the way we're interacting with non-human entities on the same planet. It's not something that you think about normally if you're just trying to get through life. But, if you're a writer [laughter], and you have a character who thinks about these things, it shifts you. It shifts your window of discourse from what isn't acceptable to what is acceptable discourse. Or it makes you think about it at least.

K: How did you research psychopaths?

E: Well, I dated one [laughter], and then became fascinated. Got stalked. Went through hell, came out the other side, and thought, "You know what, this could definitely help my writing" [laughter]. Method writer—I can't become one, but I can date one" [laughter]. No, it wasn't deliberate—I'm not that committed to my art.

K: In your experience, have you ever experienced regret over what you've published?

E: Yes. Usually it's when things are half-baked, and I've let them go. It needed more time, but I had deadlines. You sit there later and think, "Yeah, that needed a couple more months of just sitting on it and thinking about it," and you look at it later and groan.

K: Do you read your old stuff?

E: I find it really hard to read old stuff. Now, for instance, I've read *Traplines* in full Emo stage—full Emo-Goth and everything was earnest. Adjectives were my enemy and adverbs were forbidden, a sign of weakness. You needed muscular verbs and very clear nouns. I was very heavily influenced by social realists—Carver and Hemingway. Yeah, so I would have lots of screaming matches over semi-colons. So now when I read that collection, it's like reading a high school diary. That's who I was back then. I find it amusing now.

K: You said regret.

E: Yeah, not for *Traplines*, but I regret some essays and short stories that I've let loose. I'm a very slow writer, and I like time to bake and mull. I don't like writing for TV because it's too fast, and the deadlines are too tight. One of the student screenplays I wrote was *Two Bad Beautiful Babes with Big Guns*. That, I regret [laughter].

K: Have you had negative feedback related to how you represented difference in your work?

E: Yes.

K: How did you respond?

E: "Well, that's your view" [laughter].

K: So, it just doesn't register at all. You're good. You have a boundary.

E: If it's a comment about my representation of Indigenous people, usually the people making that comment don't have a complex or nuanced view of Indigenous people. If I don't fit into their parameters, that's fine. It's not something I'm concerned about. So it depends on the source. If it's an Elder, then they might be concerned that I've shown underaged sex [laughter].

K: Has that happened?

E: Yes. That was the main criticism from Elders in the village for some of the Trickster stories—the icing scene in particular, didn't go down well—especially with the more Christian Elders.

K: How'd you deal with that? That's where you live, that's your community.

E: Yes, and they're very free to tell me anything they want. And they're free to come to me with their criticisms. That's an artistic choice I've made.

K: Do they see it that way?

E: No—"You should take it out" [laughter].

K: Does that hold sway over you?

E: It would have meant more if I were younger. But now, at their age, given their circumstances, this is how they express themselves, that's their sexuality. I'm not going to edit that out, but I certainly won't read it to a class.

K: Would that prevent it from being selected as a school text?

E: Well, the very first page would prevent it from being selected [laughter]—usually they get to the bottom of the first page and they're like, "No."

K: So, in today's social context, in Canada in the fall of 2019, what's the role of literary fiction in our social context?

E: In Canada, I'm very grateful that we have a darker vision of the world [laughter].

K: What do you mean?

E: When I've tried to publish in the States, they usually say it's a little too dark. The publishing reality in the States is different than in Canada. Canada is more open to grim reality. In the States it's more of a niche market. I consider myself mid-grim. David Adams Richards' *Mercy Among the Children* was peak-grim [laughter]. Most of our fiction is at least entry-level grim. We seem suspicious of being entertained. So a lot of the mystery writers, science fiction writers, romance writers, usually have to go to the United States to get agents and publishers.

Canadian literature is full of grim fiction. And I'm so grateful, because that's my wheelhouse [laughter]. Dark and grim. One of my mentors was Icelandic, and he had a dark sense of humour, and that was where I was at, and we got along really well. I understood where his stories were funny, and he understood where my stories were funny. Whereas, other writers who didn't have such a bleak sense of humour didn't find anything in it funny [laughter]. For instance, in *Son of a Trickster*, where Maggie runs over their pit-bull, I thought it was a little funny in the blackest sense, but when I did my first reading of it, I discovered that nobody else thought it was funny, and it was not a successful reading [laughter]. Note to self: "No running over doggies in your readings."

K: Do you think fiction has a social impact?

E: I think fiction has less of a social impact than it used to, but people still read. If we want to have younger generations read, then we need to write stories that speak to them. I ask my niece and nephew to be first readers. They read sections, and their big complaint was that my character in *Son of a Trickster* was still on Facebook [laughter]. Only someone really uncool would still be on Facebook—that's what you do to keep in touch with your Gran, not to socialize with other teens. They've been really good with helping me navigate Snapchat [laughter].

K: Do you think fiction has an impact on the adult population?

E: I think it does. The impact of fiction on the adult population—not just books like *Women Talking* by Miriam Toews, where there's a specific message about the impact of the ghost rapes. When you're reading, it's one of the only ways to get out of your own head, and it's one of the only ways to see through other people's eyes that we have. We don't have psychic powers just yet [laughter]. I think with movies and television you get a sense of it, but you don't get the full experience of getting into someone else's head—seeing what they see and hearing what they think. When people are reading fiction, they go there for the immersive experience, because you're pulling on whole different parts of your brain. It's a whole different exercise from viewing a television show where it's been previewed for you.

K: What is the responsibility of writing truth in fiction? How does a writer go about doing that without obscuring important nuances of human reality?

E: The characters that you have, when you create a world for them—there's a difference between their truth and yours. If you're constantly imposing your truth on your characters, then the reader can sense that you're cheating, and they're not as invested. Whereas even if your characters believe something that you don't, even if they have experiences that you don't, the truths that your characters are revealing through their experiences in your novel should remain true to those characters, even if it's not something that you would have as truth.

I remember this one novelist—she wrote this lovely novel, and the protagonist was deeply complex, and in the end of the novel she was in the trunk of someone's car being driven into the darkness. And then this happy, friendly cop comes and rescues her. I loved it right up until that point, because you know that was really hard to believe. And she said, "Yeah, that was kind of imposed on me by the publisher, who said they wouldn't publish my novel if it didn't have an uplifting ending." I asked what ending she had intended, and it was more in keeping with that world. Sometimes I think we impose more of ourselves on our novel, and that's usually when the ending is unsatisfying.

K: So, this is the trick, right? How do we do that well? Isn't it impossible not to impose ourselves on our fiction writing?

E: Editors and readers. When you're not being true to your character, when you impose a twist or when you're trying to be super clever and have something completely unrealistic happen, your editors or first readers will usually call that out. They'll usually say, "Well, I didn't really believe that this would happen," and then you have to figure out how much of this is me imposing myself on the story—my beliefs, what I think is right—and how much of this is true to the world that I created? That's just setup and payoff. If you've set up this world, then the payoff has to match. It's the old Chekhov thing, where if you have a gun in the first chapter, you have to fire it—you can't just have a random gun.

K: Why do you write?

E: I love to read and have always wanted to read something set in my community. When I was writing *Monkey Beach*, I thought that would pretty much be the end of it, and I'd just go back to short stories. But my muse is yappy [laughter].

Chelene Knight

October 30, 2019

Chelene Knight is the author of the poetry collection Braided Skin *and the memoir* Dear Current Occupant, *winner of the 2018 Vancouver Book Award, and long-listed for the George Ryga Award for Social Awareness in Literature. Her essays have appeared in multiple Canadian and American literary journals, plus the* Globe and Mail, *the* Walrus, *and the* Toronto Star. *Her work is anthologized in* Making Room, Love Me True, Sustenance, The Summer Book, *and* Black Writers Matter.

The Toronto Star *called Knight, "one of the storytellers we need most right now." Knight was the previous managing editor at* Room *(2016 - June 2019), and programming director for the Growing Room Festival (2018, 2019), and now CEO of #LearnWritingEssentials and Breathing Space Creative. She often gives talks about home, belonging and belief, inclusivity, and community building through authentic storytelling.*

Knight is currently working on Junie, *a novel set in Vancouver's Hogan's Alley, forthcoming in 2020. She was selected as a 2019 Writers' Trust Rising Star by David Chariandy.*

K: I see that you enjoy reading Toni Morrison and Jamaica Kincaid. Did you read them from a young age, or did you find them later in life?

C: I found a lot of the books I love later in life. When I was younger, I read a lot of whatever was placed in front of me. Usually, that happened to be old, White authors. So, finally finding women of colour and Black authors in my twenties I thought, "My God, I could have been reading these things earlier on, as a teenager or as a young girl." I definitely fell into a lot of those books later.

K: How did that happen?

C: It happened through finding mentors. I started sharing my writing and my work and just having people say, "I think you'd really enjoy reading this author." Or, "You might want to check out how this person writes because I think it might help your style and your flavour," and this and that. So, it's a lot of coming from the outside, I would say. It was less me stumbling upon things and more that mentorship where someone knows my style and my tastes.

K: How did that influence you as a writer?

C: That gave me permission to write a certain way. It kind of grabbed my writing by the throat, in a way, where it was like, "You can actually do this, or you can do that, or you can have your characters live in different worlds." It really opened up a whole new idea of what writing could be.

K: Do you find that your son has more available to him or is more aware of what's out there?

C: Because of the intersections that he belongs to, he's more aware of the different literature out there. He's not a big reader anymore. He used to be when he was younger, but now he's just into different kinds of art. I'll casually throw some books his way and say, "You might be interested in this story, or the idea around this," and kind of place them there like they were placed for me. Sometimes he takes the bait and sometimes not. We talk about the types of books he reads at school for projects where he's forced to read certain things, and I'll see them and say, "Why are you reading this?" Like, why isn't he reading, not even writers of colour, but young Canadian authors who are out there now writing about current situations, versus books written a hundred and twenty-five years ago?

K: You've come to writing fiction just recently. This is the first novel that you're publishing now. On the *Running Wild* podcast with Christine Wild, you mentioned the word "authenticity" a lot. I feel that this idea of writing difference with respect has to do with authenticity. You said it's more exhausting for you to write fiction than the memoir and poetry you've already published. Can you speak to that a bit?

C: That word "authentic" or "authenticity" has a different meaning for me than it might for someone else. For me it's about looking at your story, looking at the shape of it, and being honest with yourself and being like, "This is my story. This is how it fits in my hand. The page that it falls on needs to be able to hold it." Sometimes that might mean you have to invent a new form, or it might not fit into that chronological novel form. So, for me, authenticity is just being open to the idea that your story might not fit anywhere. It might not fit into the templates that are already there, and you might have to create something new. When I think of that word "authenticity", it's more about honesty and being open and looking at creating your own house for your story.

K: That's what you did for *Dear Occupant*. What about in your fiction writing? You've chosen a traditional form—the template of the novel.

C: Exactly, I think that's what I found so exhausting. I was authentic with myself. I was very open and honest, and I realized that this story did fit into that traditional storytelling form. This is the opposite for me, so I was like, "Now I've got to make sure all of these things line up, and I have to have the characters in a particular world and stay true to some of the history I'm writing about, which is really important to me." That's a different mindset than just getting my personal story out onto the page, because now I'm building worlds, and I'm building these characters who are doing different things once I place them there. They're doing things that I'm not expecting them to do.

Part of being authentic is being open to that and saying to your characters, "You guys are in the room now. Let's see what happens." I have to document that, and I find it incredibly exhausting, but also really fun and totally new. You go into this new world yourself. The characters are in this world, but you as the writer also get to be in this space, which is exciting.

K: How do you find trying to bring authenticity to a fictional story?

C: It's kind of tough. In fiction we hold the assumption that everything is made up, but I don't think that's true. Even in fiction there's always going to be bits and pieces and glimmers of truth embedded throughout. As I'm writing, I'm realizing that one character, or all the characters, have bits and pieces of me. I should follow that, but I also want to make them their own people. I really just have to step back a bit as well and realize it's a bit like patchwork sometimes. So, one character might have bits and pieces of me. They might have bits and pieces of a friend of mine. They might have mannerisms from my mom, or something like that. Putting all of those pieces together, you're still building that fictional character. When you rip them apart, they're actually bits of truth, so it's really interesting when you deconstruct as you're constructing. It's just this really strange process.

K: So, you're writing fictional characters, yet they also feel authentic as pieces of truth from yourself and your friends. What would you say is at stake when we depart from that and dive into realms that are totally different from our own experiences?

C: I think that's when you need to be open to the idea of research and having conversations with folks. You kind of drive down this road, and you realize you're in really different terrain, and you're like, "Ooh, how do I navigate this?"

I think the best course of action is always just to stop and give yourself some space and take a breath and let things marinate. Then look at that world and at the situation and at how you're going to interpret that through your words, and then ask yourself a series of questions. You might ask, "Am I an authority to speak to this experience?" If so, continue on. If not, then you might want to stop and write down names of some folks you can think of that might be able to help you along your journey.

I always think of communication and checking in with other folks and building a community, so you can say, "Here's a story that I'm working on, and here's where it took me, but I feel like I need some help." Overall, it's just asking for help and realizing that you can't possibly have all the answers in your head. As genius as this book may be, there's always something that can be added by having a conversation with someone.

K: With Jónína Kirton and Nav Nagra you provide that kind of sensitivity reading as part of your services through Breathing Space Creative. Is that for fiction as well as memoir and poetry?

C: Yeah. For the sensitivity reading through Breathing Space Creative, I have care consultants—right now I have Nav and Jónína—and what I usually do is I'll get a manuscript from a publisher, and they have certain concerns about the manuscript. I'll look at the concerns, and I'll try to match the manuscript up with the care consultants. For example, Jónína can speak to some Indigenous issues and issues involving older women —we have a list of things they're comfortable reading and discussing— and I'll try to find a match that way. If I can't, the first thing I would do is go back and say, "We've addressed these concerns, and here's a list of additional resources, because we don't feel comfortable reading for these other concerns, and they can speak from that authority when diving into this particular manuscript." We have a lot of discussions around what we do feel comfortable speaking to and reading, just so that we're sure we're giving our authentic selves to the publisher and to the manuscript.

K: Another thing you explored with Christine on her podcast is the shifting landscape, given social media and the fact that, whereas before we might read a novel and not really know who wrote it or maybe not really care to know much about them, now we really do know a lot about the authors, and that seems to be becoming a little more important these days. How might that relate to cultural appropriation or writing difference with respect? What opportunities or limitations might our current social-media-rich world present?

C: Because most of us have this online presence, it plays a big role. We're out there. We're talking about our writing. We're talking about having a balance, so we're kind of forced to talk about our personal lives and what we're doing outside of writing, and all of that becomes this different identity. We have this need or this desire to self-identify. We say, "I'm a young mixed-race writer who's doing this, that and the other thing," and folks kind of latch onto that, and they know that about you, and they hold that close. Whereas, maybe fifty years ago, you would just write your book, and it was out there, and people weren't really questioning things.

Someone can now easily say, "I saw a twitter thread or an Instagram post where you were speaking as a keynote for whatever, and you identified yourself as this, so why are you writing this particular story?" I think those kinds of conversations can be good, but they can have this negative effect, where you're forced to defend rather than have an actual conversation about the story itself and why you're writing it and how you wanted it to exist on the page. We kind of skip over that, and we just jump to the idea of somebody needing to have that authority immediately, versus letting them talk about why they think they were the person to write this. We do a lot of jumping around because of social media and our own platforms.

Many of these terms are so loaded. We hear the word "appropriation" or "sensitivity reader", and we're like, "What does this mean?" We immediately think negatively. We need to flip that conversation, so that we can talk about the purpose of someone telling a particular story and what we want that result to be. I always ask the question, "Am I the right person to tell this story? Am I the best person to tell this story?" If the answer is, "Yes," then I should probably write it.

In | Appropriate

I think about my memoir—of course, nobody else could have written that. That's my own perspective, my own story, my own experience, and I'm the only one who could do that. But in terms of a novel, where I'm writing about a young Black female living in Vancouver—am I the best person to tell that story? There are a few people who could tell that story. I have connections to certain aspects of the novel that I want to explore and write. It's just breaking it down to its resin. Why is it existing in this form, and am I the best person to write it? Having an answer, really, is important. I don't think everyone has an answer for that. Usually, it's just, "Oh, well, I felt like writing it, so I did."

K: Is that how you came to your novel, *Junie*, and Hogan's Alley?

C: That whole thing started because I had this urge to learn more about the history of the Black community in Vancouver. I didn't have the intention of writing a novel. It just kind of happened that way. I became so obsessed with the folks who lived there and what it was like—the buildings, the businesses, all of it. What did that look like? You do your research, and you can find bits and pieces, but you can't hold all of it in your hands. I thought, "Maybe I'll just write a short story or something about this." It started really small, and then it started to grow. I thought, "Ooh, this is going to be a collection of short stories. That's what it will be," and it was one of my mentors who said, "No, this is a novel." It was this eye-opening thing where I realized I could actually create a world within a world that used to exist within an actual, real, tangible place. That's what got me excited about the whole idea of recreating that area while staying as true as I could to how it really existed in that time.

K: The city of Vancouver is a character in your novel alongside Junie, with its own simultaneously and interestingly developing trajectories. How is that part coming along?

C: It's a weird thing. I'm all about character anyway. Whether it be a novel or poem or whatever it is, I want that character to be incredibly well rounded. I want the person reading this piece to feel like they can see that person, know this person, and predict their mannerisms. As I was writing I thought, "Okay, not only do I have to amplify these characters, but I have to make sure the city is documented in a certain way." I started to think, "Well, the city has changed so much from 1930's Vancouver, like any city would. Even today, within a few months, the downtown core looks totally different to me. How do I document that change?"

I chose to have my character start in one spot, where she's going through some things and she's struggling quite a bit, but then starts to grow in this really beautiful way, right alongside the city that's cradled her and protected her. The city itself is kind of going in reverse. The community is kind of dying, and the city is slowly changing. It's been tough to write that, but if I can picture that city as a living person, as a human being, then it becomes something I can do. Not being worried about the staticness of something that just exists, and have that city be a kind of actual living breathing character that changes everyday, made it easier for me to tackle that.

K: Has your writing process led to greater understanding and empathy for what you're writing about?

C: I think so. As I'm writing, I'm having to dig around and look for even the simplest things—would there have been a laundromat? What kind of stores would have been around at that time? I'm kind of seeing the struggle, like folks didn't have things as easy as we might admit. Even the everyday interactions. One big thing that was missing from my novel, or something that I kind of danced around casually, had to do with racial tensions. What would it have been like to have been a young, Black female living in Vancouver in the 1930's and 1940's? How would it have been to navigate? How would it have been to walk down the street? These were the simplicities—the simple complexities—that I was kind of dancing around, and I had to have my mentor David Chariandy point that out. He said, "Chelene, you're missing something really important in this novel." And I'm like, "I know, I know, I'm going to add that in later." But there was a fear there of getting that wrong, because that's the biggest part of the novel. I was saving that for last [laughter], but I got called out on it.

K: In today's social context in Canada and elsewhere, do you feel like the art of literary fiction plays a role in social change?

C: Yeah, I think so. We're kind of expecting these books to tackle certain political topics. When I think of what's happening in Canada, we know that these themes and situations are going to end up in fiction. We have a responsibility to make sure that we shape these stories in a particular way, especially if we're speaking about other communities. We want to make sure we're shining an accurate light on their experience. That's where we need to have conversations, because we can't make the assumptions that we know or we can speak with authority on those experiences.

For example, can someone write an Indigenous character in their novel? There's a lot of work you'd need to do, because you'd want to make sure you're accurately documenting that character, but also, does this character need to be part of that community? If so, you'd better be prepared to explain why. Some people are accused of slapping someone with an ethnicity and saying that person will be Black or that person will be whatever without really thinking about why they're doing that. That's where there's this kind of murky ground related to appropriation and sharing stories just for the sake of sharing or creating stories. There's so much more intention that needs to take place.

K: How do you feel that intentionality can grow? You have a special perspective from where you sit in the Canadian literary landscape as an editor, festival director, author, mentor. You wear many different hats and have much in the way of experience and success. From where you sit, where do you feel this needs to go or is going?

C: A year and a half ago I was feeling really down about Canadian literature. I was feeling like there was always some fire, you know? We should definitely be speaking out about these injustices and all of that, but also, we have to balance that with care and love and making sure folks feel safe and secure in doing this work. I've been a writer, editor, festival director, all of these roles. I've gained an incredible amount of privilege, and I have to do something with that. I can't just hold onto it.

Oftentimes I'm like a fly on the wall listening to all these conversations, but also absorbing everyone's hurt. That's a lot, you know? I absorb it. I can't help but do that. I always think, "If only there was a way to take a negative situation in Canadian literature, or even a negative threat on social media, and kind of spin it toward a solution-based model where it's not just shaming, shaming, shaming, blacklisting."

I used to think that Canadian literature was very unforgiving, and once you do something wrong and make a mistake, you're out. But I'm starting to see that shift a little bit. We want to have these conversations and try to infuse solutions-based methods rather than just shaming folks. So, let's have a conversation. Let's try to find a way around this, and let's talk about how we got here, and then we'll be able to find a way out of it. I see that shift happening, and it's kind of exciting, because this is the industry that I chose, and I can't see myself doing anything else. I would like it to be sustainable for me and for folks like me who embark on this trajectory by starting down here and slowly making that climb. I would love people to feel safe doing the same thing.

K: What specifics might you be willing to share that reflect this shift you mention?

C: We used to have this call-out culture, and now I feel like we have a call-in culture. I'm seeing it on social media. It could be something like an inaccessible venue, for example, and folks are talking about that on social media. When you go back and read the threads, you'll see people sharing links to other accessible venues and saying, "Maybe try this one here," or "I was at a fabulous event here, try this one," or "Get in touch with these organizers." It's almost like we're coming out of the silos a bit and sharing resources, which is something that should have been happening a long time ago. We're so protective of our information, and we're holding it close, like there's something that's going to happen if we let that go out into the world. That's what I'm seeing now: a sharing of information and a calling-in, which I would love to see more of.

K: I read your thoughts about being mixed race, that sometimes it was like you weren't Black enough in some people's eyes. Can you speak to the process of identity formation and writing? Have you been negotiating those kinds of things as you've been writing this story as well?

C: Yes, quite a bit. With one of my characters (I don't want to spoil something here), I've been kind of playing around where I feel the most comfortable. Identifying as a Black writer or identifying as a mixed race writer, or identifying specifically as half Black and half East Indian, and what that means to me as an author is something that I've struggled with even before I dove into writing. Even within my own family, it's a tricky thing, because you want to find the spot where you fit so well that no one's going to kind of jostle you, where you're just there. I've never been able to find that. It can be that all my differences are pointed out within the family. They mean this in a good way, but it never really comes across, because I think, "Well, do I fit here? How do I do this?"

When I started writing, and the more that my writing was out there, and the more that I was out there, the more these questions came up. Having folks say, "You're speaking as a Black author, but you don't look that Black," or whatever it is, and wondering, "Can I tell this story?" I had to convince myself. And I say, "Yes. Yes, I am part of this community, and while I might not fit a particular mold, that's not my baggage to unpack."

It took a long time to figure that out and to field those questions with a certain kind of grace. It took me a long time, first getting stopped in my tracks or made to feel less than. Now I take those questions, and I say, "Yes I'm part of this community, and here are my ties to it." I can speak to my experience, but I can also speak to being part of a community that I was born into. There are all these different ties.

I want folks to get away from this idea of looking at someone and saying, "You don't look like you fit this community." There's so much more discussion that needs to happen. When we're writing stories that someone thinks are not ours, that's what we're doing—we're making assumptions. The conversation will always open doors, right? So, why not have them.

There are many ethical questions to ask as we write these stories. There are many writers who say, "I'm a writer. I'm writing fiction. These ethical questions shouldn't matter." We have to step back from that and realize that the stories we're building will exist long after us, and these are things folks will be reading for a long time. Are you creating an accurate picture of a community, or are you infusing stereotypes? Are you kind of dragging the systemic barriers and racism that started from however long ago? Are you continually pulling that forward? These are questions we have to ask ourselves.

If you're interested in change, and you want to see some of those barriers slowly melt away, then we have a responsibility to write in a certain way. Fiction, for me, is just as personal as memoir. Even though I'm writing these characters, I ask myself, "Can I say this? Can I write about a particular gender? Can I write about someone who has a ton of money and is really well-off? Can I speak to that, or can I have some conversations with folks?"

If you look at it in this positive way, where you're going to build connections and relationships with the more conversations you have, how can that be a negative thing? I mean, aside from it being time consuming. Do we really want to rush this kind of work anyway? It just comes down to doing the ethical thing and checking in with folks. So much of the problem comes from making assumptions, such as, "It must be nice just to be written about" [laughter], but what picture are you painting? Someone's going to be looking at that for hundreds of years, hopefully.

K: Do you think times have changed? Do you think we're just more aware of this now, that it's just a reflection of our political climate?

C: People feel empowered to talk about it a lot more. There are some people who aren't as touched by racism as much or who don't feel these types of microagressions who say, "This doesn't happen anymore." But, it totally does. Folks are talking about it in a really spirited way, and they can do so. Fifty or sixty years ago, what would have happened if we're having discussions like this? It's a little more out there, and social media plays a big part in that, because we can be behind the screen, saying what we want to say, without anyone seeing our faces. We have so many different media now to get these messages out there.

K: Have you ever written anything that you've regretted later?

C: I've written a lot of things I've regretted, and not because they were disrespectful, but because it wasn't polished writing, and I didn't have anyone say to me, "This is crappy, don't publish it." There are certain pieces I read now where I say, "Augh, why didn't someone stop me from publishing this?"

K: Does thinking deeply about these ethical responsibilities interfere with the art of writing fiction?

C: It can. But only if you look at it in that negative light where you think, "This is something I have to do now," versus "I'm really interested in capturing this character the best way that I can." It comes from yourself as the writer and how you approach the actual process of checking in and building characters. If you come to it with this negative feeling, of course it's going to affect your fiction.

K: What's a responsible response when something does go wrong, when an author has had feedback that indicates that some harm has been done through their writing?

C: The first step is acknowledgement. So often the first thing we do is go into our defence mechanisms—"Oh, you know, I actually… insert justification here."—whereas the first step is to say, "I'm sorry that I've done this thing." That acknowledgement, first and foremost, is going to determine how the rest of the process goes.

Then you seek assistance and seek support. If you have a publisher, you have your publisher be part of that acknowledgement, and everyone just comes together to acknowledge. Then you go behind the scenes and have a plan of attack about how to right these wrongs. How do you create an apology for the community, or how do you come back from that? Once you have that first step of acknowledgement, because that's everything, it's going to be a different process for each person after that.

K: What does the impact of the marketplace have on your writing?

C: The business of writing is something that needs to be talked about a little bit more: there's not a lot of transparency in the industry. So, once you have this book and it exists in tangible form, what happens? What's the business side of it like? I'm learning a lot about that. I find it really interesting. The biggest thing right now is more transparency, more sharing. And it comes right back to how we can come back from a negative experience. We put information out there.

In terms of marketing, we have to have realistic expectations—where our book is going to be, how it's going to be sold, and all of that. If we know a lot of that information up front, and we feel like we've got the knowledge there, then that might even affect how the book is written to begin with—knowing what markets it's going to be in, what hands it's going to be in. Having those conversations early on is important.

K: Did you know that for your novel?

C: No, I don't know that yet. I put these feelers out there, and I ask the right questions, so I kind of have an idea of what it's going to look like. Only because I'm the type of person who needs that information. I'm a nervous person, and I need to know. I don't like being in the dark for too long. Whether or not I do anything with that information, it's just good for me to have and to hold and to know. So I don't think there are going to be any surprises for me in that way, because I ask way to many questions.

K: Do you think this question about cultural appropriation is more important to people who are from marginalized communities?

C: I don't know. I feel like it's important to everybody to some extent. I just think people from marginalized communities will feel it more.

If you look at the demographics and look at who's publishing what or who's getting to write what, even in the children's book realm, there are so many stories of children of colour written by authors who aren't people of colour. So that comes right back to that question—"Are you the right person, or the best person, to tell this story?" There are so many folks who can speak to that with authority, with their experience, but they're not getting the same opportunities as maybe someone who's an established author. Publishers might tell them, "Let's run with your idea," rather than seek out someone who can really share their personal story or infuse it into fiction or whatever it is. It's more about opportunity and making sure that we're offering these opportunities to folks a little bit more evenly. All of that ties into who really grasps the idea of appropriation, who cares about it more. It's like, "I want this opportunity to tell my story, but you're telling it, and now I'm feeling that push or that nudge."

K: I find when I'm doing my research, I'm always afraid of being superficial. Even if you do research and craft a character and you feel it's really multidimensional, it's never going to represent an entire community.

C: Yeah, it's never going to do that. That's one of my fears. A lot of the talk is focused on folks outside of a particular community, but so often we're not talking about the problems that exist within a community. If I consider myself to be part of, say, the Black Canadian community, what are the struggles within that community? Often I feel more pushed in that community than I do from folks outside of it. That's just my personal experience. It ties into that idea of not fitting and having someone say, "Your work is completely devoid of Black Canadian experience," but it has my Black Canadian experience, which is a totally unique experience. All of these conversations happen too. I would love to see more conversations take place within communities, and see what it's like in there versus the exterior.

K: Have you had that kind of feedback? My thesis research is about intercultural competence and a particular theatre community, and in a recent interview I spoke with someone about this. They had an award winning workshopped piece that had toured for a while, and the company was invited to a North African country to stage the piece. When they did that, they got some pretty negative feedback, because some audience members saw it as being somewhat culturally appropriated. Part of the ensuing insight from members of the Canadian company was simply that they were staging a Canadian story. It wasn't a North African story. It was felt that their overseas audience didn't understand it, because they weren't privy to the migration experience from which the story derived. I think that relates to what you've shared about the diversity within a community.

C: It's a funny terrain, isn't it? I think about writing stories about Uganda where my father was born and grew up, but do I have claim to those stories? I've never been there. I didn't grow up with my father. I personally don't feel like I can. But I still feel that pull. There's something in the blood. There's this idea of blood memory, and so are we forced to ignore that because we don't have the physical ties to an experience while we are part of a community?

There are some really intricate details to navigate and iron out. For me, these are conversations that I want to start having. I'm really interested in that idea of diversity within a community and what that looks like in terms of sharing stories. There are so many things, we'll never run out of material [laughter].

K: Where do you think these conversations should happen?

C: They should happen all the time, everywhere. I would love to see more panels, more events that cater to or specifically talk about being of mixed race, you know? There are so many nuances. Even that idea of belonging to two separate cultures—what is that experience like? Especially when you only have exposure to one of them. Or, what is your experience like if you grow up with exposure to both of them? Has your whole life been a clash, fuelled with having to choose one over the other?

All of these experiences are super different, but being able to have those conversations is, I think, shedding light on this for folks who have no idea. Like, I've heard people say, "Well you could just fit anywhere. You can slide in." It's a terrible situation to be in, so I think we have to be talking more about these experiences.

K: David Chariandy mentioned, when he returned from the literary festival in Cape Town, South Africa, where he'd been on a panel about race and blackness, that the discussion was so much deeper than any he'd had before. It made me really reflect on context. This project is intended to be a conversation about Canadian fiction, but David's thoughts about the nuances of race and blackness being explored in perhaps a more nuanced way in Cape Town made me wonder about Canada and this topic. Does Canada have a particular stage of development with respect to this topic of writing difference and cultural appropriation that's important to be aware of and navigate? Is our context different than it might be elsewhere?

C: I think so, and I find it fascinating. I've heard people say, "I just want to be in a room full of Black writers." But what does that mean if you have Black Canadian writers, Black American writers, folks from the UK, people from all over the world put into a room? Does that guarantee us this kind of synchronicity where we're just kind of vibing? It doesn't always happen like that [laughter].

That whole idea of the nuances of blackness is fascinating. I think Canada is the place to start talking about that—to do so honestly and openly with the goal of taking away some tangible resources at the end of it and a sharing of life experiences. It's time to start doing that, and I, for one, am ready and willing—waiting for other folks to want to do that. Now is really the time.

Amanda Leduc

November 28, 2019

Amanda Leduc was born in British Columbia, and she has lived in Ontario, England, British Columbia, and Scotland. She is a disabled writer and author of The Miracles of Ordinary Men; Disfigured: On Fairy Tales, Disability, And Making Space; *and* The Centaur's Wife. *Her essays and stories have appeared in publications across Canada, the US and the UK. She lives in Hamilton, Ontario, where she serves as the communications and development coordinator for The Festival of Literary Diversity, Canada's first festival for diverse authors and stories.*

K: Can we start by talking about process? In a previous conversation, we had talked a bit about an article published on the Brockton Writer's Series website, in which you had used the word "lame", a word which you had identified in your recent workshop at Wild Writers Festival (Waterloo) as ableist language. You had said that your use of the word many years ago in that article was unintentional and unaware. So in looking at our topic more as a process than as a checkbox approach, can you dive into our subject from this point by speaking to it as more of a transformational process over time?

A: Right. Well, like we talked about before, the world is constantly changing, constantly in flux. I'd say particularly over the last, say, ten years, coinciding with the rapid increase in the use of social media, forums like twitter and that sort of thing. There's been both an increased focus and increased scrutiny on the language that people use, which is really good. It comes about as a result of increased accountability now that everybody is on this platform together, and we all have opportunities to speak and to point out when somebody may need more reflection and thinking. I think all of this is really, really good. It points to important progress we're making as a society in terms of how we care for one another and look out for one another.

I do think that sometimes we're in danger of missing some element of empathy and forgiveness and grace, if I can use that word, in this mixture as well. Just a couple of days ago I was thinking about (and I've been thinking about this for the last little while) erasing my twitter archive and just keeping the most recent tweets. There are a host of third-party apps that can be used to do that. I'm pretty sure that I haven't said terrible things in the public sphere, because I really try not to be a terrible person. But there are probably, maybe, most definitely, instances where I've used ableist language (like I used in that Brockton Writer's piece), and this isn't the right word, but I don't want to whitewash my social media past to make it look like I've never made any mistakes. I would like to be able to point to a past instance, like in the Brockton Writer's article, where I've used incorrect language, and say "No, I've changed, and it was wrong of me to say that."

However, a real point to be made in this is that even those words which we disavow, because they're on the internet, and because they sort of stay in the world's sphere, they're written in ink in a way that we haven't traditionally thought of. We don't allow that space for forgiveness anymore. There's a real question about the kind of harm those words still do. I don't think it's worth, for example, going to whoever handles the Brockton Writer's Blog and saying, "Can you please delete my article from a number of years ago because I used ableist language, and I don't want to be associated with that anymore."

However, this may still be problematic, because someone may come across that article and say, "This person who's now defined as a disability activist used ableist language." There's potential for that to be hurtful.

I would hope that the presence and personality I cultivate online and in my writing life would mean that if someone saw that (from many years ago), they would feel that they could approach me (on social media or whatever) and say, "I saw this, and it's problematic—could you speak to that?" I'd hope they'd also give me space to say, "I've grown and changed as a person."

If you look at things like Kevin Hart, earlier this year, being let go as host of the Oscars because someone had unearthed some homophobic things he had said on social media channels years ago. I don't know all the specifics of the situation, but I believe he apologized sincerely, and was still let go from the Oscars. I just don't know what kind of a society we're building if we're allowing space for accountability but not space for forgiveness and growth. I mean, growth has to happen on all sides, right?

It becomes increasingly complicated too when I consider the fact that, as a White woman who's experienced a lot of privilege in my life, it's all well and good for me to talk about forgiveness and growth. I've been disadvantaged in some ways, but also not disadvantaged in others. I'm not advocating that we forgive everyone all the time. There is a real question around the legitimate apology. But when someone shows with their words and their deeds that they've made real strides toward change, I don't think we should discount that.

K: In their book *Writing the Other*, Nisi Shawl and Cynthia Ward say,

You need to know who has privilege and who doesn't, regardless of whether your characters are modern American Blacks and Whites, or ancient Roman citizens and slaves and barbarians, or different socio-economic classes."

These authors also say, "The first sign of privilege is not knowing you have it." It's a bit of a chicken and egg situation. How do we build a relationship when we don't yet know how to speak the language, and we're going to be barbaric and offensive if we try? If we try, our awkwardness and requisite vulnerability is expressed in a general climate of division and hostility, so where do we start? How do we know who has privilege and who doesn't?

A: We don't. I've encountered this with other White people, in particular, who exist in various realms of intersection with marginalization. People who are disabled and White, or poor and White, for example, have often spoken to me, quite rightly, I think, about, "What privilege are you talking about, in my life? I've had to fight for everything," and so on. These are the kinds of arguments people bring to these discussions, and it's very true. I can look at someone like Jael, for example, who's a very successful Black woman and who grew up in an upper middle class household and has experienced very clear micro-aggressions and discriminations as a result of being Black, but who, in terms of her financial upbringing and financial stability in life has experienced a great deal more privilege than someone like myself or colleagues of mine who are disabled and White and have been working class and struggling their entire lives.

The thing that's important for people to recognize, too, is that this sort of reckoning with privilege is an ongoing thing. Recognizing your own privilege is an ongoing journey. You don't just stand in one spot and say, "I'm White. I have White privilege." I exist in a disabled body, but I also have able bodied privilege because my disability is not as severe as some. That's not one static realization. That's something that I'll continually come up against for the entirety of my life. The journey is about recognizing, each time those realizations happen, "Okay, what are the nuances here? How is it different here? How does my recognition of my White privilege intersect with my own class privileges and disadvantages?"

I grew up in a working class home. I was thinking about this with all the talk online and in social media of class distinctions, and there has recently been a twitter conversation specifically around older millennials and GenX, and how the recession in 2008 really kind of toppled a lot of people and had long-lasting effects. One of the things they talked about in that thread was the idea of owning a home as a marker of some sort of affluence. I found that comment really interesting, because I would consider myself middle class now, in terms of the kind of lifestyle that I have and things that are available to me, but I will never own a house. Is that one of those rigid distinctions? Do we say, "If you own a house you're not poor, and if you don't own a house then you are poor, even if you're able to do other things with your money and have other things?"

The point is that it's extraordinarily complicated, and there's not a one-size-fits-all approach. You have to look at privilege through those lenses that are specific to you and your own circumstance, and then try and put that varied and nuanced awareness to other people and the ways that privilege may or may not work in somebody else's life.

I come from a family that is working class, and I also come from a family that has a very significant history of mental health issues and mental health concerns. It really has taught me the idea of considering that everybody you encounter is carrying some kind of struggle. Someone might, for example, have money, but depression doesn't discriminate according to wealth and class and all those kinds of things.

The American writer Mira Jacob wrote a graphic memoir that was published earlier this year called *Good Talk*. She's an Indian American woman. Her parents immigrated from India in the late 1970's, I think. She talks about moving to New York as a young writer, and one of the first jobs that she had was ghost writing for this rich White woman who lived in a beautiful apartment somewhere in New York City. She was talking about how she was descended from the founding fathers and how this novel was going to be about their family across the generations.

One of the things Mira talks about is how the woman was very nice on the surface but also completely unaware of the class privileges and intersections that operated in Mira's own life and the assumptions that she had about Mira as an Indian-American woman. But then, also, this woman, one of the elements of her story was that she had three children, and the youngest child had died of cancer a couple of years before she met Mira and started writing the book.

One of the really wonderful parts of Mira's book is about eventually breaking off this relationship with this woman (because it became quite toxic) and then a couple of years later, Mira had her first child, her son. When he turned two, which was the same age this woman's child had been when she died, Mira said she would wake up in the middle of the night and go to his room and stand over his crib, just to see that he was there, that he wasn't going to disappear. She told me that one of the things that kept going through her head over and over again at that time was, "I'm so sorry, I didn't see you either." And it was just—I'm tearing up as I tell you this—it was just a beautiful exploration for me of that idea of how sometimes we're so focused on the fact that other people don't see us, and we don't recognize that we're also not seeing people in return. And it's that idea of privilege—yes, you don't recognize your own privilege, and you're also not recognizing the struggles that other people may be encountering when you acknowledge their privilege in return, if that makes sense. I guess it's just something that I really try and carry with me.

As writers, I think we have a real responsibility in the language we use to try to be incisive and clear and incandescent, if you will. I mean, your words are a light that's lighting the world, right? But you also need to be kind with those words.

I don't necessarily mean you need to be nice. I think those two things are separate entities. So, with ableism in language, for example, I was unaware of that five years ago. I will completely own that, and I don't think I need to disown the person that I was, because she was still trying to be a good girl. She was trying to do good in the world. I was trying to be the kind of person that would support me in the world, knowing that I needed to be supported as well as supporting other people. I don't think it's wrong to really scrutinize the language that we use, particularly as writers, and ask ourselves those questions—"Am I being kind in the language that I use?" Again, I don't necessarily need to be nice. Sometimes you need to say stark things in arresting ways that can be very unsettling for people. But unsettling people is different from hurting people.

K: Yes, it lacks the cruelty aspect of it. It's honest and probing.

A: Yes, exactly, honest and probing. I think that's what we have to work towards, as writers. And if we're continually asking ourselves these questions, obviously there will be mistakes that people make, but that's a good light to hold in front of yourself when you're writing and when you're thinking about writing the other and writing other experiences and considering these questions of privilege and how all of that intersects —"Are you being honest, and are you illuminating the world in a way that it needs to be illuminated?"

K: In your workshop, "Different Bodies, Different Stories" at Wild Writers in Waterloo, you were saying, "Many people of particular disabled communities have reclaimed certain ableist words as a means of taking back their own narrative." This idea of taking back a narrative, can you expand on that concept?

A: It's important to recognize that the idea of taking back a narrative holds within it the basic assumption that everything we do is telling a story about somebody or something else. I have a neighbour two doors down who has a real opiate addiction and struggles with that. I was at a get-together a couple of months ago, and the woman who lives across from us was speaking about the woman with the opiate addiction (who wasn't there) and referred to her offhandedly as "the crack whore". I didn't say anything then, but it's really stuck with me. You're telling yourself, the people you know, your son (who may or may not hear you offhandedly refer to this woman in this way), you're telling them a particular story about this woman that you've essentially invented, because you don't know her.

You don't know the particular circumstances that have structured this woman's life. You don't know the struggles she's encountering or undergoing. I'm not saying that this woman is necessarily entirely blameless. I don't know her either, but when we talk about taking back the narrative, what's happening there is that you have people from a particular community standing up and saying, "No, actually, you've been telling a story about me for a really long time, and I don't want to give you that power anymore. I want to tell my own story."

In my book, *Disfigured: On Fairy Tales, Disability, and Making Space*, one of the things that I do is look at my initial doctor's consult notes from when I was four and my family doctor referred me to a neurologist in

Toronto. The neurologist in Toronto did a series of tests and then wrote a whole bunch of notes back to my family doctor, just to sort of give an idea of what was happening and what surgeries might be required. I've interspersed those notes throughout the book. There are some really interesting ways that my doctor uses language, which are indicative, I think, of the social expectations that we have around certain things.

Like, at one point he talks about my skull, because I had a cyst in my head, and they had to do CAT scans and head examinations, and he said, "The skull is of a pleasing shape and circumference." It was so interesting to me, because that was standard medical terminology—"pleasing", in the sense that it looked the way a head was supposed to look. It was a "nice head". But when we say that, "This shape is pleasing," or "This looks pleasing versus that which does not," what kinds of stories are we telling about people and imposing upon them?

I didn't read these doctor's notes until earlier this year when I was doing research for the book, but that's the first thing that I twigged on, like, "Okay, so you had ideas in your head about me based on how I looked." Not bad ideas, or anything like that, but how do we as a society tell stories, even unconsciously, about people based on how they look, based on how they behave?

In my book, my aim in including the doctor's notes was to point out the preconceptions about beauty and ability and what it means to be a "successful, operating body" in the world. I could pull those out of the doctor's notes, which are supposed to be impartial, and medical and clinical, right? In braiding those questions in the story, I'm taking back the narrative of what it means to be me in my body in the world. I'm not allowing other people to tell it for me.

I had a sensitivity reader read the book, and that was one of the things they flagged. From their perspective, they were saying, "I don't think you should give your doctor the power to tell your story," even though I said I don't see it that way. I feel that I'm taking my power back by framing it in a particular way, so I disagreed, but it was very interesting to see that.

I think there's real power in stories, and stories start from a very young age when you look at something like disability and the way the disabled body is portrayed to children from a really early moment in development. It's no wonder that people grow up with these ideas that someone with a facial disfigurement or a facial difference is scary or should be avoided or things like that. It's not surprising. Stories are one of the first things that we have when we're growing as people that shape our views of the world, and that's very powerful. So, taking back the narrative, rewriting your own story or the story of your community in a way that positions you back in the centre is likewise a very powerful tool and a very powerful experience.

K: How did it show up in your life, that release of power and empowerment?

A: I was bullied a lot when I was in elementary school (I went to a Catholic school from kindergarten to grade eight). I had the surgery when I was four and went back to school when I was five, and then in grade three (I would have been eight) there was one particular girl who was new, and she sort of seized on me as the person to make fun of. She was the reality of my life for the next five years. She was a ringleader and was very cruel in the ways that kids can be cruel, where they're aware but also oblivious at the same time. They're just being cruel because they can be cruel: there's no wider, over-arching plan to it. It's just, "You're different. I don't wanna be different, so I'm gonna make fun of how you're different, and people are gonna stay away from you and come to me," kind of thing.

It destroyed my self-confidence on a romantic, sexual level—seeing myself as a sexual being, seeing myself as someone people could love, or be in a romantic relationship with. That persisted more or less until my mid-thirties, until very recently. It's only been in the last couple of years, probably since meeting Jael, that I've really come to terms with what it means to occupy a body that's maybe a little bit different. There's been an element of coming full circle and recognizing that this disability, which for so long has been seen as a marker of less for me, has been seen as some kind of flaw, is not so much a flaw as it is a superpower, because it allows me to see the world in a very specific kind of way that is crucial to the differences that the world is undergoing at this moment in time.

The world is changing quite rapidly and quite significantly. Those of us who have traditionally been on the fringes for one reason or another have unique insights into the change that is happening. I avoided considering myself a disabled person for most of my life, even though in many ways it's really obvious (my limp is visible, more at some times than others, and I pretended most of the time that it wasn't there). My actively reclaiming the narrative has been about making that shift from pretending that it's invisible to not only making it visible but making it the centre of who I really am as a person. It has made me who I am.

K: Given this greater awareness and empowerment—how would you approach writing difference? Would you even write the other, or would you simply find the Other and encourage them to write?

A: It's definitely a volatile question for me. When I was in school at the University of Victoria, (fifteen years ago) there was a creative non-fiction professor there named Lynn Van Luven, and she talked about that distinction, where she encouraged her students to write anything, and when it came time to publish, the question for her was always, is it going to hurt somebody if I publish it? She didn't care about embarrassing people, necessarily, but she didn't want to hurt people by putting it out into the world.

I went through varying reactions to this. For a long time I was thinking it made sense, and then a couple of years ago I went through a period of time where I was significantly depressed and quite angry for various reasons, and that influenced my shift in thinking. I was, like, "Nope, nope, you tell the truth whenever you can tell the truth. It doesn't matter if you're hurting somebody, because you're telling the truth, and that's what matters." Now, I'm sort of veering back to that original way of thinking. It goes back to what we were talking about earlier. That question of what you write and what you say, are you illuminating something that needs to be illuminated? If you're being unsettling, can you tell the truth in a way that tries, at least, not to hurt?

In terms of writing the Other, I'm really hesitant about it right now, to be honest. That's something that I'm trying to work through. I have this non-fiction book that's coming out, and then I have a novel that's coming out the year after (hopefully) that's written from the perspective of a disabled woman and has a number of disabled characters. I also have this idea for a new linked short story collection, which has sort of been rumbling around in my head. I'd like to explore things a little bit more in that collection. I'd like to write from a variety of different viewpoints, from people who have different jobs in the world.

I'm not wrestling with it at this stage because a lot of it hasn't been written, but I am thinking about it quite severely, because Alexander Chee wrote an article about writing difference a couple of weeks ago (I mentioned it in the workshop), and one of the things he talked about was that he'd noticed a trend in the workshops he was teaching in university, where people were beginning to write stories that just sort of had generic characters in them, where these people could be anybody (which, on some level, is a good thing, because anybody could view themselves as the character), but then he said that in many ways the stories were kind of lacking in life as a result.

I guess I have no answer for that. I'd like to explore things in this different collection I'm working on. I'd like to do it in a way that people from many different areas and many different walks of life can read the book and see themselves in there. But how do you do that in a way that doesn't make your stories flat and devoid of life and full of these robotic automatons that anybody can just jump into?

Maybe that has something to do with the traditional ideas of the western literary canon, where someone like Alice Munro (and I love Alice Munro, so this is no shame at all) can write a story that has been seen as universal. Is she universal, or is it that we've been taught for so long that the standard western canonical story is universal? This new collection that I'm talking about has main characters of a husband and wife who happen to be hyenas who walk and talk, and I struggle with how to build the world in a way that people will identify with them.

K: Yeah, I'm so glad you're doing that, it sounds amazing. It takes courage to do it. I'm curious about why, though. To bring that life into your writing, is it focused on the art of it, is that what attracts you to it? Or, are you trying to discover an empathy?

A: I'm trying to discover an empathy, but I'm also trying to avoid writing story after story about people who are either English teachers or artists or book lovers, which have predominantly occupied most of the creative sphere that I've been working in for the last ten years.

On one level, I think it's true that as writers we can and should be able to write or try to write whatever we want. It's the publisher's responsibility, actually, to ensure that everybody is writing different kinds of stories—that stories are being told carefully and appropriately, with the proper levels of attention and care. I had talked to you about Mona Awad and her novel *Bunny*, which takes place in a sorority at a university and basically it's full of White girl characters. I haven't actually read it. It's on my list, but Jael read it and loved it, and she said that one of the things she really loved about it was that Mona was just writing from the perspective of someone who wasn't her in a world that wasn't necessarily her own or what people generally think of as her own. Naben Ruthnum talks about this a lot in his work too. When he won the Journey Prize and he went and pitched a novel to Penguin Random House, he got some pushback because he wanted to write a thriller. People were, like,

"I want you to write the mango tree story of the Indian immigrant." That shouldn't be the case.

We should be giving space for people to write their own stories in a way that's authentic. People from marginalized communities have been kept away from writing their own stories for so long that we really need a long period of time where marginalized people are allowed to tell their own stories. Then, perhaps, we can move back into a space where everybody is telling any kind of story, and it doesn't become a huge issue, because as a White writer I'm not taking space from a writer from a marginalized community.

K: Are we expecting too much of a novel? I feel like, whether consciously or unconsciously, we're all aware of the needs of the time, and if a novel doesn't reflect our time in some way, we're not being awake, we're not being honest.

A: Yeah, that discussion we had about Camilla Gibb's *Sweetness in the Belly* movie backlash and all that sort of thing... if we lived in a society and in a time when everyone was telling these different kinds of stories, I don't think there would have been as much of a backlash. She lived in that community. She had that lived experience. She was writing from a particular space. She knew and consulted with the community. She did all of those things and approached the story with as much grace and respect as she could. Sometimes we're in danger of going too far on the other side of things, and that question of grace and forgiveness comes in again.

As a disabled writer, I want to see more disabled creators out there in the world, because historically we've not been able to create and get recognition for and get paid for our creations in ways that able-bodied creators have historically been able to do. But I also want to leave space within that awareness and grace for that idea that a story about a disabled person written by an abled person could still totally blow my world open and totally change my worldview. I don't want to live in a world where we don't allow that as a possibility. I just think giving space to disabled creators needs to take priority over an able-bodied writer who maybe wants to write from the perspective of somebody else.

K: Absolutely, it's about power shifts. It's tricky, and it's going to be tricky, and we just have to accept that, I think. Cynthia Erivo playing Harriet Tubman, for example.

A: Which is better than Julia Roberts playing Harriet Tubman...

K: Yeah, ridiculous, right? Just the fact that being from the United Kingdom was a problem. I was watching an interview which pointed out that with actors like Meryl Streep playing Margaret Thatcher or Daniel Day Lewis playing Abraham Lincoln there was no outcry, but then Cynthia Erivo playing Harriet Tubman is a problem?

A: I think with Cynthia Erivo, though, she had specifically made comments a number of years ago on her social media account about "the hood". She specifically made comments that were deemed anti-Black, and that's where some of the outcry has come from. Her comments were rooted in an anti-Black lens, an anti-African American lens, and that's where her trouble with it all came from. Again, though, can't we build some awareness or possibility around forgiveness into those things? I don't know, I don't know.

And that doesn't necessarily take away from the validity of the wider question, right? This is, as is everything, a spectrum. On one hand you have someone like Scarlett Johansson saying, "I should be able to step into whatever role I want." And on an objective level, she's not wrong, but the question is, "Are you stepping into whatever role you want at the expense of somebody else who is equally talented and who isn't getting the space that you get because you have access to privilege in ways that other people have not historically had the same kind of access?"

K: Yeah. There's so much to know. I feel like that's why we have to do this in groups. It's not possible for one person. There are so many things we have to take into consideration, and it's not possible for one person to do it justice.

So, what's at stake then?

A: Bringing it back to my own lens, I need to recognize things on two prongs. Firstly, I need to recognize that people will say hurtful things about disability, and that people shouldn't say some things about disability or use ableist language, because words have a real impact in the way that people go about their lives.

Secondly, who we are and what our possibilities are as human beings in the world aren't solely confined by the stories that other people tell about us. So you're shaped by stories, but you're also above stories.

As storytellers, we need to navigate both of those spaces. We have to recognize the responsibilities that we have to be thorough and kind and incandescent and illuminating with the stories that we put out into the world, and also leave space for people to grow beyond those stories we tell and to emerge stronger. It sounds cliché, but it's true at the same time. All of these things contribute to who we are as human beings, but who we are as human beings is at once all of these things and yet also more. You are not just how the world shapes you. You are also how you respond to how the world is shaping you.

These are all difficult things to hold in your head at the same time, particularly when you want to put art out into the world, particularly when you want to put art out into the world in a way that puts food on your table and allows you to survive. These are very real and difficult questions. It's a rare person who gets to put art out into the world now without having some element of this discussed or torn apart. The reason it wasn't discussed or broken apart in the previous world that we lived in is because people weren't asking these questions, because these marginalized voices weren't part of the conversation at all. No one was being asked. No one was being challenged.

K: Could you give a definition of "kindness"?

A: For me, kindness is connected to seeing, as in seeing a person. If I'm writing something about my disabled community, and I'm asking myself, "Am I being kind to you?" I think what I mean is, "Am I trying to consider various different viewpoints? Am I thinking about my disability community not just as a sort of all-encompassing community, but as a bunch of individual people who have hopes and desires and things that hurt them?" I'm trying to consider all of these things, and when I talked in that disability workshop about writing disability, it's not enough to write someone who is one-dimensional and have them as a disabled character in your book. Disabled people can be assholes. Disabled people can be mean. Disabled people can be bullies. You can write all of that stuff into your work, as long as you leave space for disabled people who can also be kind and be nice to people who are in their inner circle, or things like that.

Being kind as a writer is really trying to see that world in that three-dimensional way where you're not reducing somebody to a particular characteristic or a particular story or narrative. My neighbour, for example, the one who was referred to as the "crack whore", she's a woman, in her fifties, has three daughters. She's done a lot, and she's lived a lot in her life. You can't just reduce her to this sort of "crack whore" presence on the street. By the same token, she's also not a saint. The fact that she's done all of these things and accomplished a lot despite the hardship in her life doesn't make her Mother Theresa (who, as we know, is also a problematic figure in many ways).

People are now speaking in ways that they wouldn't have done before. Again, Mother Theresa's not a one-dimensional character, neither are you, neither am I. In being kind, am I thinking about that? In non-fiction, if I'm writing about a particular person, am I thinking about how they may or may not be hurt by various things that I say? Am I thinking about how their capacity or growth or strength as a human being can rise above what I'm saying?

K: That's a great definition. And I feel like this relates to when you mentioned Alicia Elliott's article about writing beyond empathy, writing love. How you're describing this to me also triggers the word, "fair-minded". To learn and train ourselves about what is fair and then injecting it with that love.

A: Jael is a great example of this for me. I think of Jael, and I think that she's one of the kindest people I've ever met, but it's not a kindness that coddles. I think we're in danger, especially in White cultures, of specifically conflating these two things, that kind is coddling. In actual fact, being kind is about stripping everybody to the bare essentials of what and who they are, and forcing them to recognize what it is that makes you who you are as a person, and how there's that intersection with other people.

One of the things we talk about at the Festival of Literary Diversity related to that element of kindness is that we want to make space to have those difficult conversations. It doesn't mean that we have panel discussions where we're continually placating one another and we're like nice happy bunnies hopping in a meadow. We're creating space and leaving room for empathy to grow. There's a very particular kind of power that comes from that kind of kindness, that again, isn't coddling at all. And that's something that I do think we need to be aware of.

Appendix A

*United Nations Declaration
of the Rights of Indigenous Peoples*

Resolution adopted by the General Assembly on 13 September 2007

The General Assembly,

Guided by the purposes and principles of the Charter of the United Nations, and good faith in the fulfilment of the obligations assumed by States in accordance with the Charter,

Affirming that indigenous peoples are equal to all other peoples, while recognizing the right of all peoples to be different, to consider themselves different, and to be respected as such,

Affirming also that all peoples contribute to the diversity and richness of civilizations and cultures, which constitute the common heritage of humankind,

Affirming further that all doctrines, policies and practices based on or advocating superiority of peoples or individuals on the basis of national origin or racial, religious, ethnic or cultural differences are racist, scientifically false, legally invalid, morally condemnable and socially unjust,

Reaffirming that indigenous peoples, in the exercise of their rights, should be free from discrimination of any kind,

Concerned that indigenous peoples have suffered from historic injustices as a result of, inter alia, their colonization and dispossession of their lands, territories and resources, thus preventing them from exercising, in particular, their right to development in accordance with their own needs and interests,

Recognizing the urgent need to respect and promote the inherent rights of indigenous peoples which derive from their political, economic and social structures and from their cultures, spiritual traditions, histories and philosophies, especially their rights to their lands, territories and resources,

Recognizing also the urgent need to respect and promote the rights of indigenous peoples affirmed in treaties, agreements and other constructive arrangements with States,

Welcoming the fact that indigenous peoples are organizing themselves for political, economic, social and cultural enhancement and in order to bring to an end all forms of discrimination and oppression wherever they occur,

Convinced that control by indigenous peoples over developments affecting them and their lands, territories and resources will enable them to maintain and strengthen their institutions, cultures and traditions, and to promote their development in accordance with their aspirations and needs,

Recognizing that respect for indigenous knowledge, cultures and traditional practices contributes to sustainable and equitable development and proper management of the environment,

Emphasizing the contribution of the demilitarization of the lands and territories of indigenous peoples to peace, economic and social progress and development, understanding and friendly relations among nations and peoples of the world,

Recognizing in particular the right of indigenous families and communities to retain shared responsibility for the upbringing, training, education and well-being of their children, consistent with the rights of the child,

Considering that the rights affirmed in treaties, agreements and other constructive arrangements between States and indigenous peoples are, in some situations, matters of international concern, interest, responsibility and character,

Considering also that treaties, agreements and other constructive arrangements, and the relationship they represent, are the basis for a strengthened partnership between indigenous peoples and States,

Acknowledging that the Charter of the United Nations, the International Covenant on Economic, Social and Cultural Rights and the International Covenant on Civil and Political Rights, as well as the Vienna Declaration and Programme of Action, affirm the fundamental importance of the right to self-determination of all peoples, by virtue of which they freely determine their political status and freely pursue their economic, social and cultural development,

Appendix A

Bearing in mind that nothing in this Declaration may be used to deny any peoples their right to self-determination, exercised in conformity with international law,

Convinced that the recognition of the rights of indigenous peoples in this Declaration will enhance harmonious and cooperative relations between the State and indigenous peoples, based on principles of justice, democracy, respect for human rights, non-discrimination and good faith,

Encouraging States to comply with and effectively implement all their obligations as they apply to indigenous peoples under international instruments, in particular those related to human rights, in consultation and cooperation with the peoples concerned,

Emphasizing that the United Nations has an important and continuing role to play in promoting and protecting the rights of indigenous peoples,

Believing that this Declaration is a further important step forward for the recognition, promotion and protection of the rights and freedoms of indigenous peoples and in the development of relevant activities of the United Nations system in this field,

Recognizing and reaffirming that indigenous individuals are entitled without discrimination to all human rights recognized in international law, and that indigenous peoples possess collective rights which are indispensable for their existence, well-being and integral development as peoples,

Recognizing that the situation of indigenous peoples varies from region to region and from country to country and that the significance of national and regional particularities and various historical and cultural backgrounds should be taken into consideration,

Solemnly proclaims the following United Nations Declaration on the Rights of Indigenous Peoples as a standard of achievement to be pursued in a spirit of partnership and mutual respect:

Article 1

Indigenous peoples have the right to the full enjoyment, as a collective or as individuals, of all human rights and fundamental freedoms as recognized in the Charter of the United Nations, the Universal Declaration of Human Rights and international human rights law.

Article 2

Indigenous peoples and individuals are free and equal to all other peoples and individuals and have the right to be free from any kind of discrimination, in the exercise of their rights, in particular that based on their indigenous origin or identity.

Article 3

Indigenous peoples have the right to self-determination. By virtue of that right they freely determine their political status and freely pursue their economic, social and cultural development.

Article 4

Indigenous peoples, in exercising their right to self-determination, have the right to autonomy or self-government in matters relating to their internal and local affairs, as well as ways and means for financing their autonomous functions.

Article 5

Indigenous peoples have the right to maintain and strengthen their distinct political, legal, economic, social and cultural institutions, while retaining their right to participate fully, if they so choose, in the political, economic, social and cultural life of the State.

Article 6

Every indigenous individual has the right to a nationality.

Article 7

    1. Indigenous individuals have the rights to life, physical and mental integrity, liberty and security of person.

    2. Indigenous peoples have the collective right to live in freedom, peace and security as distinct peoples and shall not be subjected to any act of genocide or any other act of violence, including forcibly removing children of the group to another group.

Article 8

    1. Indigenous peoples and individuals have the right not to be subjected to forced assimilation or destruction of their culture.

    2. States shall provide effective mechanisms for prevention of, and redress for:

    (a) Any action which has the aim or effect of depriving them of their integrity as distinct peoples, or of their cultural values or ethnic identities;

    (b) Any action which has the aim or effect of dispossessing them of their lands, territories or resources;

(c) Any form of forced population transfer which has the aim or effect of violating or undermining any of their rights;

(d) Any form of forced assimilation or integration;

(e) Any form of propaganda designed to promote or incite racial or ethnic discrimination directed against them.

Article 9

Indigenous peoples and individuals have the right to belong to an indigenous community or nation, in accordance with the traditions and customs of the community or nation concerned. No discrimination of any kind may arise from the exercise of such a right.

Article 10

Indigenous peoples shall not be forcibly removed from their lands or territories. No relocation shall take place without the free, prior and informed consent of the indigenous peoples concerned and after agreement on just and fair compensation and, where possible, with the option of return.

Article 11

1. Indigenous peoples have the right to practise and revitalize their cultural traditions and customs. This includes the right to maintain, protect and develop the past, present and future manifestations of their cultures, such as archaeological and historical sites, artefacts, designs, ceremonies, technologies and visual and performing arts and literature.

2. States shall provide redress through effective mechanisms, which may include restitution, developed in conjunction with indigenous peoples, with respect to their cultural, intellectual, religious and spiritual property taken without their free, prior and informed consent or in violation of their laws, traditions and customs.

Article 12

1. Indigenous peoples have the right to manifest, practise, develop and teach their spiritual and religious traditions, customs and ceremonies; the right to maintain, protect, and have access in privacy to their religious and cultural sites; the right to the use and control of their ceremonial objects; and the right to the repatriation of their human remains.

2. States shall seek to enable the access and/or repatriation of ceremonial objects and human remains in their possession through fair, transparent and effective mechanisms developed in conjunction with indigenous peoples concerned.

Article 13

1. Indigenous peoples have the right to revitalize, use, develop and transmit to future generations their histories, languages, oral traditions, philosophies, writing systems and literatures, and to designate and retain their own names for communities, places and persons.

2. States shall take effective measures to ensure that this right is protected and also to ensure that indigenous peoples can understand and be understood in political, legal and administrative proceedings, where necessary through the provision of interpretation or by other appropriate means.

Article 14

1. Indigenous peoples have the right to establish and control their educational systems and institutions providing education in their own languages, in a manner appropriate to their cultural methods of teaching and learning.

2. Indigenous individuals, particularly children, have the right to all levels and forms of education of the State without discrimination.

3. States shall, in conjunction with indigenous peoples, take effective measures, in order for indigenous individuals, particularly children, including those living outside their communities, to have access, when possible, to an education in their own culture and provided in their own language.

Article 15

1. Indigenous peoples have the right to the dignity and diversity of their cultures, traditions, histories and aspirations which shall be appropriately reflected in education and public information.

2. States shall take effective measures, in consultation and cooperation with the indigenous peoples concerned, to combat prejudice and eliminate discrimination and to promote tolerance, understanding and good relations among indigenous peoples and all other segments of society.

Article 16

1. Indigenous peoples have the right to establish their own media in their own languages and to have access to all forms of non-indigenous media without discrimination.

2. States shall take effective measures to ensure that State-owned media duly reflect indigenous cultural diversity. States, without prejudice to ensuring full freedom of expression, should encourage privately owned media to adequately reflect indigenous cultural diversity.

Appendix A

Article 17

1. Indigenous individuals and peoples have the right to enjoy fully all rights established under applicable international and domestic labour law.

2. States shall in consultation and cooperation with indigenous peoples take specific measures to protect indigenous children from economic exploitation and from performing any work that is likely to be hazardous or to interfere with the child's education, or to be harmful to the child's health or physical, mental, spiritual, moral or social development, taking into account their special vulnerability and the importance of education for their empowerment.

3. Indigenous individuals have the right not to be subjected to any discriminatory conditions of labour and, inter alia, employment or salary.

Article 18

Indigenous peoples have the right to participate in decision-making in matters which would affect their rights, through representatives chosen by themselves in accordance with their own procedures, as well as to maintain and develop their own indigenous decision-making institutions.

Article 19

States shall consult and cooperate in good faith with the indigenous peoples concerned through their own representative institutions in order to obtain their free, prior and informed consent before adopting and implementing legislative or administrative measures that may affect them.

Article 20

1. Indigenous peoples have the right to maintain and develop their political, economic and social systems or institutions, to be secure in the enjoyment of their own means of subsistence and development, and to engage freely in all their traditional and other economic activities.

2. Indigenous peoples deprived of their means of subsistence and development are entitled to just and fair redress.

Article 21

1. Indigenous peoples have the right, without discrimination, to the improvement of their economic and social conditions, including, inter alia, in the areas of education, employment, vocational training and retraining, housing, sanitation, health and social security.

2. States shall take effective measures and, where appropriate, special measures to ensure continuing improvement of their economic and social

conditions. Particular attention shall be paid to the rights and special needs of indigenous elders, women, youth, children and persons with disabilities.

Article 22

1. Particular attention shall be paid to the rights and special needs of indigenous elders, women, youth, children and persons with disabilities in the implementation of this Declaration.

2. States shall take measures, in conjunction with indigenous peoples, to ensure that indigenous women and children enjoy the full protection and guarantees against all forms of violence and discrimination.

Article 23

Indigenous peoples have the right to determine and develop priorities and strategies for exercising their right to development. In particular, indigenous peoples have the right to be actively involved in developing and determining health, housing and other economic and social programmes affecting them and, as far as possible, to administer such programmes through their own institutions.

Article 24

1. Indigenous peoples have the right to their traditional medicines and to maintain their health practices, including the conservation of their vital medicinal plants, animals and minerals. Indigenous individuals also have the right to access, without any discrimination, to all social and health services.

2. Indigenous individuals have an equal right to the enjoyment of the highest attainable standard of physical and mental health. States shall take the necessary steps with a view to achieving progressively the full realization of this right.

Article 25

Indigenous peoples have the right to maintain and strengthen their distinctive spiritual relationship with their traditionally owned or otherwise occupied and used lands, territories, waters and coastal seas and other resources and to uphold their responsibilities to future generations in this regard.

Article 26

1. Indigenous peoples have the right to the lands, territories and resources which they have traditionally owned, occupied or otherwise used or acquired.

2. Indigenous peoples have the right to own, use, develop and control the lands, territories and resources that they possess by reason of traditional ownership or other traditional occupation or use, as well as those which they have otherwise acquired.

3. States shall give legal recognition and protection to these lands, territories and resources. Such recognition shall be conducted with due respect to the customs, traditions and land tenure systems of the indigenous peoples concerned.

Article 27

States shall establish and implement, in conjunction with indigenous peoples concerned, a fair, independent, impartial, open and transparent process, giving due recognition to indigenous peoples' laws, traditions, customs and land tenure systems, to recognize and adjudicate the rights of indigenous peoples pertaining to their lands, territories and resources, including those which were traditionally owned or otherwise occupied or used. Indigenous peoples shall have the right to participate in this process.

Article 28

1. Indigenous peoples have the right to redress, by means that can include restitution or, when this is not possible, just, fair and equitable compensation, for the lands, territories and resources which they have traditionally owned or otherwise occupied or used, and which have been confiscated, taken, occupied, used or damaged without their free, prior and informed consent.

2. Unless otherwise freely agreed upon by the peoples concerned, compensation shall take the form of lands, territories and resources equal in quality, size and legal status or of monetary compensation or other appropriate redress.

Article 29

1. Indigenous peoples have the right to the conservation and protection of the environment and the productive capacity of their lands or territories and resources. States shall establish and implement assistance programmes for indigenous peoples for such conservation and protection, without discrimination.

2. States shall take effective measures to ensure that no storage or disposal of hazardous materials shall take place in the lands or territories of indigenous peoples without their free, prior and informed consent.

3. States shall also take effective measures to ensure, as needed, that programmes for monitoring, maintaining and restoring the health of indigenous peoples, as developed and implemented by the peoples affected by such materials, are duly implemented.

Article 30

1. Military activities shall not take place in the lands or territories of indigenous peoples, unless justified by a relevant public interest or otherwise freely agreed with or requested by the indigenous peoples concerned.

2. States shall undertake effective consultations with the indigenous peoples concerned, through appropriate procedures and in particular through their representative institutions, prior to using their lands or territories for military activities.

Article 31

1. Indigenous peoples have the right to maintain, control, protect and develop their cultural heritage, traditional knowledge and traditional cultural expressions, as well as the manifestations of their sciences, technologies and cultures, including human and genetic resources, seeds, medicines, knowledge of the properties of fauna and flora, oral traditions, literatures, designs, sports and traditional games and visual and performing arts. They also have the right to maintain, control, protect and develop their intellectual property over such cultural heritage, traditional knowledge, and traditional cultural expressions.

2. In conjunction with indigenous peoples, States shall take effective measures to recognize and protect the exercise of these rights.

Article 32

1. Indigenous peoples have the right to determine and develop priorities and strategies for the development or use of their lands or territories and other resources.

2. States shall consult and cooperate in good faith with the indigenous peoples concerned through their own representative institutions in order to obtain their free and informed consent prior to the approval of any project affecting their lands or territories and other resources, particularly in connection with the development, utilization or exploitation of mineral, water or other resources.

3. States shall provide effective mechanisms for just and fair redress for any such activities, and appropriate measures shall be taken to mitigate adverse environmental, economic, social, cultural or spiritual impact.

Article 33

1. Indigenous peoples have the right to determine their own identity or membership in accordance with their customs and traditions. This does not impair the right of indigenous individuals to obtain citizenship of the States in which they live.

2. Indigenous peoples have the right to determine the structures and to select the membership of their institutions in accordance with their own procedures.

Article 34

Indigenous peoples have the right to promote, develop and maintain their institutional structures and their distinctive customs, spirituality, traditions, procedures, practices and, in the cases where they exist, juridical systems or customs, in accordance with international human rights standards.

Article 35

Indigenous peoples have the right to determine the responsibilities of individuals to their communities.

Article 36

1. Indigenous peoples, in particular those divided by international borders, have the right to maintain and develop contacts, relations and cooperation, including activities for spiritual, cultural, political, economic and social purposes, with their own members as well as other peoples across borders.

2. States, in consultation and cooperation with indigenous peoples, shall take effective measures to facilitate the exercise and ensure the implementation of this right.

Article 37

1. Indigenous peoples have the right to the recognition, observance and enforcement of treaties, agreements and other constructive arrangements concluded with States or their successors and to have States honour and respect such treaties, agreements and other constructive arrangements.

2. Nothing in this Declaration may be interpreted as diminishing or eliminating the rights of indigenous peoples contained in treaties, agreements and other constructive arrangements.

Article 38

States in consultation and cooperation with indigenous peoples, shall take the appropriate measures, including legislative measures, to achieve the ends of this Declaration.

Article 39

Indigenous peoples have the right to have access to financial and technical assistance from States and through international cooperation, for the enjoyment of the rights contained in this Declaration.

Article 40

Indigenous peoples have the right to access to and prompt decision through just and fair procedures for the resolution of conflicts and disputes with States or other parties, as well as to effective remedies for all infringements of their individual and collective rights. Such a decision shall give due consideration to the customs, traditions, rules and legal systems of the indigenous peoples concerned and international human rights.

Article 41

The organs and specialized agencies of the United Nations system and other intergovernmental organizations shall contribute to the full realization of the provisions of this Declaration through the mobilization, inter alia, of financial cooperation and technical assistance. Ways and means of ensuring participation of indigenous peoples on issues affecting them shall be established.

Article 42

The United Nations, its bodies, including the Permanent Forum on Indigenous Issues, and specialized agencies, including at the country level, and States shall promote respect for and full application of the provisions of this Declaration and follow up the effectiveness of this Declaration.

Article 43

The rights recognized herein constitute the minimum standards for the survival, dignity and well-being of the indigenous peoples of the world.

Article 44

All the rights and freedoms recognized herein are equally guaranteed to male and female indigenous individuals.

Article 45

Nothing in this Declaration may be construed as diminishing or extinguishing the rights indigenous peoples have now or may acquire in the future.

Article 46

1. Nothing in this Declaration may be interpreted as implying for any State, people, group or person any right to engage in any activity or to perform any act contrary to the Charter of the United Nations or construed as authorizing or encouraging any action which would dismember or impair, totally or in part, the territorial integrity or political unity of sovereign and independent States.

2. In the exercise of the rights enunciated in the present Declaration, human rights and fundamental freedoms of all shall be respected. The exercise of the rights set forth in this Declaration shall be subject only to such limitations as are determined by law and in accordance with international human rights obligations. Any such limitations shall be non-discriminatory and strictly necessary solely for the purpose of securing due recognition and respect for the rights and freedoms of others and for meeting the just and most compelling requirements of a democratic society.

3. The provisions set forth in this Declaration shall be interpreted in accordance with the principles of justice, democracy, respect for human rights, equality, non-discrimination, good governance and good faith.

Appendix B

United Nations Declaration of the Rights of Disabled Persons

Proclaimed by General Assembly resolution 3447 (XXX) of 9 December 1975

The General Assembly,

Mindful of the pledge made by Member States, under the Charter of the United Nations to take joint and separate action in co-operation with the Organization to promote higher standards of living, full employment and conditions of economic and social progress and development,

Reaffirming its faith in human rights and fundamental freedoms and in the principles of peace, of the dignity and worth of the human person and of social justice proclaimed in the Charter,

Recalling the principles of the Universal Declaration of Human Rights, the International Covenants on Human Rights, the Declaration of the Rights of the Child and the Declaration on the Rights of Mentally Retarded Persons, as well as the standards already set for social progress in the constitutions, conventions, recommendations and resolutions of the International Labour Organisation, the United Nations Educational, Scientific and Cultural Organization, the World Health Organization, the United Nations Children's Fund and other organizations concerned,

Recalling also Economic and Social Council resolution 1921 (LVIII) of 6 May 1975 on the prevention of disability and the rehabilitation of disabled persons,

Emphasizing that the Declaration on Social Progress and Development has proclaimed the necessity of protecting the rights and assuring the welfare and rehabilitation of the physically and mentally disadvantaged,

Bearing in mind the necessity of preventing physical and mental disabilities and of assisting disabled persons to develop their abilities in the most varied fields of activities and of promoting their integration as far as possible in normal life,

Aware that certain countries, at their present stage of development, can devote only limited efforts to this end,

Proclaims this Declaration on the Rights of Disabled Persons and calls for national and international action to ensure that it will be used as a common basis and frame of reference for the protection of these rights:

1. The term "disabled person" means any person unable to ensure by himself or herself, wholly or partly, the necessities of a normal individual and/or social life, as a result of deficiency, either congenital or not, in his or her physical or mental capabilities.

2. Disabled persons shall enjoy all the rights set forth in this Declaration. These rights shall be granted to all disabled persons without any exception whatsoever and without distinction or discrimination on the basis of race, colour, sex, language, religion, political or other opinions, national or social origin, state of wealth, birth or any other situation applying either to the disabled person himself or herself or to his or her family.

3. Disabled persons have the inherent right to respect for their human dignity. Disabled persons, whatever the origin, nature and seriousness of their handicaps and disabilities, have the same fundamental rights as their fellow-citizens of the same age, which implies first and foremost the right to enjoy a decent life, as normal and full as possible.

4. Disabled persons have the same civil and political rights as other human beings; paragraph 7 of the Declaration on the Rights of Mentally Retarded Persons applies to any possible limitation or suppression of those rights for mentally disabled persons.

5. Disabled persons are entitled to the measures designed to enable them to become as self-reliant as possible.

6. Disabled persons have the right to medical, psychological and functional treatment, including prosthetic and orthotic appliances, to medical and social rehabilitation, education, vocational training and

rehabilitation, aid, counselling, placement services and other services which will enable them to develop their capabilities and skills to the maximum and will hasten the processes of their social integration or reintegration.

7. Disabled persons have the right to economic and social security and to a decent level of living. They have the right, according to their capabilities, to secure and retain employment or to engage in a useful, productive and remunerative occupation and to join trade unions.

8. Disabled persons are entitled to have their special needs taken into consideration at all stages of economic and social planning.

9. Disabled persons have the right to live with their families or with foster parents and to participate in all social, creative or recreational activities. No disabled person shall be subjected, as far as his or her residence is concerned, to differential treatment other than that required by his or her condition or by the improvement which he or she may derive therefrom. If the stay of a disabled person in a specialized establishment is indispensable, the environment and living conditions therein shall be as close as possible to those of the normal life of a person of his or her age.

10. Disabled persons shall be protected against all exploitation, all regulations and all treatment of a discriminatory, abusive or degrading nature.

11. Disabled persons shall be able to avail themselves of qualified legal aid when such aid proves indispensable for the protection of their persons and property. If judicial proceedings are instituted against them, the legal procedure applied shall take their physical and mental condition fully into account.

12. Organizations of disabled persons may be usefully consulted in all matters regarding the rights of disabled persons.

13. Disabled persons, their families and communities shall be fully informed, by all appropriate means, of the rights contained in this Declaration.

Selected Bibliography

Abdou, Angie. *In Case I Go.* Arsenal Pulp Press, 2017.

Abdou, Angie. "On seeking permission to use a First Nations character." *Quill & Quire.* September 12, 2017. https://quillandquire.com/omni/angie-abdou-on-seeking-permission-to-use-first-nations-stories/.

Ali, Monica. *Brick Lane.* Scribner, 2003.

Anwar, Arif. *The Storm.* Harper Collins, 2018.

Awad, Mona. *Bunny.* Viking, 2019.

Babstock, Ken. "Review: *River of Thieves* by Michael Crummey." *Quill & Quire.* March 19, 2004. https://quillandquire.com/review/river-thieves/.

Balderson, Lauren. *The Revolutionists.* Dramatist's Play Service, 2018.

Carlson-Wee, Anders. "How-To." *The Nation.* July 5, 2018. https://www.thenation.com/article/archive/how-to/.

Chariandy, David. *Brother.* McClelland & Stewart, 2017.

Chee, Alexander. "How to Unlearn Everything: When it comes to writing the "other," what questions are we not asking?" *Vulture.* October 30, 2019. https://www.vulture.com/2019/10/author-alexander-chee-on-his-advice-to-writers.html.

Crummey, Michael. "Most of what follows is true: Michael Crummey on writing and the relationship between fact and fiction." *CBC.* July 4, 2019. https://www.cbc.ca/radio/ideas/most-of-what-follows-is-true-michael-crummey-on-writing-and-the-relationship-between-fact-and-fiction-1.4814202.

Crummey, Michael. "Afterwords: An Introduction to Poetry." *The New Quarterly.* 134 (Spring 2015): 133-135.

Crummey, Michael. *River Thieves.* Anchor, 2001.

Crummey, Michael. *The Wreckage.* Anchor, 2006.

Crummey, Michael, and Lisa Moore. "Two faces of the Rock." *Quill and Quire.* August, 2005. https://quillandquire.com/authors/two-faces-of-the-rock/.

Doctor, Farzana. *All Inclusive.* Dundurn, 2015.

Doctor, Farzana. *Seven.* Dundurn, 2020.

Doctor, Farzana. *Six Metres of Pavement.* Dundurn, 2011.

Dooley, Danette. "Getting up close with Annie Proulx." *The Telegram.* August 12, 2017. https://www.thetelegram.com/news/local/getting-up-close-with-annie-proulx-67453/.

Elliott, Alicia. *A Mind Spread Out on the Ground.* Doubleday Canada, 2019.

Elliott, Alicia. "Tracks." *The New Quarterly.* 141 (Winter 2017). https://tnq.ca/issues/issue-141/.

Gibb, Camilla. *Sweetness in the Belly.* Anchor, 2005.

Grady, Wayne. *Up From Freedom.* Doubleday Canada, 2018.

Hill, Jeremy Luke. "Interview: Claire Tacon." *Queen Mob's Teahouse.* June 30, 2018. https://queenmobs.com/2018/06/interview-claire-tacon/.

Jacob, Mira. *Good Talk: A Memoir in Conversations.* One World, 2019.

Jago, Robert. "Canada's Hollow Concern for First Nations Democracy." *The Walrus.* February 21, 2019. https://thewalrus.ca/canadas-hollow-concern-for-first-nations-democracy/.

Johnson, Adam. *The Orphan Master's Son.* Random House, 2012.

Selected Bibliography

Kay, Jonathan. "Seeing Lili Elbe." *The Walrus*. January 7, 2016. https://thewalrus.ca/seeing-lili-elbe/.

Keeshig [Tobias], Lenore. "Stop Stealing Native Stories." *Introduction to Indigenous Criticism in Canada*. Heather Macfarlane and Armand Garnet Ruffo, editors. Broadview, 2016.

Knight, Chelene. *Dear Current Occupant*. Book*hug Press, 2018.

Knight, Chelene. *Junie*. Book*hug Press, 2020.

Leduc, Amanda. *Disfigured: On Fairy Tales, Disability, and Making Space*. Coach House Books, 2020.

Leduc, Amanda. "Public Freaking." *Brockton Writers Series*. May 14, 2007. https://brocktonwritersseries.wordpress.com/2014/04/09/bws-07-05-14-amanda-leduc/.

Leroux, Darryl. *Distorted Descent: White Claims to Indigenous Identity*. University of Manitoba Press, 2019.

Marshall, Ingeborg. *A History and Ethnography of the Beothuk*. McGill-Queen's University Press, 1998.

Marshall, Ingeborg. *The Beothuk*. Breakwater Books, 2009.

McNichol, Kat. "An Interview with Angie Abdou." *Dreamer's Magazine*. April 4, 2019. https://www.dreamerswriting.com/angie-abdou/.

Mohammad, Ibtihaj. *Proud: My Fight for an Unlikely American Dream*. Hachette Books, 2018.

Moore, Lisa. *Degrees of Nakedness*. House of Anansi Press, 2005.

Norman, Howard. *The Bird Artist*. Picador, 1995.

Norris, Dennis, Joe Osmundson, Tommy Pico, and Fran Tirado. "Bonus!! You is Kind, You is Smart, You is Problematic." *Food 4 Thot*. July 29, 2018. https://player.fm/series/food-4-thot-2094158/bonus-you-is-kind-you-is-smart-you-is-problematic.

NourbeSe Philip, M. "The Disappearing Debate; or, How the Discussion of Racism Has Been Taken Over by the Censorship Issue." *Borrowed Power: Essays on Cultural Appropriation*. Bruce Ziff and Pratima V. Rao, editors. Rutgers University Press, 1997.

Novick, Miriam. "Impostures: Subjectivity, Memory, and Untruth in the Contemporary Memoir." Unpublished dissertation. University of Toronto, 2011.

O'Connell, Grace. *Be Ready for The Lightening*. Penguin Random House, 2017.

Palmer, Dorothy. *Falling for Myself*. Wolsak & Wynn, 2019.

Plett, Casey. "Before you write about a transgender character, read this." *CBC*. January 03, 2017. https://www.cbc.ca/arts/before-you-write-about-a-transgender-character-read-this-1.3919848.

Plett, Casey. "More fear, more love, more honesty: A call for intimacy in works from marginalized writers." *CBC*. May 04, 2017. https://www.cbc.ca/arts/more-fear-more-love-more-honesty-a-call-for-intimacy-in-works-from-marginalized-writers-1.4095248.

Plett, Casey. "Rise of the Gender Novel." *The Walrus*. March 18, 2015. https://thewalrus.ca/rise-of-the-gender-novel/.

Proulx, Annie. *The Shipping News*. Scribner, 1993.

Rice, Waubgeshig. *Midnight Sweatlodge*. Theytus Books, 2011.

Rice, Waubgeshig. *Moon on the Crusted Snow*. ECW Press, 2018.

Richardson, Jael. *Gutter Child*. Forthcoming, 2021.

Richardson, Jael. *Stone Thrower*. Dundurn, 2012.

Robinson, Eden. *Monkey Beach*. Penguin Random House, 2000.

Robinson, Eden. *Son of a Trickster*. Penguin Random House, 2017.

Robinson, Eden. *Traplines*. Vintage Canada, 1996.

Robinson, Eden. *Trickster Drift*. Penguin Random House, 2018.

Roth, Phillip. *Exit Ghost*. Houghton Mifflin Harcourt, 2007.

Sebastian, Troy. "Misrepresentation and the truth of Ktunaxa consent: A response from Ktunaxa Nation Council." *Quill & Quire*. January 11, 2018. https://quillandquire.com/omni/misrepresentation-and-the-truth-of-ktunaxa-consent-a-response-from-ktunaxa-nation-council/.

Selected Bibliography

Shawl, Anisi and Cynthia Ward. *Writing the Other.* Aqueduct Press, 2005.

Sturm, Circe. *Becoming Indian: The Struggle over Cherokee Identity in the Twenty-First Century.* SAR Press, 2011.

Sur, Sanchari. "Get to Know Sanchari Sur." *PRISM International.* October 15, 2018. https://prismmagazine.ca/2018/10/15/issue-57-1-teaser-get-to-know-sanchari-sur/

Sur, Sanchari. "Mistaken Longings: When I Write of Calcutta, I Don't Write of 'Home'." *Invisible Publishing.* November 8, 2018. https://invisiblepublishing.com/author/sanchari-sur/.

Tacon, Claire. *In Search of the Perfect Singing Flamingo.* Wolsak & Wynn, 2018.

Toews, Miriam. *Women Talking.* Penguin Random House, 2018.

Tsabari, Ayelet. *The Art of Leaving.* Penguin Random House, 2019.

Tsabari, Ayelet. *The Best Place on Earth.* Random House, 2013.

Tsabari, Ayelet. "How to lose friends and alienate readers." *The National Post.* March 21, 2013. https://nationalpost.com/entertainment/books/ayelet-tsabari-how-to-lose-friends-and-alienate-readers.

Whitehead, Colson. *The Underground Railroad.* Doubleday, 2016.

Wild, Christine. "Learn Writing Essentials with Chelene Knight." *Running Wild.* January 25, 2019. https://www.stitcher.com/podcast/christine-wild/running-wild-with-christine/e/58380076.

Williams, Ian. *Not Anyone's Anything.* Freehand Books, 2011.

Williams, Ian. *Reproduction.* Penguin Random House, 2019.

Writers Trust Canada. "Michael Crummey, Writers' Trust Fellow (2015)." *YouTube.* November 26, 2015. https://www.youtube.com/watch?v=KGPIBdkfGyk.